VOYAGEUR  CS

BOOKS THAT EXPLORE CANADA

Michael Gnarowski — Series Editor

The Dundurn Group presents the Voyageur Classics series, building on the tradition of exploration and rediscovery and bringing forward time-tested writing about the Canadian experience in all its varieties.

This series of original or translated works in the fields of literature, history, politics, and biography has been gathered to enrich and illuminate our understanding of a multi-faceted Canada. Through straightforward, knowledgeable, and reader-friendly introductions the Voyageur Classics series provides context and accessibility while breathing new life into these timeless Canadian masterpieces.

The Voyageur Classics series was designed with the widest possible readership in mind and sees a place for itself with the interested reader as well as in the classroom. Physically attractive and reset in a contemporary format, these books aim at an enlivened and updated sense of Canada's written heritage.

VOYAGEUR CLASSICS

BOOKS THAT EXPLORE CANADA

EMPIRE AND COMMUNICATIONS

HAROLD A. INNIS

GENERAL INTRODUCTION
BY ALEXANDER JOHN WATSON

DUNDURN PRESS
TORONTO

Editor: Michael Carroll
Design: Alison Carr
Printer: Marquis

Library and Archives Canada Cataloguing in Publication

Innis, Harold A., 1894-1952.
    Empire and communications / Harold A. Innis; introduction by Alexander John Watson.
Includes bibliographical references.
ISBN 10: 1-55002-662-3
ISBN 13: 978-1-55002-662-7

    1. Communication--History. I. Watson, A. John (Alexander John), 1948- II. Title.

P90.I5 2006   302.209   C2006-904492-9

1   2   3   4   5   11   10   09   08   07

Conseil des Arts du Canada   Canada Council for the Arts   Canada

ONTARIO ARTS COUNCIL
CONSEIL DES ARTS DE L'ONTARIO

We acknowledge the support of the Canada Council for the Arts and the Ontario Arts Council for our publishing program. We also acknowledge the financial support of the Government of Canada through the Book Publishing Industry Development Program and The Association for the Export of Canadian Books, and the Government of Ontario through the Ontario Book Publishers Tax Credit program, and the Ontario Media Development Corporation.

Care has been taken to trace the ownership of copyright material used in this book. The author and the publisher welcome any information enabling them to rectify any references or credits in subsequent editions.

J. Kirk Howard, President

www.dundurn.com

Dundurn Press
3 Church Street, Suite 500
Toronto, Ontario, Canada
M5E 1M2

Gazelle Book Services Limited
White Cross Mills
High Town, Lancaster, England
LA1 4XS

Dundurn Press
2250 Military Road
Tonawanda, NY
U.S.A. 14150

To GVF

CONTENTS

PUBLISHER'S NOTE

Harold Innis's *Empire and Communications* was originally published by Oxford University Press in 1950 and then reissued by the University of Toronto Press in 1972 in an edition edited by Innis's widow, Mary Quayle Innis. A third, illustrated edition of the book was published by Press Porcépic (later Beach Holme Publishing) in 1986. The University of Toronto Press edition boasted a foreword by Marshall McLuhan and reproduced marginalia that Innis had written in a copy of the Oxford edition of his book before he died in 1952. These margin notes — allusions to new quotations, notions, references, ideas — are often fragmentary, even cryptic, and were meant to be incorporated in the footnotes of a second edition of the book.

Mary Innis and University of Toronto Press published these marginalia substantially the way Harold Innis had written them. In some cases, the sources for quotations in the marginalia were updated, and anything that was added or expanded was indicated by enclosing it in square brackets, a practice maintained in this edition. Parentheses and question marks found in the present marginalia are those employed by the author. Mary Innis also added punctuation to the marginalia whenever the pursuit of clarity made it necessary. In his annotated copy of the Oxford edition of his book, Harold Innis had also specified a few changes in the main text of the work. These were made by his wife without comment.

In the present text, as with the University of Toronto Press edition, many marginalia notes are indicated in the main text with a letter. Both these and other marginalia that are merely fragments are referenced to the page or pages in this edition that they allude to. In order to make it easier to read the main text, Innis's original edition notes (indicated by numerals) and the marginalia have been removed from the foot of the page to the back of the book.

Except for the aforementioned reorganization of the notes, a few minor stylistic changes (treatment of dashes, quotation marks, ellipses, block quotations), and the addition of a suggested reading list and an incisive new general introduction by Innis's recent biographer, Alexander John Watson, the text of this classic work remains the way its author wrote it.

GENERAL INTRODUCTION
BY ALEXANDER JOHN WATSON

Concentration on a medium of communication implies a bias in the cultural development of the civilization concerned either towards an emphasis on space and political organization or towards an emphasis on time and religious organization. Introduction of a second medium tends to check the bias of the first and to create conditions suited to the growth of empire.

— Harold A. Innis, *Empire and Communications*

Shortly after the end of World War II, Harold Innis (1894–1952), whose reputation was founded on his work on the development of Canada, was invited to give the prestigious Beit Lectures on Imperial History at Oxford University. *Empire and Communications* was the written version of what he said during that lecture series.

As Canada's pre-eminent scholar/statesman, he had come a long way from his background as a poor farm boy of a Baptist family in Southwestern Ontario. Fundamental to understanding both the personality and the thought of Innis is that, unlike many others who travelled the road to intellectual success starting from a poor background, he never became deracinated. He continued to insist that his experience as a child on a farm that was being buffeted by the changeover from wheat to mixed farming as a result of the opening of prairie agriculture was the foundation that allowed him to construct his understanding of empire.

Along with many of his generation, he volunteered for service in World War I motivated by Christian and democratic ideals.

His experience in the trenches came close to killing him and scarred him emotionally for life. He returned to Canada with religious sentiment knocked out of him. Reason, not revelation, would underpin his life's work. The accomplishment of Canadians during the war, exemplified by the taking of Vimy Ridge where so many others had failed, saved him from the typical veteran's disease of cynicism. Instead he would remain a lifelong skeptic of the metropolitan paradigms that had led to the slaughter in the first place. He believed that the very lack of intellectual sophistication on the periphery created an environment that provided a comparative advantage for the development of critical thought. In Innis's view, the margin, not the centre, was the cornerstone for the renewal of Western civilization. He lived his life accompanied by the ghosts of so many of the bright minds that did not return from the conflict. This outlook, in turn, saddled him with a mind-numbing intellectual work ethic as he attempted to overcome the loss of his war-depleted generation.

The first stage of his intellectual journey was a collective effort to revise the understanding of Canadian history using a perspective developed by the first generation of indigenous intellectuals. He grew up in an educational system whose upper echelons were still staffed by British scholars. Their story of Canada, not surprisingly, was a transplanted version of their story of Britain — the long struggle between parliament and the crown that led to the responsible government of parliamentary democracy. When this paradigm applied to Canada, the story emerged as a country in which political ideals had triumphed against the grain of geography.

Against this paradigm, Innis and his colleagues in economic history pursued exhausting "dirt" research across the breadth of Canada. They mined the archives, but they also travelled to all corners of the country talking to everyone along the way — from industry leaders to ordinary folk — in an effort to understand what made it tick.

The result of this intellectual effort was a new paradigm that presented a material underpinning as central to the development of the country. Canada existed because of geography, not in spite of it. It was defined by the river drainage basins down which the fur trade was pursued. In Innis's hands this was not a rigidly deterministic model but a subtle and nuanced one that factored in the characteristics of staples products, the nature of metropolitan demand, geographical factors, and the structure and interaction of two cultural constellations — that of the indigenous peoples and that of the European settlers. It was a remarkable collective achievement carried out in the two decades of the interwar period when Canada was coming of age. To this day, in my opinion, the last chapter of Innis's *The Fur Trade in Canada* still represents the most concentrated and profound single piece of writing for anyone seeking to understand the nature of Canada.

But Innis's intellectual goal was never so parochial. He had always insisted that the perspective of peripheral intellectuals was essential to the renewal of Western civilization as a whole. He underwent a multilevel crisis towards the end of the Great Depression and the beginning of World War II that launched him on the second half of his intellectual journey. Although there were personal, institutional, and historical elements to this crisis, I will concentrate on the intellectual logic of this crossover period that eventually led to his composition of *Empire and Communications*.

Innis and his colleagues had fixed on explaining the history of Canada in terms of the characteristics of the succession of staple products that were demanded by the metropolis of empire from this peripheral region, its geography, and the cultural interaction of the peripheral peoples that exploited them. This chronicle was a story of phased and overlapping development in which the fisheries were succeeded by the fur trade, timber, mining, wheat, oil, hydroelectric power, and so on.

When Innis came to the study of pulp and paper, however, he shifted his attention. Instead of applying the paradigm he had developed to better understand an area peripheral to empire (Canada), he sought to gauge its effect on the centre. The reason for this change was that the demand for pulp and paper grew out of the rise of mass-circulation daily newspapers and their impact on public opinion in cities like London and New York.

At this point Innis made an intellectual leap to examine imperial history using the characteristics of media as the staples of empire. For his final decade, Innis embarked on an exhausting and lonely analysis of historical empires and the mix of media that had allowed them to flourish and ultimately stagnate. The present book, *Empire and Communications*, is the fruit of that intense labour. His intellectual endeavours on this book would have been enough, in themselves, to challenge a normal scholar. But we should remember that aside from his ongoing research, Innis was at the height of his professional career. Never before or since has a single scholar exerted such an influence on the social sciences in Canada. His control of appointments, research funding, publications, and professional associations was further increased as he recommitted himself to university work while many of his peers went into war service. In the end, he became known in the international scholarly world not as Professor Innis of the Department of Political Economy, University of Toronto, but simply as "Innis of Canada."

Not one of his economic history colleagues accompanied him on his intellectual journey into the distant past. Indeed, they were of the opinion that he had gone seriously off track. Their skepticism was understandable. Innis had no facility with any of the ancient languages and therefore all his work during this stage was based on secondary source material. Yet the specialist scholars who produced this source material did not accept him as a colleague. It was a one-way influence only, with Innis mining their work and them oblivious to his contribution and dismissive if it came to their attention. The Beit Lectures were not a contemporaneous success. Audiences had expected a world-class presentation on an aspect of colonial history; they received what they judged to be an inferior colonial perspective on world history. Not surprisingly, the numbers fell off dramatically as one lecture succeeded another. The reviews were condescending, and the original edition of *Empire and Communications* sold so slowly that Oxford's Clarendon Press declined to re-issue it. Given the intellectual solitude in which Innis pursued his communications studies and the negativity with which they were received, it is perhaps not surprising that when he died in 1952 this line of inquiry died with him. Two decades would elapse before University of Toronto Press republished *Empire and Communications*.

Two developments took place in the intervening period that rekindled an interest in Innis's work. Ironically, the first was the fragmentation of academic disciplines into specialized areas — a trend about which Innis himself forewarned. With communications studies now being pursued as a discrete discipline, scholars returned to an examination of earlier scholarly texts, and Innis's work was imbued with a canonical significance.

Second, Marshall McLuhan was recognized as a popular intellectual, and interest in McLuhan in turn led to interest in Innis as a precursor to McLuhan's thought. McLuhan was always clear about his debt to Innis, and indeed, his facility with a turn of phrase had the effect of popularizing some of Innis's key ideas — "the medium is the message," for example. So when *Empire and Communications* returned to print it did so largely on the basis of McLuhan's reputation and with a foreword by him interpreting Innis.

But McLuhan's intellectual voyage to communications came via literary criticism and fine art, not through economic history and politics. There was very little intellectual or personal chemistry between the two men. Innis did put McLuhan's first book, *The Mechanical Bride*, on the reading list for his graduate students. However, a personal introduction of the two academics arranged by a mutual colleague quickly descended into fundamental disagreement between the skeptical ex-Baptist Innis and the Catholic McLuhan over the nature of the Spanish Inquisition.

Not surprisingly, McLuhan's "take" on Innis tended to reflect his own thought rather than that of Innis. He stressed the bias of media in terms of sensory factors — whether the various media were eye- or ear-oriented — and pointed out inconsistencies in

Innis's argument based on this interpretation of the concept of bias. In so doing, he largely de-politicized Innis and replaced his pessimistic outlook on the impasse we are currently experiencing with what communications scholar and media critic James Carey had evocatively termed "the celebration of the electrical sublime."

Innis's methodology during the communications period lent itself to this interpretation by McLuhan. He was very much aware that he was open to attack from specialized scholars in archaeology, ancient history, and the classics. He was also running out of time to complete the scholarly path he had set for himself. Under these pressures, Innis developed an unusual methodology that allowed him to distil vast amounts of secondary sources and combine them in a literal "cut and paste" fashion into blocks of new text that formed much of the content for his communications books and essays.

As he pursued his research, he made textual deposits in three separate "accounts" — one for quotations; a second for ideas, aphorisms, and anecdotes; and a third for précised reading notes of the secondary sources he was scouring. Innis made withdrawals from these accounts to construct a massive 2,400-page manuscript entitled "A History of Communications." This process was facilitated by a grant he received that allowed him to make primitive photocopies (white on black) of these various notes out of which he could then clip sections to build text.

It may have been that Innis had originally intended to publish "A History of Communications" as a massive tome that would be his magnum opus. In any event, he decided during the 1940s that the days of the "big book" were numbered and that he himself was running out of time. For this reason, he released his communications work in speeches and lectures, later gathered into a series of short books, in the late 1940s and early 1950s. What is clear is that the first three chapters of "A History of Communications" are missing. They appear to have been used to produce the final text represented by the present book, *Empire and Communications*.

By adopting this methodology, Innis increased his publication productivity tremendously and, he thought, kept himself less exposed to the attacks of specialist scholars by staying close to the (précised) words of the authorities in the field he was studying. It was also consistent with the terrible symmetry of his thought on communications. One of Innis's central ideas was that consciousness was in large part structured by the technologies that were used to express thought. We should not be surprised then that Innis, in trying to break through the limitations of the worldview of his time, was experimenting with the oral presentation and material production of the ideas he was formulating. In many ways, he was anticipating the possibilities that the Internet, word-processing software, and search engines would bring into being only two generations after his death.

But, overall, his adoption of this research methodology undercut his work. I suspect that he was well aware that it left him open to the charge of plagiarism. He therefore never wrote or talked about his methodology. For this reason, there were no young scholars ready to pick up the loose ends of his research in the 1950s. Furthermore, the text produced through the methodology had a cryptic and elusive character whose obscurity came to be celebrated by communications scholars as a precursor to McLuhan's own style. Decades later, Innisian scholars were plagued with the belief that there might be some sort of key that could be discovered through which the obscure nature of Innis's texts would suddenly become clear. This dream will never be accomplished. Reading Innis will always remain as much work for the reader as it was for Innis, the author.

What Innis was attempting to do in the social sciences was to develop a grand synthesis akin to the quest to develop a "unified field theory" in post-relativity science. He was attempting to develop and merge a theory of politics or imperialism (drawing largely on the work of classics scholars) with a theory of consciousness (drawing on scholars researching the concept of time and space) and a theory of technology (based on an understanding of the biases of media of communications). In so doing, he hoped to overcome the persistent problem of objectivity in the social sciences and provide a means of escape from the limitations of contemporary worldviews.

Although Innis did not successfully complete this grand synthesis, his work in my opinion does not represent a dead end but a rich scholarly vein that has been abandoned long before it is exhausted. Innis offers an immensely suggestive way forward in a world dominated by "spin," punditry, and commercialism. I can think of no better inoculation against the rampant disease of present-mindedness in the contemporary world than a careful reading of his classic, *Empire and Communications*. This book was the foundation on which he built his understanding of the contemporary world, in particular his view of the United States of America, its foreign policy, and its effects on other cultures. At the time of Innis's death in 1952, his perspective on the contemporary world seemed radical and farfetched. When we read his work anew over a distance of more than fifty years, it seems fresh and, indeed, prophetic.

PREFACE
BY HAROLD A. INNIS

In this preface I must express my thanks to Sir Reginald Coupland for his kindness in extending to me an invitation to deliver the Beit lectures on Imperial economic history. I am grateful to him for his consistent encouragement. To his name I must add those of Professor W.K. Hancock, Sir Henry Clay, and Humphrey Sumner, Warden of All Souls College, for innumerable kindnesses. I have been greatly encouraged also by Professor and Mrs. John U. Nef and the Committee on Social Thought and Professor F.H. Knight of the University of Chicago. An interest in the general problem was stimulated by the late Professor C.N. Cochrane and the late Professor E.T. Owen. Professor Grant Robertson, Professor W.T. Easterbrook, Mr. R.H. Fleming, and Mr. D.Q. Innis have read the manuscript in whole or in part. I am under heavy obligations to Mr. W.S. Wallace and his staff in the library of the University of Toronto and to my colleagues in the department of political economy.

No one can be oblivious to the work of Kroeber, Mead, Marx, Mosca, Pareto, Sorokin, Spengler, Toynbee, Veblen, and others in suggesting the significance of communication to modern civilization. I have attempted to work out its implications in a more specific fashion and to suggest the background of their volumes. The twentieth century has been conspicuous for extended publications on civilization which in themselves reflect a type of civilization. It is suggested that all written works, including this one, have dangerous implications to the vitality of an oral tradition and to the health of a civilization, particularly if they thwart the interest of a people in culture and, following Aristotle, the cathartic effects of culture. "It is written but I say unto you" is a powerful directive to Western civilization.

See S.H. Butcher, *Some Aspects of the Greek Genius* (London, 1891), 234 *ff.*

1 — INTRODUCTION

The twentieth century has been notable in the concern with studies of civilizations. Spengler, Toynbee, Kroeber, Sorokin, and others have produced works, designed to throw light on the causes of the rise and decline of civilizations, which have reflected an intense interest in the possible future of our own civilization. In the title of these lectures on imperial economic history it is clear that in our civilization we are concerned not only with civilizations but also with empires and that we have been seized with the role of economic considerations in the success or failure of empires. Recognition of the importance of economic considerations is perhaps characteristic of the British Empire and it will be part of our task to appraise their significance to the success or failure of the British Empire and in turn to the success or failure of Western civilization. We may concede with Mark Pattison that

> ... In one department of progress the English development has indeed been complete, regular, and from within. In commerce and manufactures England may be said to have conducted, on behalf of the world, but at her own risks and perils, the one great commercial experiment, that has yet been made. Our practice has been so extended and diversified, that from it alone, with but little reference to that of the other trading nations of antiquity, or of modern times, the laws of economics have been inferred, and a new science constructed on a solid and indisputable basis ...[1]

We are immediately faced with the very great, perhaps insuperable, obstacle of attempting in this University, located so near a centre which has been the heart of an economic empire, to appraise economic considerations by the use of tools that are in themselves products of economic considerations. A citizen of one of the British Commonwealth of Nations, which has been profoundly influenced by the economic development of empires, who has been obsessed over a long period with an interest in the character of that influence, can hardly claim powers of objectivity adequate to the task in hand. It is an advantage, however, to emphasize these dangers at the beginning so that we can at least be alert to the implications of this type of bias. Obsession with economic considerations illustrates the dangers of monopolies of knowledge and suggests the necessity of appraising its limitations. Civilizations can survive only through a concern with their limitations and in turn through a concern with the limitations of their institutions, including empires.

We shall try to take heed of the warning of John Stuart Mill who

> believed that, though the science's method of investigation was still applicable universally, "it is, when not duly guarded against, an almost irresistible tendency of the human mind to become the slave of its own hypotheses; and when it has once habituated itself to reason, feel, and conceive, under certain arbitrary conditions, at length to mistake these convictions for laws of nature."[2]

And we shall try to escape his strictures on English political economists whom he felt were in danger of becoming enemies of reform.

> They revolve in their eternal circle of landlords, capitalists, and labourers, until they seem to think of the distinction of society into those three classes, as if it were one of God's ordinances, not man's, and as little under

human control as the division of day and night. Scarcely any one of them seems to have proposed to himself as a subject of inquiry, what changes the relations of those classes to one another are likely to undergo in the progress of society; to what extent the distinction itself admits of being beneficially modified, and if it does not even, in a certain sense, tend gradually to disappear.[3]

I shall find sympathy in these warnings in this University though it is perhaps easier for one trained in the universities of North America to be alert to them, but this is scarcely the time to appear boastful.

In paying heed to these warnings I do not intend to concentrate on microscopic studies of small periods or regions in the history of the British Empire, important as these are to its understanding. Nor shall I confine my interest to the British Empire as a unique phenomenon, since it is to an important extent a collection of odds and ends of other empires represented by the French in Quebec and the Dutch in South Africa. I shall attempt rather to focus attention on other empires in the history of the West, with reference to empires of the East, in order to isolate factors which seem important for purposes of comparison. Immediately one is daunted by the vastness of the subject and immediately it becomes evident that we must select factors that will appear significant to the problem.

It has seemed to me that the subject of communication offers possibilities in that it occupies a crucial position in the organization and administration of government and in turn of empires and of Western civilization. But I must confess at this point a bias which has led me to give particular attention to this subject. In studies of Canadian economic history or of the economic history of the French, British, and American empires, I have been influenced by a phenomenon strikingly evident in Canada, which for that reason I have perhaps over-emphasized. Briefly, North America is deeply penetrated by three vast inlets from the Atlantic — the Mississippi, the St. Lawrence, and

Hudson Bay, and the rivers of its drainage basin. In the northern part of the continent or in Canada extensive waterways and the dominant Pre-Cambrian formation have facilitated concentration on bulk products the character of which has been determined by the culture of the aborigines and by the effectiveness of navigation by lake, river, and ocean to Europe.[a] Along the north Atlantic coast the cod fisheries were exploited over an extensive coast-line; decentralization was inevitable; and political interests of Europe were widely represented. The highly valuable small-bulk furs were exploited along the St. Lawrence by the French and in Hudson Bay by the English. Continental development implied centralization. Competition between the two inlets gave the advantage in the fur trade to Hudson Bay, and after 1821 the St. Lawrence region shifted to dependence on the square timber trade. Monopoly of the fur trade held by the Hudson's Bay Company checked expansion north-westward from the St. Lawrence until Confederation was achieved and political organization became sufficiently strong to support construction of a transcontinental railway, the Canadian Pacific, completed in 1885. On the Pacific coast the discovery of placer gold was followed by rapid increase in settlement, exhaustion of the mines, and the development of new staples adapted to the demands of Pacific Ocean navigation such as timber. The railway and the steamship facilitated concentration on agricultural products, notably wheat in western Canada and, later on, products of the Pre-Cambrian formation such as precious and base metals and pulp and paper. Concentration on the production of staples for export to more highly industrialized areas in Europe and later in the United States had broad implications for the Canadian economic, political, and social structure. Each staple in its turn left its stamp, and the shift to new staples invariably produced periods of crises in which adjustments in the old structure were painfully made and a new pattern created in relation to a new staple. As the costs of navigation declined, less valuable commodities emerged as staples — precious metals, dried fish exported to Spain to secure precious metals, timber to support defence, in the words of Adam

Smith "perhaps more important than opulence," and finally wheat to meet the demands of an industrialized England. An attempt has been made to trace the early developments elsewhere but little has been done to indicate clearly the effects of the development of the pulp and paper industry. The difficulty of studying this industry arises partly from its late development and partly from the complexity of the problem of analysing the demand for the finished product. Concentration on staple products incidental to the geographic background has involved problems not only in the supply area but also in the demand area, to mention only the effects of specie from Central America on European prices, the effects of the fur trade on France, of wheat production on English agriculture, the impact on Russia of the revolution, and of pulp and paper production on public opinion in Anglo-Saxon countries. The effects of the organization and production on a large scale of staple raw materials were shown in the attempts by France to check the increase in production of furs, in the resistance of English purchasers to the high price of timber ending in the abolition of the Navigation Acts, in the opposition of European agriculture to low-cost wheat, and in the attempt to restrain the sensationalism of the new journalism, which followed cheap newsprint.

In this reference to the problem of attack it will be clear that we have been concerned with the use of certain tools that have proved effective in the interpretation of the economic history of Canada and the British Empire. It may seem irreverent to use these tools in a study of public opinion and to suggest that the changing character of the British Empire during the present century has been in part a result of the pulp and paper industry and its influence on public opinion, but I have felt it wise to proceed with instruments with which I am familiar and which have proved useful. The viewpoint is suggested in a comment of Constable to Murray: "If you wish to become a great author your chance will be bye and bye when paper gets cheaper."[4] In any case I have tried to present my bias in order that you may be on your guard.

I shall attempt to outline the significance of communication in a small number of empires as a means of understanding its role in a general sense and as a background to an appreciation of its significance to the British Empire. Bryce has stated that

> from the time of Menes down to that of Attila the tendency is generally towards aggregation: and the history of the ancient nations shows us, not only an enormous number of petty monarchies and republics swallowed up in the Empire of Rome, but that empire itself far more highly centralized than any preceding one had been. When the Roman dominion began to break up the process was reversed and for seven hundred years or more the centrifugal forces had it their own way ... From the thirteenth century onwards the tide begins to set the other way ... neither Democracy nor the principle of Nationalities has, on the balance of cases, operated to check the general movement towards aggregation which marks the last six centuries.[5]

In attempting to understand the basis of these diverse tendencies, we become concerned with the problem of empire, and in particular with factors responsible for the successful operation of "centrifugal and centripetal forces." In the organization of large areas, communication occupies a vital place, and it is significant that Bryce's periods correspond roughly first to that dominated by clay and papyrus, second to that dominated by parchment, and third to that dominated by paper. The effective government of large areas depends to a very important extent on the efficiency of communication.

The concepts of time and space reflect the significance of media to civilization. Media that emphasize time are those that are durable in character, such as parchment, clay, and stone. The heavy materials are suited to the development of architecture and sculpture. Media that emphasize space are apt to be less durable and light in character, such as papyrus and paper. The latter are suited to wide areas in administration and trade. The conquest of Egypt by Rome gave access to supplies of papyrus, which became the basis of a large administration empire. Materials that emphasize time favour decentralization and hierarchical types of institutions, while those that emphasize space favour centralization and systems of government less hierarchical in character. Large-scale political organizations such as empires must be considered from the standpoint of two dimensions, those of space and time, and persist by overcoming the bias of media which over-emphasize either dimension. They have tended to flourish under conditions in which civilization reflects the influence of more than one medium and in which the bias of one medium towards decentralization is offset by the bias of another medium towards centralization.[6]

We can conveniently divide the history of the West into the writing and the printing periods. In the writing period we can note the importance of various media such as the clay tablet of Mesopotamia, the papyrus roll in the Egyptian and in the Graeco-Roman world, parchment codex in the late Graeco-Roman world and the early Middle Ages, and paper after its introduction in the Western world from China. In the printing period we are able to concentrate on paper as a medium, but we can note the introduction of machinery in the manufacture of paper and in printing at the beginning of the nineteenth century and the introduction of the use of wood as a raw material in the second half of that century.

It would be presumptuous to suggest that the written or the printed word has determined the course of civilizations, and we should note well the warning of Mark Pattison that "writers with a professional tendency to magnify their office have always been given to exaggerate the effect of printed words." We are apt to overlook the significance of the spoken word and to forget that it has left little tangible remains. We can sense its importance[7] even in contemporary civilization and we can see its influence in the great literature of the heroic age[8] of the Teutonic peoples and of Greece and in the effects[9] of its discovery in the sagas of

Europe in the late eighteenth century on the literature of the north. Prior to the introduction of writing, music played its role in emphasizing rhythm and metre, which eased the task of memory. Poetry is significant as a tribute to the oral tradition. Sapir has noted that "many primitive languages have a formal richness; a latent luxuriance of expression that eclipses anything known to languages of modern civilization." The written tradition has had a limited influence on them.

It is scarcely possible for generations disciplined in the written and the printed tradition to appreciate the oral tradition. Students of linguistics have suggested that the spoken word was in its origins a half-way house between singing and speech, an outlet for intense feelings rather than intelligible expression.[10] Used by an individual, it was in contrast with language described as the sum of word-pictures stored in the mind of all individuals with the same values. In the words of Cassirer[11] language transformed the indeterminate into the determinate idea and held it within the sphere of finite determinations. The spoken word set its seal on and gave definite form to what the mind created and culled away from the total sphere of consciousness. But the speech of the individual continued in a constant struggle with language and brought about constant adjustment. "The history of language when looked at from the purely grammatical point of view is little other than the history of corruptions" (Lounsbury).[12] Herbert Spencer wrote that "language must be regarded as a hindrance to thought, though the necessary instrument of it, we shall clearly perceive on remembering the comparative force with which simple ideas are communicated by signs."[13] Perhaps it is a tribute to the overwhelming power of printed words that Maeterlinck could write: "It is idle to think that, by means of words, any real communication can ever pass from one man to another ... from the moment that we have something to say to each other we are compelled to hold our peace."[14] *"Ils ne se servent de la pensée que pour autoriser leurs injustices, et n'emploient les paroles que pour déguiser leurs pensées"* (Voltaire).

The significance of a basic medium to its civilization is difficult to appraise since the means of appraisal are influenced by the media, and indeed the fact of appraisal[15] appears to be peculiar to certain types of media. A change in the type of medium implies a change in the type of appraisal and hence makes it difficult for one civilization to understand another. The difficulty is enhanced by the character of the material, particularly its relative permanence. Pirenne has commented on the irony of history in which as a result of the character of the material much is preserved when little is written and little is preserved when much is written. Papyrus has practically disappeared, whereas clay and stone have remained largely intact, but clay and stone as permanent material are used for limited purposes and studies of the periods in which they predominate will be influenced by that fact. The difficulties of appraisal will be evident, particularly in the consideration of time. With the dominance of arithmetic and the decimal system, dependent apparently on the number of fingers or toes, modern students have accepted the linear measure of time. The dangers of applying this procrustean device in the appraisal of civilizations in which it did not exist illustrate one of numerous problems. The difficulties will be illustrated in part in these six lectures in which time becomes a crucial factor in the organization of material and in which a lecture is a standardized and relatively inefficient method of communication with an emphasis on dogmatic answers rather than eternal questions.

I have attempted to meet these problems by using the concept of empire as an indication of the efficiency of communication. It will reflect to an important extent the efficiency of particular media of communication and its possibilities in creating conditions favourable to creative thought. In a sense these lectures become an extension of the work of Graham Wallas and of E.J. Urwick.

Much has been written on the developments leading to writing and on its significance to the history of civilization, but in the main studies have been restricted to narrow fields or to broad generalizations. Becker[16] has stated that the art of writing provided man with a transpersonal memory. Men were given an artificially extended and verifiable memory of objects and events not present to sight or recollection. Individuals applied their minds to symbols rather than things and went beyond the world of concrete experience into the world of conceptual relations created within an enlarged time and space universe. The time world was extended beyond the range of remembered things and the space world beyond the range of known places. Writing enormously enhanced a capacity for abstract thinking which had been evident in the growth of language in the oral tradition. Names in themselves were abstractions. Man's activities and powers were roughly extended in proportion to the increased use and perfection of written records. The old magic was transformed into a new and more potent record of the written word. Priests and scribes interpreted a slowly changing tradition and provided a justification for established authority. An extended social structure strengthened the position of an individual leader with military power who gave orders to agents who received and executed them. The sword and pen worked together. Power was increased by concentration in a few hands, specialization of function was enforced, and scribes with leisure to keep and study records contributed to the advancement of knowledge and thought. The written record signed, sealed, and swiftly transmitted was essential to military power and the extension of government. Small communities were written into large states and states were consolidated into empire. The monarchies of Egypt and Persia, the Roman empire, and the city-states were essentially products of writing.[17] Extension of activities in more densely populated regions created the need for written records which in turn supported further extension of activities. Instability of political structures and conflict followed concentration and extension of power. A common ideal image of words spoken beyond the range of personal experience was imposed on dispersed communities and accepted by them. It has been claimed that an extended social structure was not only held together by increasing numbers of written records but also equipped with an increased capacity to change ways of living. Following the invention of writing, the special form of heightened language, characteristic of the oral tradition and a collective society, gave way to private writing. Records and messages displaced the collective memory. Poetry was written and detached from the collective festival.[18] Writing made the mythical and historical past, the familiar and the alien creation available for appraisal. The idea of things became differentiated from things and the dualism demanded thought and reconciliation. Life was contrasted with the eternal universe and attempts were made to reconcile the individual with the universal spirit. The generalizations which we have just noted must be modified in relation to particular empires. Graham Wallas has reminded us that writing as compared with speaking involves an impression at the second remove and reading an impression at the third remove. The voice of a second-rate person is more impressive than the published opinion of superior ability.

Such generalizations as to the significance of writing tend to hamper more precise study and to obscure the differences between civilizations insofar as they are dependent on various media of communication. We shall attempt to suggest the roles of different media with reference to civilizations and to contrast the civilizations.

2 — EGYPT

The Nile, with its irregularities[a] of overflow, demanded a co-ordination of effort. The river created the black land which could only be exploited with a universally accepted discipline and a common goodwill of the inhabitants. The Nile acted as a principle of order and centralization, necessitated collective work, created solidarity, imposed organizations on the people, and cemented them in a society. In turn the Nile was the work of the Sun, the supreme author of the universe. Ra — the Sun — the demiurge was the founder of all order human and divine, the creator of gods themselves. Its power was reflected in an absolute monarch to whom everything was subordinated. It has been suggested that such power followed the growth of astronomical knowledge[b] by which the floods of the Nile could be predicted, notably a discovery of the sidereal year in which the rising of Sirius coincided with the period of floods. Moret has argued that as early as 4241 BC a calendar was adopted which reconciled the lunar months with the solar year, and that the adoption marked the imposition of the authority of Osiris and Ra, of the Nile and the Sun, on Upper Egypt. The great gods of the fertile delta imposed their authority on the rest of Egypt and their worship coincided with the spread of political influence. Universal gods emerged in certain centres, their influence was extended by theologians, and diffusion of worship supported the growth of kingdoms. The calendar became a source of royal authority. Detachment of the calendar from the concrete phenomena of the heavens and application of numbers which provided the basis of the modern year has been described by Nilsson as the greatest intellectual fact in the history of time reckoning.

Achievement of a united monarchy by material victories and funerary beliefs and practices centring in the person of the king produced a social situation of which the invention of writing was the outcome. The position of the monarch was strengthened by development of the idea of immortality. The pyramids and the elaborate system of mummification carried with them the art of pictorial representation as an essential element of funerary ritual.

The divine word was creative at the beginning of the universe and acted on gods, men, and things in a fashion reminiscent of Genesis and the Gospel of St. John. "I created all shapes with what came out of my mouth,ᶜ in the time there was neither heaven nor earth."[1] In fixing the tradition of magic rites and formulae in the Old Kingdom the God Thoth,[2] as the friend, minister, scribe, and keeper of the divine book of government of Ra became the Lord of ritual and magic. He represented creation by utterance and production by thought and utterance. The spoken word possessed creative efficiency and the written word in the tomb perpetuated it.[3] The magical formulae of the pyramids assumed the productive and creative power of certain spoken words.

In the handbooks of temple structure and adornment of sacred shrines, which probably made up a large part of temple libraries, Thoth was the framer of rules of ecclesiastical architecture. No essential difference existed between pictorial decorations and hieroglyphic script. Thoth represented intelligence and was "Lord of the Divine Word." He was the unknown and mysterious, the lord of scribes and of all knowledge, since the setting down of words in script suggested the possession of mysterious and potent knowledge in the scribe who "brought into being what was not." Formulae of sacred ritual, collections of particularly effective formulae, and books of divine words were attributed to Thoth as the inventor of language and script. Beginning with drawing and literature in the decoration of temples and tombs in the use of figures as definitions of living beings and objects, the pictorial principle was extended and adapted to the need of expressing non-pictorial elements into a hieroglyphic system by 3500 BC. Hieroglyphics was the Greek name for sacred engraved writing. From about 4000 BC the names of kings, wars, political events, and religious doctrines were written. The earliest documents were names and titles on sealings and vases, notes of accounts or inventories, and short records of events. Seals and wooden tablets with primitive script recorded the outstanding events of the Abydos reign. Writing gradually developed towards phoneticism and by the time of Menes (about 3315 BC)[4] many picture signs had a purely phonetic value and words were regularly spelled out.

As the founder of the first dynasty at Thinis, Menes developed the theory of the absolute power of kings. A new capital was built at Memphis at the balance of the two lands to the north and to the south.[d] As the successor of Horus and Osiris and as their living image the king was identified with them in every possible way in order to ensure eternal life. From about 2895 BC to 2540 BC autocratic monarchy was developed by right divine. The pyramids of about 2850 BC suggested that the people expected the same miracles from the dead as from the living king. All arable land became the king's domain. After 2540 BC royal authority began to decline and the power of the priests and the nobles to increase. The difficulties of the sidereal year in which a day was gained each year may have contributed to the problems of the absolute monarch and hastened the search for a solar year possibly discovered by the priests. The Sun Ra cult was exalted to the rank of chief God and the king was lowered from the Great God to the Son of Ra and to the Good God. The king as a Sun-god was a man who did not work with his hands but merely existed and, like the sun, acted on environment from a distance. The Sun was law and imposed it on all things, but law was distinct from the Sun as it governed even him. Recognition of this fact has been described as implying the discovery of government.[5] In Heliopolis as the centre of priestly power, the doctrine was developed in which God was conceived of as an intelligence which has thought the world and expresses itself by the word, the organ of government, the instrument of continuous creation, and the herald of law and justice. An order of the king was equivalent to an act of creation of the same kind as that of the demiurge. The command of the superior obeyed by dependents was reinforced by the mystery of writing as a reflex of the spoken word. Centralization of the gods favoured the growth of political ideas.

After a period of political confusion from 2360 BC to 2160 BC a new political order emerged in which the absolute monarch was replaced by the royal family. The clergy of Heliopolis established a new calendar and imposed it on Egypt. Extension of privileges to the priestly class brought a transition to oligarchy. The royal domain was broken up in favour of a feudal clergy and royal officials. The Theban kings (2160–1660 BC) restored order and prosperity. After 2000 BC religious equality was triumphant. The masses obtained religious rights and corollary political rights. The Pharaohs gave up their monopoly and accepted the extension of rights to the whole population. Admission of the masses to religious rights and to everlasting life in the next world was recognized along with civic life in this world. Power was essentially religious and extension of direct participation in worship brought increased participation in the administration of stock and the ownership of land. The management of royal lands was farmed, partial ownership of houses and tombs was permitted, and free exercise of trades and administrative offices was conceded. Peasants, craftsmen, and scribes rose to administrative posts and assemblies.

The profound disturbances in Egyptian civilization involved in the shift from absolute monarchy to a more democratic organization coincides with a shift in emphasis on stone as a medium of communication or as a basis of prestige, as shown in the pyramids, to an emphasis on papyrus.ᵉ Papyrus sheets dated from the first dynasty and inscribed sheets from the fifth dynasty (2680–2540 BC or 2750–2625 BC). In contrast with stone, papyrus as a writing medium was extremely light. It was made from a plant (*Cyperus papyrus*) that was restricted in its habitat to the Nile delta and was manufactured into writing material near the marshes where it was found. Fresh green stems of the plant were cut into suitable lengths and the green rind stripped off. They were then cut into thick strips and laid parallel to each other and slightly overlapping on absorbent cloth. A similar layer was laid above and across them and the whole covered by another cloth. This was hammered with a mallet for about two hours and the sheets welded into a single mass which was finally pressed and dried. Sheets were fastened to each other to make rolls, in some cases of great length. As a light commodity it could be transported over wide areas.[6] Brushes made from a kind of rush (*Funcus maritimus*) were used for writing. Lengths ranging from 6 to 16 inches and from one-sixteenth to one-tenth of an inch in diameter were cut slantingly at one end and bruised to separate the fibres.[7] The scribe's palette had two cups, for black and red ink, and a water-pot. He wrote in hieratic characters from right to left, arranging the text in vertical columns or horizontal lines of equal size, which formed pages. The rest of the papyrus was kept rolled up in his left hand.[8]

Writing on stone was characterized by straightness or circularity of line, rectangularity of form, and an upright position, whereas writing on papyrus permitted cursive forms suited to rapid writing. "When hieroglyphs were chiselled on stone monuments they were very carefully formed and decorative in character. When written on wood or papyrus they became simpler and more rounded in form ... The cursive or hieratic style was still more hastily written, slurring over or abbreviating and running together ... they ceased to resemble pictures and became script."[9] "By escaping from the heavy medium of stone" thought gained lightness. "All the circumstances arouse interest, observation, reflection."[10] A marked increase in writing by hand was accompanied by secularization of writing, thought, and activity. The social revolution between the Old and the New Kingdom was marked by a flow of eloquence and a displacement of religious by secular literature.

Writing had been restricted to governmental, fiscal, magical, and religious purposes. With increase in use of papyrus, simplification of hieroglyphic script into hieratic characters in response to the demands of a quicker cursive hand, and growth of writing and reading, administration became more efficient. Scribes and officials charged with the collection and administration of revenues and of rents and tributes from the peasants became members of an organized civil service, and prepared accounts intelligible to their colleagues and to an earthly god, their supreme master. After 2000 BC the central administration employed an army of scribes, and literacy was valued as a stepping-stone to prosperity and social rank. Scribes became a restricted class and writing a privileged profession. "The scribe comes to sit among the members of the assemblies ... no scribe fails to eat the victuals of the king's house."[11] "Put writing in your heart that you may protect yourself from hard labour of any kind and be a magistrate of high repute. The scribe is released from manual tasks."[12] "But the scribe, he directeth the work of all men. For him there are no taxes, for he payeth tribute in writing, and there are no dues for him."[13]

The spread of writing after the democratic revolution was accompanied by the emergence of new religions in the immortality cult of Horus and Osiris. Ra worship had become too purely political and individuals found a final meaning and a fulfilment of life beyond the vicissitudes of the political arbitrator.[14] Osiris, the god of the Nile, became the Good Being slain for the salvation of men, the ancestral king and model for his son Horus. As an agricultural god he had faced death and conquered it. His wife Isis, the magician, made codes of law and ruled when Osiris was conquering the world. She persuaded the Sun-god Ra to disclose his name, and since knowledge of a person's name[15] gave to him who possessed it magical power over the person himself she acquired power over Ra and other gods. In the twelfth dynasty Osiris became the soul of Ra, the great hidden name which resided in him. With Ra he shared supremacy in religion and reflected the twofold influence of the Nile and the Sun. Night and day were joined as complementary —

Osiris, yesterday and death, Ra, to-morrow and life. Funerary rites invented by Isis were first applied to Osiris. Conferring immortality they have been described by Moret as "the most precious revelation which any Egyptian god had ever made to the world."[f]

Osiris was served by Thoth as vizier, sacred scribe, and administrator. As the inventor of speech and writing, "Lord of the creative voice, master of words and books,"[g] he became the inventor of magic writings. Osiris became the centre of a popular and priestly literature to instruct people in the divine rights and duties. Words were imbued with power. The names of gods were part of the essence of being, and the influence of the scribe was reflected in the deities. Since religion and magic alike were sacred they became independent. The priest used prayers and offerings to the gods, whereas the magician circumvented them by force or trickery. Family worship survived in the Osirian cult, and because of a practical interest magic was used by the people. Since to know the name of a being was to have the means of mastering him, to pronounce the name was to fashion the spiritual image by the voice, and to write it especially with hieroglyphics was to draw a material image. In the manifold activity of the creative word magic permeated metaphysics. Polytheism persisted, and names were among the spiritual manifestations of the gods. Magical literature and popular tales preserved the traditions of the great gods of the universe.

The king gained from the revolution as the incarnation of the king gods, Falcon, Horus-Seth, Ra, Ra-Harakhti, Osiris, Horus, son of Isis, and Amon-Ra, who ruled Egypt. The king's devotion created a great wave of faith among the people. Ritual enabled him to appoint a proxy to act as prophet. Power was delegated to professional priests who first incarnated themselves in the king and performed the ceremonies in every temple every day. The worship of Ra and the celestial gods was confined to priests and temples. The priests of Atum condensed revelation in the rituals of divine worship, and a cult supplied the needs of living images in statues in the temple.

The shift from dependence on stone to dependence on papyrus and the changes in political and religious institutions imposed an enormous strain on Egyptian civilization. Egypt quickly succumbed to invasion from peoples equipped with new instruments of attack. Invaders with the sword and the bow and long-range weapons broke through Egyptian defence, dependent on the battle-axe and the dagger. With the use of bronze and possibly iron weapons, horses and chariots, Syrian Semitic peoples under the Hyksos or Shepherd kings captured and held Egypt from 1660 to 1580 BC. Egyptian cultural elements resisted alien encroachments and facilitated reorganization and the launching of a counter-attack. The conquerors adopted hieroglyphic writing and Egyptian customs, but complexity enabled the Egyptians to resist and to expel the invaders. They probably acquired horses[16] and light four-spoked chariots from the Libyans to the west, and after 1580 BC the Nile valley was liberated. In a great victory at Megiddo in 1478 BC[h] Thutmose III gave a final blow to Hyksos power. Under rulers of the eighteenth dynasty (1580–1345 BC) the New Theban Kingdom was established.

In the New Kingdom, the Pharaohs at Thebes, as the capital and metropolis of the civilized east, had resumed their sovereign rights, taken possession of the goods of the temples and brought clerical vassalage to an end. Monarchical centralization was accompanied by religious centralization. The gods were "solarized," and Amon the God of the Theban family as Amon-Ra reigned over all the gods of Egypt after 1600 BC. As a result of the success of war in imperial expansion, the priests became securely established in territorial property and assumed increasing influence. Problems of dynastic right in the royal family gave them additional power.

The use of papyrus rapidly increased after the expulsion of the Hyksos. The cult of Thoth had played an important role in the expulsion of the Hyksos and in the New Kingdom. Thoth became the god of magic. His epithets had great power and strength, and certain formulae were regarded as potent in the resistance to, or in the expulsion of, malicious spirits. To about 2200 BC medicine and surgery had advanced since mummification had familiarized the popular mind with dissection of the human body and had overcome an almost universal prejudice, but after the Hyksos invasion medicine became a matter of rites and formulae[17] and opened the way to Greek physicians and anatomists in Alexandria.

Military organization essential to expulsion of the invaders became the basis of expansion and the growth of an Egyptian empire. Protectorates were established beyond the borders as a means of economy in the use of soldiers and in administrative costs. Syria and Palestine became part of the empire. Reinforcements were brought by sea and control extended to Carchemish on the Euphrates by 1469 BC. During the period of the Egyptian hegemony, from about 1460 to 1360 BC, the Pharaohs employed directive authorities found in conquered countries, and made them effective by a process of Egyptianization. Under Amenophis II and Thutmose IV (1447–1415 BC) control was extended through marriage alliances with Mitannian princes and by intrigue and bribery implied in the sending of gold to the Kassites. Union in marriage took the place of unity derived from blood kinship. The system of amalgamating gods as a means of uniting groups into a nation was supplemented by union through marriage.

Under Amenophis III the Egyptian empire reached the zenith of wealth and power. A postal service was established between the capital and the cities of the empire, but cuneiform was appropriated as a simpler medium of communication than hieroglyphics. Akhnaton (1380–1362 BC), son of Amenophis III, possibly with the support of learned Egyptian priests, who held higher beliefs as philosophers in an exalted idea of the one and only God, attempted to introduce a system of worship which would provide a religious basis for imperial development. The worship of Aten, the solar disk, was a device for creating a united Orient. Religious monopoly of the solar disk was designed to provide a common ideal above political and commercial interests, and above distinctions between Egyptians and foreigners.

These internationalist tendencies were resisted by the priests of Amon and the sacerdotal class supported by popular feeling. The priesthood defeated an attempt to impose a single cult in which duty to the empire was the chief consideration. It has been suggested that the rise of a middle-class bureaucracy under anti-aristocratic kings was accompanied by increased democratization of the cult of Osiris.[18] Desperate attempts of the heretic kings to free themselves from the growing domination of Theban priests were defeated, and Tutankhaten, the son-in-law of Akhnaton, returned to the worship of Amon, restored the gods to all their privileges, and changed his name to Tut-ankh-Amen. Akhnaton had failed to gain emotional support from the people, and they returned to the private worship of Osiris and the enjoyment of Osirian privilege.

Successful wars had also created a military nobility, holding land, enjoying certain privileges, and becoming an hereditary privileged class, which supported the restoration of Amon. About 1345 BC[i] Horemheb, a general, raised himself to power, received the crown of Thebes from Amon, and re-established the old order in favour of priests and soldiers. From the nineteenth dynasty (1345–1200 BC) the gods intervened more and more in private affairs. Royal authority and lay justice were weakened by the influence of the priests and the popularity of the gods. After Rameses II (1300–1234 BC) the first prophet of Amon became the highest personage in the royal administration. In the twentieth dynasty an invasion of people of the seas was followed by the loss of the Syrian provinces. By the end of that dynasty in the twelfth century the royal heredity, which had lain in the queen,[19] was included among the privileges of the family of the first prophet. On the death of Rameses XII kingship was assumed by the royal priests, and royal decrees were those of Amon. A priestly theocracy had replaced human kingship. The weakness of a theocratic society was shown in the invasions of the Assyrians, the Persians, and the Greeks, but its strength was evident in the periodic outbreaks against foreign domination and in the difficulties of Assyrians and Persians in attempts to establish empires in Egypt. Nectanebo (359–342 BC) was the last Egyptian king claiming descent from the god Amon.

The dominance of stone as a medium of communication left its stamp on the character of writing, and probably checked its evolution after the introduction of papyrus and the brush. "The earliest form of writing seems to have been picture writing ... when the same fixed set of pictures were used over and over again to represent not merely ideas and objects but also words and sounds."[20] As a result of the significance of writing to religion, and ample supplies of papyrus, Egypt never took the logical step of discarding the cumbersome methods of representing consonantal sounds or of creating an alphabet. With purely pictorial and artistic characters eye-pictures were used with ear-pictures and the script never passed to the use of fixed sign for certain sounds. Consonantal values were represented by single signs, principally for foreign names and words, but the older pictographic writing was maintained as a shorter and more convenient form of abbreviation, particularly after the scribes had learned a large number of signs. The Egyptians succeeded with consonants but failed with vowels, in contrast with the Sumerians, and enormously reduced the number of signs needed for the phonetic representation of the word.[21] But their language exhibited a distinction between consonants expressing the notion or conception of a root and vowels marking the form of roots and changes in their meaning, and opened the way to the splitting up of words and syllables into component elements which was denied to the Akkadians through their use of syllables.[22] Twenty-four signs emerged with the value of single consonants.

The effects of restricted development in writing were evident in literature. Freshness depended on the degree of accord between the art of writing and actual speech.[23] With the use of papyrus the didactic or reflective form had apparently been invented before 2000 BC, but literary forms reached a high point after that date. Flinders Petrie, in illustrating his pattern of evolution of civilizations, suggests that Egyptian sculpture passed from archaism about 1550 BC, painting became free and natural about 1470 BC, literature witnessed freedom in style about 1350 BC, mechanics became important about 1280 BC, and wealth was dominant about 1140 BC.[24] The attempt of Akhnaton to break the power of the priesthood and to remodel the religion of the people was accompanied by attempts to bring the written and the spoken language into accord, and to bring about an improvement of speech and writing.[j] The Hymn to the Disk, about 1370 BC, was the "earliest truly monotheistic hymn which the world has produced."[25] Dominance of the priesthood from the thirteenth to the tenth centuries brought a separation of speech and literary language and artificial composition. Egypt has been described as the first consciously literary civilization to cultivate literature for its own sake, but style outlived its first freshness and gave way to artificiality and bombast, with little regard for content.

The special position of the scribe meant that prophets in the Hebrew sense failed to emerge. The Egyptian loved to moralize, and the highest literary distinction was reached in wisdom literature.[26] Since the development of script out of a series of picture drawings was based on the pun, the Egyptian was an "inveterate punster." The Egyptians had no great body of national epic but were successful in the profane lyric, an art "entirely neglected by the Babylonians."[27] Egypt gave to the world "what are, as far as we know, its earliest love poems."[28] She was the home of the short story in which tales were told for the joy of story-telling.

The Egyptians had no record of laws comparable to Deuteronomy. In the Old Kingdom a strictly absolute monarch was sole legislator. With the use of papyrus the system of administration became one of numerous officials. Administration and its dependence on writing implied religious sanctions, which meant encroachments on law. Lawsuits occupied a large place in Egyptian literature and great interest was shown in legal decisions, and in the nineteenth and later dynasties a consistent attempt was made to build up a law of procedure on the basis of omniscience of duty. The treatment of eternal property as a legal personality may have had its influence on Roman law and on the law of corporations.

Writing was a difficult and specialized art requiring long apprenticeship, and reading implied a long period of instruction. The god of writing was closely related to the leading deities and reflected the power of the scribe over religion. The scribe had the full qualifications of a special profession and was included in the upper classes of kings, priests, nobles, and generals, in contrast with peasants, fishermen, artisans, and labourers. Complexity favoured increasing control under a monopoly of priests and the confinement of knowledge to special classes. Monopoly of knowledge incidental to complexity coincided with the spread of magical writings among the people.[k] Short cuts of magic and religion were entrenched in writing as the occupation of a respectable learned profession in the ruling class. Attempts of kings to escape were defeated by the power of monopoly. A monopoly control of communication defeated attempts to construct empires. The limitations of the Egyptian empire were in part a result of the inflexibility of religious institutions supported by a monopoly over a complex system of writing.

The demands of the Nile required unified control and ability to predict the time at which it overflowed its banks. Possibly the monarchy was built up in relation to these demands, and strengthened its position by construction of the pyramids, which reflected the power of the monarchy over space and time. But a monopoly of knowledge in relation to stone imposed enormous burdens on the community, and was possibly accompanied by inability to predict the date of floods through dependence on the sidereal year. A new competitive medium, namely the papyrus roll, favoured the position of religion, and possibly its advantages coincided with the discovery of a more efficient method of predicting time by dependence on the sun. In the period of confusion which accompanied the introduction of papyrus, Egypt was subjected to invasion. A fusion between the monarchy and the priesthood became the basis of a successful counterattack and emergence of an Egyptian empire. Inability to maintain the fusion and to develop a flexible religious and political organization was in part a result of a monopoly of knowledge which had been built up in relation to the papyrus roll and a complex system of writing. A successful empire required adequate appreciation of problems of space that were in part military and political, and of problems of time that were in part dynastic and biological and in part religious. Dependence on stone as a medium provided the background of an absolute monarchy, but its monopoly position invited competition from papyrus and the development of a new monopoly dominated by religion and control over writing in the complex hieroglyphics. The new monopoly presented problems to an Egyptian empire and to other empires that attempted to exercise control over Egypt. Monopoly over writing supported an emphasis on religion and the time concept, which defeated efforts to solve the problem of space.

3 — BABYLONIA

In Egypt ability to measure time and to predict the dates of floods of the Nile became the basis of power. In the Tigris and Euphrates valleys in southern Mesopotamia the rivers[a] were adapted to irrigation and organized control, and less exacting demands were made on capacity to predict time. Sumer was a land of small city-states in which the chief priest of the temple was the direct representative of the god. The god of the city was king, and the human ruler was a tenant farmer with the position and powers of a civil governor.

It has been suggested that writing was invented in Sumer to keep tallies and to make lists and hence was an outgrowth of mathematics. The earliest clay tablets include large numbers of legal contracts, deeds of sale, and land transfers, and reflect a secular and utilitarian interest. Lists, inventories, records, and accounts of temples and small city-states suggest the concerns of the god as capitalist, landlord, and bank. Increased revenues necessitated complex systems of accounting and writing intelligible to colleagues and successors. Temple offices became continuing and permanent corporations. Growth of temple organizations and increase in land ownership were accompanied by accumulation of resources and differentiation of functions. Specialization and increased wealth brought rivalry and conflict.

Alluvial clay found in Babylonia and Assyria was used for the making of brick, and as a medium in writing. Modern discoveries of large numbers of records facilitate a description of important characteristics of Sumerian and later civilizations, but they may reflect a bias incidental to the character of the material used for communication. On the other hand, such a bias points to salient features in the civilization. In preparation for writing, fine clay was well kneaded and made into biscuits or tablets. Since moist clay was necessary and since the tablet dried quickly it was important to write with speed and accuracy.[b] Pictographs of fine lines made by an almost knife-sharp reed were probably followed by linear writing such as might be easily cut on stone records. But the making of straight lines tended to pull up the clay, and a cylindrical reed stylus was stamped perpendicularly or obliquely on the tablet. A triangular stylus of about the size of a small pencil with four flat sides and one end bevelled was introduced, probably in the second half of the third millennium. It was laid on a sharp edge, and if the tip was pressed deeply a true wedge or cuneiform appeared on the tablet. If the stylus was pressed lightly a large number of short strokes was necessary to make a single sign. Economy of effort demanded a reduction in the number of strokes, and the remnants of pictorial writing disappeared. As a medium clay demanded a shift from the pictograph to formal patterns. "The gap between picture and word is bridged."[1] Cuneiform writing was characterized by triangles and the massing of parallel lines. The complexity of a group of wedges of different sizes and thicknesses and an increase in the size of the tablets which changed the angle at which they were held in the writer's hand hastened the tendency towards conventionalization. A change in the direction of the angle[c] meant a change in the direction of the strokes or wedges and hastened the transition from pictographs to signs.[2] Conventionalization of pictographs began with signs most frequently used and advanced rapidly with the replacement of strokes by wedges. Pictographic expression became inadequate for the writing of connected religious or historical texts and many signs were taken to represent syllables. By 2900 BC the form of the script and the use of signs had been fully developed, and by 2825 BC the direction of writing and the arrangement of words according to their logical position in the sentence had been established. Signs were arranged in compartments on large tablets. The writing ran from left to right and the lines followed horizontally. Cylinders could be rolled on wet clay to give a continuous impression, and cylinder seals of hard stone were introduced. Engraved with various designs they served as personal symbols and were used as marks of identification of ownership in a community in which large numbers were unable to read and write. Seals were carried around the neck and served to stamp signatures to contracts concerning property and ownership.

Concrete pictographs involved an elaborate vocabulary with large numbers of items. To show modifications of the original meaning signs were added to the pictures and as many as 2,000 signs were in use. By 2900 BC the introduction of syllabic signs in a vocabulary which was largely monosyllabic had reduced the number of signs to about 600. Of these signs about 100 represented vowels, but no system was devised for representing single consonantal sounds or creating an alphabet. Cuneiform writing was partly syllabic and partly ideographic or representative of single words. Many of the signs were polyphonic or had more than one meaning. Sumerian had no distinctions of gender, and often omitted those of number, persons, and tenses. An idea had not fully developed to the symbol of a word or syllable. Pictographs and ideograms took on abstract phonetic values, and the study of script became linked to the study of language.

Sun-dried tablets could be altered easily and this danger was overcome by baking in fire. Indestructibility assured inviolability for commercial and personal correspondence. Though admirably adapted by its durability to use over a long period of time, clay as a heavy material was less suited as a medium of communication over large areas. Its general character favoured the collection of permanent records in widely scattered communities. Adaptability to communication over long distances emphasized uniformity in writing and the development of an established and authorized canon of signs. Extensive commercial activity required a large number of professional scribes or of those who could read and write. In turn the difficulties of writing a complex language implied a long period of training and the development of schools. Temple accounts and sign lists with the names of priests inventing the signs were made into school texts. In order to train scribes and administrators, schools and centres of learning were built up in connection with temples and special emphasis was given to grammar and mathematics. Since the art of writing as the basis of education was controlled by priests, scribes, teachers, and judges assumed the religious point of view in general knowledge and in legal decisions. Scribes kept the voluminous accounts of the temples and recorded the details of regulations in priestly courts. Practically every act of civil life was a matter of law which was recorded and confirmed by the seals of contracting parties and witnesses. In each city decisions of the courts became the basis of civil law. The growth of temples and extension in power of the cult enhanced the power and authority of priests. The characteristics of clay favoured the conventionalization of writing, decentralization of cities, the growth of continuing organization in the temples, and the religious control. Abstraction was furthered by the necessity of keeping accounts and the use of mathematics particularly in trade between communities.

The accumulation of wealth and power in the hands of the priests and the temple organizations, which accompanied the development of mathematics and writing, was probably followed by ruthless warfare between city-states and the emergence of military specialization and mercenary service. It has been suggested that the control of religion over writing and education entailed a neglect of technological change and military strength. Temple government or committees of priests were unable to direct organized warfare and temporal potentates appeared beside the priest. The latter enjoyed a prerogative and led the prince into the presence of the deity. Priests were organized in hierarchies but war increased the power of kings because of the need for a unified command. "Armies are essentially monarchist." As a leader in war the king commanded a nucleus of organized specialists. The army opened a career to ability, but the head of an army concerned with the advancement of talent was constantly exposed to dangers from rivals. Success implied an emphasis on territorial control in which jurisdiction was given to army leaders and the danger of rivalry lessened. Extension of territory and delegation of authority necessitated an interest in the administration of justice. The king checked the extensive rigour of law and injustice which characterized religious control.[3] About 2450 BC Urukagina rescued classes of the population from exactions of the priests, restrained the lavishness of funeral rites, and made serfs free men. Civil law was slowly developed with less regard to the small city-state with its laws, constitution, ruler, and god.

The supreme merit of monarchy was its intelligibility. "Men are governed by the weakness of their imaginations" (Bagehot). The influential chief became a man god. The age of magic had passed to the age of religion but left the magician who became a divine king. Dynasties of absolute monarchs tended to become unstable, not only because of threats from rivals in the army but also because of problems of succession and the difficulties of securing popular support. Destruction of old capitals as a means of destroying the prestige of conquered rulers and creation of new capitals were accompanied by attempts to reorganize the system of deities by admitting the gods of conquered peoples to the pantheon. Attempts were made to make religion flexible and suited to the needs of political units based on force. The difficulties contributed to the downfall of the first dynasty of Ur and later to successful resistance against Semitic invaders.

The Sumerians had used archers effectively and had introduced chariots drawn by four asses, but the Akkadians succeeded in conquering them. Under Sargon of Agade (about 2568–2513 BC) they built up an empire probably extending to Asia Minor and the Mediterranean. The dynasty was brought to an end probably by the resistance of the conquered and a new invasion from Gutium. Sumerian opposition finally succeeded and the third dynasty was founded by Ur-Nammu about 2474 BC. The power of city governors was weakened by expansion of a bureaucracy and the concentration of authority in a centralized government.

Under the second king of this dynasty a system of laws was developed to ensure the uniformity of business and scribal custom. The practice of Semitic invaders in making themselves deities was followed by Dungi,[d] who disregarded the Sumerian practice of making the chief god the real ruler of the city-state and the king merely a vice-regent, and took the final step of deifying the reigning monarch. The cult of the sovereign was designed to achieve religious unity as a foundation for political unity. Under the Sumerians land had been vested in the god and rent was paid, but the Semites established the practice of allowing land to be held in fee simple on which taxes were exacted.

The emergence of kings and a unitary economic system in contrast with decentralized temples were followed by interminable dynastic wars reflected in the concern of documents with wars and treaties. The moral and cultural superiority of Sumerian civilization and the Sumer-Akkadian empire were destroyed by the savagery of the Elamites about 2187 BC. The Amorite Sumer-Abum had himself proclaimed king of Babylon about 2125 BC and by 2007 BC the dynasty controlled a large part of Akkad. The Elamites were defeated by Hammurabi about 1955 BC and the empire was greatly extended.

The subordination of Sumerian civilization by Semitic peoples had an important effect on the conventionalization of writing. Sumerian was apparently an agglutinative language to which the conquerors would not adapt themselves. The difficulty of uniting languages with different structures involved supplanting the older language. The Sumerians had limited need for signs representing syllables, but the Babylonians were compelled to spell out every single word by syllables. The basis of the Sumerian system was word values and of the Akkadian system, syllable values.[4] The Akkadians developed a syllabary of 275 signs in which the welding of consonants and vowels checked the possibility of an alphabet. The conquerors abandoned their proto-Elamite script, adapted the signs and characters of the conquered, and wrote inscriptions in cuneiform. Sumerian became a dead language preserved largely by priests in religious writing, but signs which had been used as single syllables free of relationship to pictographs were taken over by the conquerors, as were those that had been used to represent objects or ideas, and were read as ideographs with Semitic translations. The Sumerian pronunciation of the more important ideographs was followed. Contact with Sumerian written texts brought an appreciation of abstract symbols such as became the basis for symbolic algebra.[5] Hammurabi completed the change from Sumerian to Akkadian and made the Semitic language official. The Amorites reinforced the Akkadians and their language became the popular speech and the official medium. The Babylonians wrote words in non-Semitic form but in the main pronounced them as Semitic. Influenced by Sumerian script they never developed an alphabet and at the most expressed one vowel and one consonant by a sign.

Though Sumerian was no longer spoken and became the fossilized sacred language of priests, its decline was marked by defiance of the conquerors and by intense literary and historical activity. Cultural pre-eminence was emphasized by religious scribes who made fresh copies of ancient texts which were arranged and stored in the library of the god, and prepared hymns, books, and litanies for the temple services. Priests trained in the Sumerian tradition and with the scholastic attitude emphasized the systematic organization of knowledge. Grammars and huge dictionaries of "syllabaries" were prepared for the translation of Sumerian literature for the Semitic reader. Oral traditions were written down and literature became the bond slave of religion. The epic was invented as a means of "working up the story of the demigods and heroes for use in the service of religion."[6] Lyric poetry was entirely devoted to the service of religion and reached a standard of composition "very close to the best work" of the psalms.[7] Though contributing little to wisdom literature and showing little evidence of writing for writing's sake,[8] Babylonia reached "a high point of aesthetic excellence of hymns to deities, of prayers in lyric form, and of psalms of penitence."[9]

Though religion became less important following the consolidation of power, it was reduced to a system and acquired
pontifical authority in the minds of the conquered. Sumerian
gods continued but with Semitic names. The number of gods
was reduced and impetus given to monotheism. Anu the sun
god had a centre of worship in Uruk and Er the water deity in
Eridu. Enlil, the chief god of Nippur and head of the pantheon
under the Sumerians, was a storm-god who absorbed the attributes of the solar and agricultural deities. His consort Ninlil
became the mother goddess. He was made subordinate to
Marduk,ᵉ who became the god of Babylon and assumed the
powers and attributes of other gods in the empire and as sun-
god became the god of heaven and earth. A threefold division of
heaven, earth, and water was developed and a deity given to each
division. Nabu, the son of Marduk, was the god of writing who
gave understanding and wisdom and had the stylus of the scribe
as a symbol.

Sumerian influence evident in script, religious rights and
beliefs, and military organization of the conquerors was also
apparent in law. Expansion of trade in a united Babylonia was
followed by an elaborate system of administration and compli-
cations of social life, which required higher and lower courts and
assured a decline in the authority of priests. Temples continued
as extensive organizations and centres of justice, but the palaces
as large undertakings favoured the growth of private business.
Hammurabi claimed to have received the lawsᶠ from the god of
justice and subordinated ecclesiastical to civil courts. The king
was the servant and not the source of law. Law guided the ruler
and protected the subject. Law was regarded as a divine decree,
the oracular decision of a deity, and was adapted to old laws in
a system of legislation rather than a code. Under centralized
power the administration of justice was reorganized. The rights
and prerogatives established by priests in earlier codes of law
were arranged in patrician order. Civil laws and customs of conquered cities were arranged in a system and were entirely freed
from religious formulae. Adoption had been prevalent among

the Sumerians possibly as a result of the practice of temple prostitution where the fathers were unknown, but paralleling religious prostitution Sumerian laws carefully regulated domestic life and tended to uphold the rights of individuals. Hammurabi apparently attempted to stamp out religious influence and introduced much more severe penalties against violations of the sacredness of the family tie. Marriage rested essentially on a written document. The family was a unit endowed with rigid cohesion by rules laid down to govern succession and division of goods. Family solidarity was assumed in a complete indefeasible right over the family estate. Rights were devolved to individuals as they formed new family units, but rights amounting to a strict entail were retained.

In checking the vices of corruption and indolence, Hammurabi centralized and perfected the system of administration, organized the direction of affairs, and supervised even minute details. Babylonia became a political reality, a unified nation with a common capital, a common code of written law, a common calendar, and a permanent system of government. The city-state was absorbed in the territorial state. For the marking and distinction of months, ideograms were borrowed from the Sumerian calendar and a fixed series of months was arranged by a selection of 354 days in a lunar year. The priests concerned with extensive administration of landed property owned by the temples had adapted religious ceremonies, festival seasons, and time reckoning to practical occupations. In an agricultural society religion was faced with the problem of predicting important dates to determine the seasonal round of activities. The Semites apparently introduced worship of the moon as a deity suited to a hot climate and providing a fixed measure of time in continuous time reckoning. Astronomy was studied in order to determine seasons and festival dates and results of observations were recorded in writing. Man was able to arrest time. Under the Semites the calendar was determined by a central authority and one calculation for the whole empire enabled the king to decide when it became necessary to add a month to the current year. The duo-decimal system of the zodiac was developed and hours of daylight were divided into twelve as were the hours of night.

Mathematics and time reckoning facilitated the development of meteorology and the establishment of the sexagesimal system, "the invention of which is to their eternal glory,"[10] which spread far beyond Mesopotamia and dominates the currency of Great Britain to the present day. Its superiority over the decimal system followed its ease in the handling of fractions. The royal or king's weight was adopted by royal proclamation throughout the empire. Fixed standards of weights and measures for grain and metal over large areas facilitated trade. The development of mathematics followed the demands of expanding trade in a large centre of a unified empire. Mathematics was studied in relation to accounts, field plans, and calendars. Mathematical texts were used as supplements to oral instruction and were in the form of concrete examples. Apprentices followed their masters in handling problems of architecture, engineering, and business, notably the calculation of interest. Multiplication tables were apparently used before 2000 BC, but reckoning was chiefly by addition and subtraction. Fractional quantities were mastered and figures were given a definite value according to position in a number, but the zero sign was not used consistently. Measurement assumed abstract thinking and led eventually to problems of Euclidian space, but mathematical symbolism was not highly developed and geometry was chiefly significant in decorative art.

The development of writing, mathematics, the standardization of weights and measures, and adjustments of the calendar were a part of an urban revolution. Rules for writing and systems of notation were involved in business transactions and the administration of revenues. Writing has been regarded as the "unforeseen outgrowth of a social order which was founded on a recognition of personal rights,"[11] and scientific advance[g] as dependent on "a concept of society whereby the powers of the state are restricted and the rights of the individual receive a corresponding emphasis" (E.A. Speiser).[12]

The accumulated wealth of an empire that followed an urban revolution attracted the attention of invaders with more efficient means of warfare. Success in the art of horsemanship, the care and breeding of horses, and ability to use chariots in mountainous regions enabled Aryan groups to dominate the empire. The Hittites attacked Babylon probably between 1950 BC and 1926 BC, and though repulsed probably brought the first dynasty to an end. They were followed by the Kassites. Gandash probably proclaimed himself king of Babylon about 1746 BC and established a dynasty that persisted to the end of the thirteenth century. It is probably that the Semites were checked in expansion to the north and compelled to turn towards Egypt under the Hyksos or Shepherd kings. In turn the Hittites,[13] including probably the Mitanni, the Vanni,[14] and the Kassites, overran regions to the north in Cappadocia to which traders had introduced cuneiform writing by about 2000 BC. The latter was apparently overwhelmed by the Hittite hieroglyphic system but, used for governmental purposes in the capital at Boghaz-keui and elsewhere, it restricted the development of Hittite pictographic writing.

Without a consistently efficient system of writing and the stabilizing conservative influence of religion, the Hittite empire was exposed to difficulties from within and without. The priest king represented the sun and the priestess the mother goddess. A territorial deity was queen but religion was not supported by traditions of learning and by an abundance of writing material such as clay. The Mitanni were attacked by the Egyptians under Amenhotep II (1470–1420 BC) and came under their influence through an alliance strengthened by the marriage of Thutmose II to a daughter of the king lasting from 1440 to 1380 BC. About 1370 BC Suppiluliuma, king of the Hittites, succeeded in dominating the Mitanni and created a highly organized imperial and central administration whose officials took the oath of allegiance and met the demands of increasing complexity in state and imperial affairs. A strong imperial capital, a system of radiating communications, and the use of iron gave the Hittites important advantages in the consolidation of power. Egyptian provinces in Syria became exposed to Hittite intrigue, but about 1272 BC Hattusil, king of the Hittites[h] concluded a treaty with Rameses II,[i] conceding to him Syria and all western Asia from the Euphrates to the sea. Shortly after this date Shalmaneser I (1280–1250 BC) of the Assyrians subjugated the Mitanni, and the Cappadocian empire of the Hittites collapsed about 1200 BC. About 1150 BC the Hittites attacked Babylon but were defeated by Nebuchadnezzar I of the dynasty which followed the Kassites, about 1180 BC. Expansion of the sea-rovers (Achaeans) in the fourteenth century was followed by maritime invasion of the countries of the eastern Mediterranean and about 1184[j] the Greeks probably defeated allies of the Hittites at Troy.[15] Resistance of the Hittite power to encroachment from the south and east fostered the growth of Ionian states and its contraction gave an opportunity for fresh expansion.

In spite of the success of Tiglath-Pileser (1090–1060 BC) in breaking up the Hittite federation and in laying the foundations of an efficient imperial organization, contraction of Assyrian power as a result of encroachments from Arameans who were pushed into Assyrian territory to the left bank of the Euphrates from the fourteenth to the twelfth centuries enabled the Hittites[k] to establish Carchemish as a bridgehead on the Euphrates about 1050 BC. After the first phase of Assyrian expansion the Arameans probably absorbed Hittite culture and established the supremacy of their customs and language. Driven into north Syria they probably introduced Mitanni-Hittite art, including the practice of engraving Semitic script in relief, to Zenjuli. A simplified script, developed at Carchemish to meet the demands of trade in the tenth century, spread to Asia Minor in the ninth century. These importations probably strengthened the tendencies in the period of comparative peace and expansion of trade in north Syria in the twelfth and eleventh centuries in which the relieved pictographic characters of the Hittites were reduced to a purely linear system. In contrast with Cappadocia, where pictographic writing was checked in its development by cuneiform, Hittite characters followed an independent line of development. Both relieved and incised Hittite characters were used simultaneously in engraving, and the more elaborate script was preserved for expensive monuments. In central Syria Egyptian influence was more important and by about 900 BC Hittite script was not far from the Phoenician in that it was partly in alphabetic form. With the script of the Vannic people[j] that of the Hittites disappeared in competition with the Phoenician alphabet. As a result of the scarcity of suitable clay in northern regions and the development of a linear script with curved strokes on papyrus or parchment, an alphabet of twenty-two linear signs appeared in north Syria[16] in about the tenth century.

The Assyrians made the most persistent attempts to build up an imperial organization. Administration was emphasized as a basis of imperialism. Provinces were in existence by 1500 BC, but under Shalmaneser III provincial government was elaborated and governors were appointed to collect tribute. Subject kings were replaced by Assyrian officials and the policy of earlier empires in which personal union was achieved by allowing the king to rule in each state by a separate title was abandoned. The Assyrians lacked an interest in trade and captured commercial cities, never as rivals, but for booty, taxes, and strategic reasons. In the second wave of expansion military success was dependent on more extensive use of iron, as it had been developed by the Hittites, on the employment of more efficient breeds of horses, and on the evolution of an efficient military organization. Coarse thickset horses of Upper Asia and Europe which appeared in Babylonia about 2000 BC were crossed with light Libyan horses, which were being exported by the Egyptians to western Asia in the tenth century. By 1000 BC King Solomon and the kings of the Hittites and Assyrians were acquainted with African horses. The crossing of Libyan horses of great speed with Asiatic horses of great strength produced an animal which enabled horse-driving peoples to become horse-riding peoples. The charioteers remained an *élite* corps among the Assyrians, but Ashur-nasir-pal II[m] (885–860 BC) used large numbers of cavalry obtained chiefly from allies to supplement chariots, as well as a strong core of native Assyrian infantry. Battering-rams and tanks became effective means of attack against southern cities built largely of brick. Success was evident in the capture of Carchemish in 877 BC. Its importance was reduced in 740 BC, and it became part of an Assyrian province in 717 BC. In 729 BC Tiglath-Pileser III became king of Babylon. Dynastic difficulties emerged and after Shalmaneser V (728–722 BC) Sargon, an Assyrian general, seized the crown. He replaced a low by a high chariot capable of carrying three instead of two men and used cavalry more extensively. A standing army with bowmen as an important element in the infantry was created. The army was brought to its greatest efficiency.

Spectacular military success probably accentuated difficulties of control over conquered peoples, particularly through religion. In Babylon the temple and the palace were separate, whereas the Assyrians combined them and the kings were their own chief priests. The god-king was the centre of power. The temples never attained an independent position and power of the priesthood was restricted. Religious imperialism centred around Ashur, a solar god, though Ishtar, his consort, had her own cult and temples. After the capture of Babylonia, Ashur displaced Marduk and Enlil[n] and occupied the first place in the pantheon. Ashur became the father of the gods and Shamash appeared to represent the sun. Nabu, the Babylonian god of knowledge, became more important and probably reflected the influence of the powerful guild of professional scribes of which he was the patron deity. "The cuneiform script, the beginning of kingship"[17] became the means of advancing to high positions of Babylon in 709 BC. Later difficulties led to the destruction of Babylon by Sennacherib in 689 BC, but again priestly influence secured its reconstruction by his son Esarhaddon.

Babylonian religious ceremonies played an important role in reducing the despotism of the king. The monotheistic and cosmopolitan religion of the Assyrians gradually gave way to the flood of Babylonian deities. Attempts to offset the influence of Babylon paradoxically increased its power. Sargon built a palace at Dur-Sharukin and started a library, which was continued by his son, who added volumes of ancient dialects of Sumerian and built a new palace at Nineveh. Instructions were given to search for documents and to make copies for its collection. Copying of Babylonian literature by Assyrian scribes enhanced the position of Nineveh as a religious and political centre but increased Babylonian influence. The Sumerian classics were translated and studied. Babylonian practices[18] in hepatology or the divining of the future by studying the liver of sacrificial sheep were continued. The temple tower was brought from the south and passed on to the west as the church steeple. A renaissance of art and literature followed the conquest of Egypt and transmission of the wisdom of Babylonia in copies, compilations, and revisions from the originals to the royal library and archives under Ashurbanipal (668–626 BC). The language of the Assyrians varied in details from that of the Akkadians and the cuneiform signs of Hammurabi were used, though conservatism in writing brought greater complexity than that of the script that had been modified by Babylonian merchants. As a result of Babylonian influence Assyria was unable to develop a powerful literary tradition.° Native religious literature centred entirely about Ashur. The royal annals alone were purely Assyrian in style and followed invention of the cylinder or hexagon on which crowded lines of script permitted longer narratives. They were fully developed in the inscription of Tiglath-Pileser I.

Egypt became an Assyrian province following invasion in 674 BC, the capture of Memphis in 671 BC, and the sack of Thebes in 668 BC.ᴾ The additional strains imposed by expansion brought disaster. The burden of military campaigns had been evident in a weakening of administration under Esarhaddon. Only strong rulers had been able from time to time to unite the north and south Euphrates and the cultural and religious strength of Babylon proved too powerful. To this was added the task of including the cultural and religious centre of Egypt.

Flexibility was introduced in the imperial structure through the rise of imperial free cities in Babylonia. Cities were given a certain measure of freedom and in Ashur townsmen were given charters with clearly defined special privileges. But without the strength of organized continuity characteristic of religious organizations, the problem of succession was never satisfactorily solved. Royal families reached periods of degeneracy and dynasties were overthrown. The most energetic rulers refused to build palaces in old capitals and built new capitals as a means of avoiding the enemies of an old court and of strengthening their prestige. The building of new and expensive capitals with stone, in contrast with use of clay and brick in the south, imposed heavy drains on the energies of the people. At the end of the eighth century a new wave of horsemen of Indo-European speech began to pour into Asia Minor. The Cimmerians attacked Lydia in 652 BC and Scythians, Medes, and Babylonians joined to destroy Nineveh in 612 BC.

Expansion of the Assyrian empire facilitated the growth of trade conducted by Arameans, who carried the products of Egypt, Syria, and Babylonia eastward by land, and by the Phoenicians, who built up the coast cities of Tyre, Sidon, and Byblos in relation to trade by sea. Phoenicians and Arameans, the commercial peoples of the empire, used the alphabet. Peace within an enlarged empire brought increased industrial efficiency. The culture of Assyria was imperial and rested on the subjugation and incorporation of peoples of different languages, races, and cultures. A system of deportation was used on a large scale as a means of blotting out nationalistic and narrowly local cultures. The political decay of Aramean states was followed by the cultural and economic supremacy of Aramaic by the end of the seventh century. The Aramean city-states were destroyed and the people turned to trade in the vast territory within the Assyrian imperial structure. Domestication of the camel about the end of the twelfth century was followed by the growth of a caravan trade. Babylonian weights and measure were used on a larger scale. Refined silver, stamped with the image of the god whose temple guaranteed its fineness, marked the beginnings of an efficient coined money. By the middle of the ninth century the alphabet was extensively used in Syria. Arameans used the Phoenician characters and languages in north Syrian inscriptions. After Sennacherib Aramaic characters alone were used for weights. Cuneiform was used in business documents but Aramaic dockets were kept. By the middle of the eighth century Assyrian records were being kept in Aramaic. Ink was used on the margins of clay tablets and on potsherds. Two scribes were shown in drawings, the chief with a stylus and a tablet and the assistant with the pen and parchment or papyrus. Skins first appeared in the reign of Tiglath-Pileser and were used by the priests of Gula and Ishtar. Since papyrus was easily broken it spread less rapidly than pen and ink and the alphabet.[9] With the development of writing and the use of parchment, officials in the empire could be kept under close supervision. They acted under detailed orders and were subject to immediate recall. Daily communication was established with the capital. The introduction of a new language and a new medium of communication was followed by more efficient administration.

The spread of a more efficient system of writing which followed the discovery of the alphabet had profound implications for imperial organization. Babylonian and Egyptian civilizations and the empires which grew out of them were associated with great rivers in which the demand for centralization was imperative. Priestly colleges held a monopoly of knowledge through which they dominated successive organizations of political power. But the very success of the monopolies contributed to the destruction of empires.

Dominance of monopolies of knowledge in the centre of civilizations implied limitations on the fringes, particularly with new languages compelled to emphasize simplicity rather than complexity in writing. Marginal classes as well as marginal regions demanded simplicity and weakened the position of elaborate systems of the scribes. From a study of the inscriptions of Sinai discovered by Flinders Petrie at Serabit in 1905 it has been suggested by A.G. Gardiner,[19] that since the Egyptians were interested in this region from 1887 to 1801 BC, Semitic workmen had used devices for keeping records which evaded the intricacies of the Egyptian system and that they probably borrowed the simplest signs of the alphabet and abandoned the remainder of the complicated system. In any case, Semitic peoples in contact with Egyptians at some time before 1500 BC apparently invented an alphabet which was developed in Palestine and perfected on the Phoenician coast. Papyrus and the alphabet prevailed over clay in regions in which the latter was difficult to find and to which it was difficult to transport. The invasion of the Hyksos[r] apparently imposed a barrier between the south and the north of Arabia and led to the development of divergent systems of writing.

About the tenth century the northwest Semitic alphabet was used to write the Aramaic language. Aramaic writing developed as a traders' script[s] with a concise conventional alphabet, which was free from the complexities of cuneiform writing, and could be written quickly. It included numbers which had been introduced from India. It was probably developed in relation to parchment as a new medium. As a result of the influence of Arameans on Semitic trade over the land routes to the north, Aramaic spread to Syria and far beyond. Towards the end of the eighth century it prevailed in Asia Minor and among the Phrygians. After 500 BC it became the most important script of the Near East, the diplomatic script of the Persian empire, and the official script for the western provinces of Persia. By about 400 BC it succeeded Hebrew as a spoken language.

The discovery of cuneiform texts[20] at Ras Shamra-Ugarit, a centre for the manufacture of copper brought from Cyprus into bronze, has shown that the alphabet was used at least as early as 1500 BC. Nigmed, probably a Mitannian prince of about that date, had a college of learned priests and scribes who built up a library of clay tablets chiefly concerned with religion. Inclusion of the poetical works of the Canaanites suggests the existence of a literary tradition at least by the fourteenth century. Myths were concerned with the mysteries of nature — death in the approach of winter and revival with the approach of spring. None of the literature was concerned with the experiences of individuals. Animal representations were rare and secondary and the pantheon was essentially anthropomorphic. The supremacy of El pointed towards a tendency to monotheism. The chief merchants used the Babylonian scripts in correspondence and book-making, but the scribes had a cuneiform alphabet of twenty-nine signs in contrast with the twenty-four consonants of Egypt and the twenty-two signs of the Hebrews and the Canaanites.

The decline of Mycenean civilization after the Dorian[t] invasion opened the road to Phoenician expansion in the Aegean area. Control over Phoenicia from Egypt was apparently followed by the shipment of quantities of papyrus through Byblos (hence the name Bible) and its use by Phoenicians by the end of the eleventh century and possibly by the Assyrians[21] in the eighth century. The Canaanite Phoenician alphabet was possibly influenced by cuneiform writing in the emphasis on short straight lines and by the papyrus and the brush in the emphasis on curving lines. Brush forms ran to long, vague strokes as in the tails of Phoenician letters. The dryness of the strokes eliminated the danger of blotting peculiar to the pen and facilitated crossing of the strokes. It seems doubtful that the use of the pen in relation to parchment could be adapted to papyrus. The contact between papyrus and the brush and cuneiform writing probably contributed to the process of analysing out of an alphabet of twenty-two consonants.[22] Distinctiveness was combined with simplicity of form. Sounds of human speech were analysed into primary elements each represented by a separate visual symbol.

The Phoenicians had no monopoly of knowledge in which religion and literature might hamper the development of writing. The necessities of an expanding maritime trade demanded a swift and concise method of recording transactions and the use of a single shortened type of script. Surplus signs and cumbersome determinatives were discarded in the interest of speed and brevity. Commerce and the alphabet were inextricably interwoven, particularly when letters of the alphabet were used as numerals. Phoenician cities rather than capitals of empires reflected a concern with trade. Submission to overlords was tolerated so long as they were allowed to trade. Sidon was lost to Philistines[11] in the twelfth century but Tyre became important after 1028 BC. Sidon was recaptured in the eighth century but Assyrian advance and declining sea-power favoured independent colonies such as Carthage, founded in 814 BC and Gades (Cadiz) in the eighth century.

A flexible alphabet in contrast with cuneiform and hieroglyphic or hieratic writing facilitated the crystallization of languages and favoured the position of cities and smaller nations rather than empires. The oral tradition in these languages could be written down, particularly the myths, which had reached the fringes of the Egyptian and the Babylonian empires. Hebrew and Phoenician were dialects of a common language and Hebrew was probably spoken in Palestine after 1200 BC. The influence of Egypt[23] on the Hebrews was suggested in the emphasis on the sacred character of writing and on the power of the word which when uttered brought about creation itself. The word is the word of wisdom. Word, wisdom, and God were almost identical theological concepts.

With a restricted written tradition in the empires of Babylonia and Egypt emphasis was given to architecture and sculpture in the round, in temples, palaces, and pyramids. In the south Sumerian plain, dwellers[24] used the column, arch, vault, and dome, and constructed ziggurats of solid brickwork in their temples. Sculpture of the Sumer-Akkadians representing nature was replaced under the Kassites by an art emphasizing the human form. In the north the use of stone favoured centralized power and it was used to a larger extent in sculpture, as a medium of writing, particularly of laws, and in architecture. Since sculpture occupied a prominent place in the support of religious and political institutions it was prohibited in images by the Hebrews. "Thou shalt not make unto thee any graven image, or any likeness of *any thing* that *is* in heaven above, or that *is* in the earth beneath, or that *is* in the water under the earth" (Exodus xx.4). The written letter replaced the graven image as an object of worship. "The omission or the addition of one letter might mean the destruction of the whole world" (Talmud). Denunciation of images and concentration on the abstract in writing opened the way for advance from blood relationship to universal ethical standards and strengthened the position of the prophets in their opposition to absolute monarchical power. The abhorrence of idolatry of graven images implied a sacred power in writing, observance of the law, and worship of the one true God.[v]

As the alphabet had developed by conventionalization through adaptation to the language of conquerors, religion was probably more easily conventionalized by use of the alphabet and by absorption from the conquered. The Hebrews took over the Canaanite religion and purified and cleansed it to their own purposes. Stories of the creation and the Deluge of Babylonia were adopted by the Hebrew prophets and the mystical element reduced to a minimum.[25] In the creation the blood of gods was mixed with clay and man was created. Man was brought into association with gods. The naturalistic conception of creation was replaced by a monotheistic interpretation of divine rule. More primitive laws of the Mosaic code were probably Israelite and descended from old nomadic custom and more advanced laws were gradually assimilated from Canaanite sources. The laws of Moses[w] were probably based on Sumerian laws such as were collected by Hammurabi. The Book of the Covenant was relatively immature[26] compared to the laws of Hammurabi.

The decline of Egypt permitted the growth of nationalism in Israel. Resistance of David and Saul against the Philistines from 1090 to 1085 BC was followed by the union of Israel and Judah under a Hebrew monarchy and a brief period of glory under Solomon. Egyptian policy favoured distrust and division and the stirring up of religious and racial enmity between Israel and Judah. Political weakness was offset by the power of the priesthood, which had been strengthened during the period of resistance against the Philistines. Elijah protested against the natural religion of Baal and insisted on the moral religion of Jehovah with its absolute and binding demands on king and peasant for righteousness.

Literature was mobilized in the interests of religion. About 850 BC stories in oral or written form[x] which had been polished for generations were collected and given a literary stamp in a great work by J. Poems as the earliest form of literary production recited orally from generation to generation reflected the power of a rich oral tradition. Settled life in Palestine and spread in the use of a flexible alphabet and of writing enabled writers to capture and preserve poetry in the form of quotations in books of prose. The work of J was the first comprehensive history ever written and reflected the interest of a powerful mind which thought of history as the working out of the purpose of God, but the religious objective of the narratives was often transcended by delight in the story and the skill of handling it. Hebrew has been described as the only Semitic language before Arabic to produce an important literature characterized by simplicity, vigour, and lyric force. With other Semitic languages it was admirably adapted to the vivid, vigorous description of concrete objects and events. Poor in abstracts, they abounded in synonyms with fine shades of meaning for deeds and things and provided the vocabulary of the poet rather than the philosopher. Though vivid, ingenious simile was hampered by monotony and over-elaboration of detail, Patrick Carleton[27] has described the victory of the Semitic group of languages as carrying the imposition of a mental outlook and a way of thinking that had greater influence than that of Greece and Rome.

About 750 BC Elohist in the work of E emphasized the theocratic point of view and made the history of Israel more definitely a vehicle for his religious ideas. King and people were warned to be loyal to Jahweh. Monarchy was regarded as inherently wicked. The influence of theocracy was offset in the latter part of the eighth century by the emergence of literary prophets who attacked its limitations. Amos as the first exponent of ethical monotheism emphasized universal righteousness and justice to man and not gifts to God. From 745 to 735 BC Hosea attacked the local shrines and incurred the enmity of the priests. Isaiah flourished after 738 BC. After beginning as an orator and a man of affairs, because of opposition he became a writer, teaching faith in the holiness of God. The prophets held that divine power acted from self-imposed laws of righteousness tempered with mercy. Religion was transformed into the worship of one God, the creator and ruler of all things, the God of social justice, mercy, and finally love.

In 732 BC the Assyrians captured Damascus and in 721 BC Samaria. After 734 BC Israel became a vassal to Assyria and in 701 BC Judah was devastated. Under Manasseh (692-638 BC) Assyrian influence dominated politics and religion. Jerusalem[y] alone remained the single sanctuary and exercised its influence on centralization of worship and the unity of God. The work of J and E was combined. A compromise between prophetic and priestly views in a purified sacrificial system met the demands of a true social morality and whole-hearted worship. After the death of Ashurbanipal a movement for independence began in Judah and achieved success in 621 BC. A new law code gave religion an authoritative book and tended to create a religion of the book and a written tradition. The Deuteronomic code established a single sanctuary and the Pentateuch included the material provided in 621 BC. Where formerly a priestly oracle had been the final resort, Deuteronomy added a lay judge. The value of the individual with separate rights and obligations was recognized in criminal law. The work was permeated with a conscious didactic purpose and a spirit of expurgation in which the sagas of Semitic pagans were converted into monotheism. Foreign companion of Jahweh were expelled.

Collapse of the Assyrian empire led to new efforts of organization. In Babylonia Nebopolassar threw off the Assyrian yoke about 625 BC and was succeeded by Nebuchadnezzar, 605–562 BC. Jerusalem was captured in 587 BC, but Babylonian expansion was checked by the rise of the Medes and the Persians. The Medes were an Aryan people who migrated in the general movement to the Iranian plateau and the Hindu peninsula before the end of the fifteenth and fourteenth centuries. They emphasized patriarchal authority in the family and polygamy. Media had been ravaged by the Assyrians in 737 BC and Deioces (708–655 BC) attempted to unify the Medes in the interests of self-defence. After 632 BC Cyaxares built up an army on the Assyrian model and to 615 BC succeeded in pushing back an invasion of the Scythians. The Medes declined in importance after the fall of Nineveh and were defeated by Cyrus who had been named king of Ashan in 558 BC. The latter captured Sardis, capital of Lydia, in 546 BC and was named king of Persia. With the use of new weapons, such as the long bow and the long pike, the Persians achieved notable military success. As a result of the opposition of the priests to Nabonidus, who introduced new gods in Babylonia, Cyrus was consecrated king in 536 BC. He left the cult of Babylonian gods undisturbed and restored the statues to their owners in Babylon. In 529 BC Cambyses succeeded to the throne and in 525 BC added Egypt to the Persian empire.[28] He adopted the ceremonial, royal costume, and double cartouche of the Pharaohs but incurred religious hostility by his treatment of the priests. Darius I succeeded to the throne in 522 BC and in order to gain the support of the Egyptian priests reversed the policy of Cambyses. In 521 BC he gained more effective control over Babylonia. In 494 BC he encroached on the Greeks and captured Miletus.

Darius restored order throughout the empire and became a great oriental administrator. A system of communication was built up in which the horse played a dominant role. A road was built over a distance of 1,500 miles from Susa to Sardis and a system of posts to the capital established. The empire was divided into satrapies, each governed by a satrap, a military commander, and a secretary of state who acted independently of each other and received orders direct from the capital. Concentration of power in a single hand was thus avoided. The satraps and generals had no scribes and Babylonian civil servants were employed. The cuneiform script was taken over and reduced to thirty-six characters each with one value. This syllabary was adapted to the Indo-Persian language by scribes familiar with Aramaic. The Persian language was written in Aramaic characters and the Pahlavi or Parthian script was created.[29] The changes assumed the use of papyrus and the brush or of parchment and the pen. Croesus of Lydia had introduced precious metals as a medium of exchange and Darius followed his example in using gold coins on a large scale.

A single master, the Great King, dominated political and cultural life, and loyalty of the subjects to the reigning house[z] became the basis of empire. Imposition of the Achaemenid monarchy of Persia on the Babylonian and Egyptian empires implied a dominance of Aryans over Semitic peoples and it became necessary to give autonomy to alien nationalities within a military and tribute-collecting organization. In contrast with the Assyrians, who transported people in large numbers and carried off the plastic images of the gods of the conquered, the Persians recognized the significance of two separate religious centres in Babylonia and Egypt by a policy of toleration in which subject peoples were allowed to keep their religions. The Jews were released from captivity in Babylonia in 539 BC. Judah as a Persian province under tolerant rule became the centre of an independent and effective religious organization.

The position of the king in the Persian empire implied enormous demands on administrative capacity. Darius died in 485 BC and Xerxes his successor proved less competent. The complexity of the task of controlling powerful religious centres became more evident. Egypt revolted in 486 BC but was suppressed in 484 BC. Xerxes renounced his title "King of Babel" and removed the statue of Bel-Marduk from its temple. Insurrections followed in Babylon, probably in 484 and in 479 BC, but were quickly suppressed. The Persians were defeated by the Greeks at Marathon in 484 BC. Later kings were faced with continued difficulties in Egypt, which declared independence in 404 BC, but was reconquered in 342 BC.[aa] Conflicts with Greek city-states accentuated decline of the empire. The defeat of

Darius III by Alexander at Issus in 333 BC and at Arbela in 331 BC brought the Persian empire to an end. The Persian empire, like the Assyrian, failed to solve the problems of religion accentuated by a more flexible alphabet. Persian religion was unable to resist the influences of Babylonia. Ahura-Mazda, possibly the successor of the Assyrian Ashur, was the highest god who had created heaven and earth. About the seventh or sixth centuries Zarathustra carried out a revolution[bb] in favour of Ahura-Mazda, which purified worship and abolished blood sacrifices. The whole of creation was divided into the kingdom of darkness and the kingdom of light. The dualism of nature was projected into ethics in the division between good and evil. Revelation of a future life and judgment was developed as a substitute for miasma in the enforcement of moral laws. Every evil thought, word, and deed bound man to the kingdom of darkness. Mithraism was introduced to provide a doctrine of redemption. Common ancestors of Persians and Hindus celebrated the name of Mithra and in the later Vedic hymns of India and the *Avesta* of Persia he had similar characteristics, but Indians became more concerned with mystic absorption in the divine and Persians with the goal of practical duty free from antagonism to the world and human life. With the difficulties of divergent theological systems Ahura-Mazda established Mithra "to maintain and watch over all this moving world."[30] As an ever victorious warrior he enabled the Supreme Being to destroy all demons and to cause even Ahriman to tremble. He was introduced in the special religion of the kings at the end of the fifth century.[cc] A system of unified administration with peace and property and intercommunication between nations and tribes demanded a synthetic religious movement and favoured ceremonial religions. The religious conceptions of the Achaeminides took on a simpler form than those of Zoroastrianism.

Mazdean beliefs came under the influence of the erudite theology of the Chaldeans of Babylonia. In the eighth century the Babylonians adopted an exact system of chronology and began the measurement of time in the era of Nabonassar in 747 BC. Scientific

71

astronomy became possible and the periodic character of celestial phenomena was discovered and reduced to a numerical expression by which repetitions could be predicted. In recognizing the unchangeable character of celestial revolutions they imagined they had discovered laws of life. The influence of the stars was formulated in dogmas of absolute rigidity and a cosmic religion was based on science. Human activity and relations with astral divinities were brought into a general harmony of organized nature. During the short-lived restoration of the second Babylonian empire in the sixth century astral religion became established and acted as a powerful force in the dissolution of older beliefs.[31] The sacerdotal character of these conceptions laid the basis for a learned theology which had its influence on Persian religion in the addition of other deities, including Anahita or the planet Venus, and destroying the exclusive position of Ahura-Mazda.

In Persia speculative monotheism possibly became a starting-point for revealed religion, but the organization of an empire attempting to dominate Egypt and Babylonia prevented religion from becoming too strongly nationalized. The toleration of Persian rule and the advantage of a flexible alphabet on the other hand favoured an intensely nationalized form of religion as it was revealed or consciously constructed by priests of the Jewish theocratic state. The God of the universe was nationalized and not the national god universalized.[32] During the Babylonian captivity, after the fall of Jerusalem in 587 BC, Ezekiel subordinated the political state to the religious community and attempted to turn from intense nationalism to a more cosmopolitan personalism. Jeremiah had spiritualized religion and separated it from all outward institutions, even from the nation. It was discovered that religion could be practised in Babylonia as well as in Judah. The strong solidarity of society was broken into atoms. Life was composed of countless single acts. Contact with other religions, including Chaldean astrology during the captivity, possibly strengthened the concept of duality and of the devil, and a belief in immortality, but it accentuated the distinction of a culture which kept Israel apart from the world and preserved a moral standard and an ethical god. The unconditional omnipotence of God created the problem of evil.

After return from the exile, reaction favoured exclusive particularism. It has been suggested that the priests returned from Babylonia with the idea of a universal god and with no king or nobility arranged a compact with the people.[33] The temple became a rallying ground for the community. Music assisted in consolidation as psalms were sung by a temple choir. The Jewish ideal of direct government by God implied opposition to the deification of kings who were never recognized as divine by nature but were subject to law and threatened by the prophets if they disregarded it. A covenant god gave the prophets an enormous advantage over kings. Jahweh was a God not because of blood relationship but because of a definite agreement. Monopoly of the scriptures rigidly maintained by the priesthood strengthened the position of the prophet as a threat to the prestige of the king and a check to the abuse of absolute power.

The prophets of the seventh and sixth centuries reduced a multitude of gods to one and transformed Judaism by giving religion an ethical basis. With few abstract terms and without powers of rationalization the Judaism of antiquity produced no philosophers. Religion was made ethical by "a personal, direct, vivid vision." The great prophets conceived duty as righteous and made righteousness the most effective way of gaining the favour of God. Spirit and conduct rather than cult was emphasized. Righteousness alone could save people. The conception of a supreme god was expressed in terms of spiritual power and the ethical content of the monotheistic view of divine government of the universe. The pentateuchal works breathed the spirit of ethical monotheism and with the historical books emphasized absolute obedience. In the fifth century, under the influence of Ezra and Nehemiah, religion was purified and the law was revised. The teaching of the prophets was an intensified form of group morality. Israel remained a group united by blood relationship but with an ethical code imposed by a covenant God and entered on a spiritual mission.

The universal demands of the covenant put special emphasis on ceremonials of attainment. The prophets emphasized morality and the priests ritual holiness. The age of Deuteronomists was followed by the age of priests. The document P with its chief interest in the temple, showed how religion could be practised without sacrifices. The Priests' code[dd] was probably completed about 500 BC and became the norm of Jewish life after 444 BC. A theocratic organization strengthened ritual.[34] Religion became the sole cause of all history and historical narratives a device for religious education. History illuminated the truths of religion and was used to teach the origin and sanctity of various writers and institutions. Political and economic forces were subordinated. The Priests' code with the heavy economic burdens of a cultic system left no place for a king. With these tendencies Hebrew ceased as a spoken language about 400 BC and became the language of religion and of the schools. The priests were concerned with the interpretation of the scriptures in a sacred language. The growth of exclusiveness in turn brought conflict with the Persian empire and illustrated again the problem of religion and empires.

4 — THE ORAL TRADITION AND GREEK CIVILIZATION

A flexible alphabet contributed to the spread of Aramaic, of Phoenician, and of Hebrew. It facilitated the development of effective expression in literature in Indo-European languages. In part it was responsible for the rise and fall of the Persian empire. The problems of later political empires in the West followed its adaptability to languages.

In adaptation to the demands of new languages, script was conventionalized into the alphabet. Trade followed a conventionalized alphabet suited to the demands of large areas dominated by armed force supported by technological advances in improved breeds of horses, and the use of bronze and iron. Religion became conventionalized and monotheistic following adaptation of animistic religions dependent on agriculture. Finally, political organization became conventionalized as empires were compelled to recognize the religions of diverse centres. Conventionalization of script, religion, and political organization in Asia and Africa facilitated transmission across the Mediterranean to Europe. Separated from earlier civilizations by a body of water, the Greeks escaped their full cultural impact and adopted cultural features suited to their needs. The alphabet escaped from the implications of sacred writing. It lent itself to an efficient representation of sounds and enabled the Greeks to preserve intact a rich oral tradition. The ancient world troubled about sounds.

The concept of empire in Babylonia arose in part from a conflict between a civilization based on clay and the stylus and a civilization based on stone and the chisel. In the north the use of stone[a] in architecture, sculpture, and writing emphasized the importance of monarchy and centralized power. Religious organization in relation to the use of clay with an emphasis on time and continuity came into conflict with military organization in relation to the use of stone and technological advance represented by the use of iron and improved breeds of horses with an emphasis on space. Conflict between the Semitic king and Sumerian priest contributed to the growth of law evident in the work of Hammurabi. Religion became malleable and adapted to the demands of force. The gods were reduced to order and in turn laws dependent on the gods. An emphasis on military organization and space demanded uniformity of laws. Dominance of political organization over vast areas and control over religious organization facilitated the spread of writing and the use of the alphabet as a more efficient instrument. In turn the spread of Aramaic hastened the growth of trading cities and the development of trading oligarchies under the shelter of the Assyrian imperial structure. The monopoly power over writing exercised by religious institutions in Egypt and Babylonia was destroyed by the development of a new simplified type of writing which became the basis of new developments in communication and political organization shown in the Assyrian and the Persian empires. The development of political organization in relation to improved means of communication led to the growth of trade and trading cities as interstitial institutions between political and religious organizations and to the development of trading oligarchies such as emerged in Carthage. The problem of political organization was in part that of efficiency incidental to the mobility with which ability was attracted to administrative positions. In part such efficiency was dependent on the success with which writing linked the written to the spoken word. A breach between the written and the spoken word accompanied the growth of monopoly incidental to complexity of writing and invited invasion from regions in which such breaches were not in evidence and in which technological advance was unchecked. Invasion involved compromise with the conquered in which the language of the conquered becomes sacred and a centre of appeal to the conquered and in the use of which religious institutions tempered the influence of the conquerors. In turn the administrative bureaucracy of military conquerors becomes linked to the ecclesiastical hierarchy and monopolistic, the breach between the written and the spoken word is widened and invasion from new peoples is invited. The efficiency of the alphabet and its adaptability to languages provided a temporary means of escape in facilitating, on the one hand, the expansion and development of empires by the Assyrians and the Persians and the growth of trade under the Arameans and Phoenicians, and on the other hand the intensification of religion in Palestine. The power of religion based on monopolies of complex systems of writing implied an emphasis on continuity and time, but the alphabet facilitated the growth of political organizations which implied an emphasis on space. The commercial genius of the peoples of Syria and Palestine "borrowed what was essential in the Sumero-Acadian or Egyptian systems, and adapted it to their own urgent needs."[1] An alphabet became the basis of political organization through efficient control of territorial space and of religious organization through efficient control over time in the establishment of monotheism.

The task of understanding a culture built on the oral tradition is impossible to students steeped in the written tradition. The outlines of that culture can be dimly perceived in the written records of poetry and prose and in the tangible artefacts of the excavator. Recognition of its significance has been evident in the concern of scholars over centuries with interpretations of records.[2] But the similarity of the Greek alphabet to the modern alphabet and the integral relation of Greek civilization to Western civilization implies dependence on the complex art of introspection. Individuals in different ages and nations have looked into the pool of classical civilization and seen precise reproductions of themselves.[3] Renan wrote that "progress will eternally consist in developing what Greece conceived." Grote described the democratic tendencies of Grecian civilization and E.A. Freeman stated that "the democracy of Athens was the first great instance which the world ever saw of the substitution of law for force." More recently Marxian interpretation[4] has received its expected reward. The fundamental solipsism of Western civilization presents an almost insuperable barrier to objective interpretation of Greek culture.

Greek civilization was a reflection of the power of the spoken word. Socrates in *Phaedrus* reports a conversation between the Egyptian god Thoth, the inventor of letters, and the god Amon in which the latter remarked that

> this discovery of yours will create forgetfulness in the learners' souls, because they will not use their memories; they will trust to the external written characters and not remember of themselves. The specific you have discovered is an aid not to memory, but to reminiscence, and you give your disciples not truth but only the semblance of truth; they will be hearers of many things and will have learned nothing; they will appear to be omniscient and will generally know nothing; they will be tiresome company, having the show of wisdom without the reality.

Socrates continues:

> I cannot help feeling, Phaedrus, that writing is unfortunately like painting; for the creations of the painter have the attitude of life, and yet if you ask them a question, they preserve a solemn silence, and the same may be said of speeches. You would imagine that they had intelligence, but if you want to know anything and put a question to one of them, the speaker always gives one unvarying answer.

He continued with a plea for a better kind of word or speech and one having far greater power. "I mean an intelligent word graven in the soul of the learner which can defend itself, and knows when to speak and when to be silent."

The character of Socrates worked through the spoken word. He knew that "the letter is destined to kill much (though not all) of the life that the spirit has given."[5] He was the last great product and exponent of the oral tradition. Plato attempted to adapt the new medium of prose to an elaboration of the conversation of Socrates by the dialogue with its question and answer, freedom of arrangement, and inclusiveness. A well-planned conversation was aimed at discovering truth and awakening the interest and sympathy of the reader. The dialogues were developed as a most effective instrument for preserving power of the spoken word on the written page and Plato's success was written in the inconclusiveness and immortality of his work. His style was regarded by Aristotle as half-way between poetry and prose. The power of the oral tradition persisted in his prose in the absence of a closely ordered system. Continuous philosophical discussion aimed at truth. The life and movement of dialectic opposed the establishment of a finished system of dogma. He would not surrender his freedom to his own books and refused to be bound by what he had written. "The Platonic dialogue was as it were the boat in which the shipwrecked ancient poetry saved herself together with all her children" (Nietzsche). Plato attacked the pedagogical value of poetry[b] and of Homer by pointing to the contrast between philosophy and poetry, truth and sham, and expelled poets from the state. The medium of prose was developed in defence of a new culture. In opposition to the highest authority of the gods and the poets and with no examples to which he could appeal he worked out a new position through the use of dialogues, allegories, and illustrations. His later work reflected the growing power of the written word and of prose.

In Aristotle the power of the spoken word declined sharply and became a source of confusion. The dialogue form was used but with an important change in which he made himself the interlocutor. In the main, literary activity was practically abandoned and the *Politics* appears to have been made up from notes of his lectures. Carefully integrated work written in more popular style and probably intended for publication was followed by treatises, which became a basis for teaching and lecturing. "The scientific spirit no longer feels itself bound to put itself under the protection of its elder sister the literary spirit."[6] Extension of the written tradition under the influence of Aristotle was evident in a movement to collect and preserve books which corresponded roughly with the founding of his school in 335 BC.[c] But neither Aristotle nor Plato appears to have regarded a library among the requirements of an ideal state.

The conquest of prose over poetry assumed a fundamental change in Greek civilization. The spread of writing destroyed a civilization based on the oral tradition, but the power of the oral tradition as reflected in the culture of Greece has continued throughout the history of the West, particularly at periods when the dead hand of the written tradition threatened to destroy the spirit of Western man.

Plato and Aristotle wrote in a period after the great tragedy of the oral tradition had been witnessed in the fall of Athens and the execution of Socrates. These were symptoms of the collapse of a culture and of the necessity of starting from a new base that emphasized a medium other than poetry. "The earlier the language the richer it is — masterpieces only make their appearance when it is already in its decline" (Burckhardt). Plato and Aristotle had no alternative but to search for the basis of another culture in the written tradition. After Aristotle "the Greek world passed from oral instruction to the habit of reading."

In contrast with the Aryans in Asia Minor the Greeks were less exposed to the influence of those whom they had conquered. Minoan civilization with its maritime empire had escaped the full impact of continental civilizations and in turn was less able to impose its culture on the immigrants of the northern mainland. The complexity of the script of Minoan civilization and its relative restriction to Crete left the Greeks free to develop their own traditions. Successive waves of Greek immigrants checked the possibility of conservative adaptation of cultural traits. The existence of a powerful court and later of a number of feudal courts favoured the growth of an oral tradition and resistance to complete acceptance of other cultures. The Greeks took over the conventional Phoenician Semitic consonantal alphabet and the Cypriote syllabary[d] and adapted them to the demands of a rich oral tradition possibly as late as the beginning of the seventh century.[7] The Greek archaic alphabet was not cursive in form but of the type used by Phoenicians about the middle of the ninth century. The earliest Greek inscriptions dated from about the middle of the eighth century and writing was used for public inscriptions from about the seventh century. An alphabet of twenty-four letters which represented consonants to Semitic peoples proved exportable and adaptable to Greek demands. A different language structure and systems of sounds led the Greeks to use Semitic consonantal characters, which were useless to their language, as vowels which were indispensable to them. Since vowels were of equal value with consonants, they had to be represented in each written word. They permitted the expression of fine distinctions and light shades of meaning. The Greek language "responds with happy elasticity to every demand of the Greek intellect ... the earliest work of art created by the spontaneous working of the Greek mind."[8] Woolner described the change as one of the greatest triumphs of the human intellect.

The power of the oral tradition implied the creation of a structure suited to its needs. Minstrels developed epic poems in hexameter which involved rigidities but permitted elasticities facilitating adaptation to the demands of vernacular speech. Epic technique involved the use of a particular language with forms, words, and stock expressions bound up with the metre. Epic poetry apparently began before the Dorian invasion and after the breakup of the Achaeans was preserved by their northern branch, the Aeolians, and carried by them to the Ionians in Asia Minor. A traditional epic language was built up first in the Aeolian dialect and secondly in the Ionic dialect. Ionian minstrels took over the Aeolian epic and developed their own epic language. The Homeric poems appeared in the Ionian language with a substantial mixture of archaic forms appropriate to epic style in Aeolic which were retained particularly because of their adaptability to versification. The fixed epithet was used repeatedly because of its metrical convenience. A noun epithet of a certain metrical value was used as a convenient expression to the exclusion of all other formulae by generations of singers. Stock expressions and phrases persisted as aids. Audiences regarded the ornamental gloss as an element of heroic style.[9]

Nilsson describes the epic style as a conventionalized outcome of a long evolution extending from the thirteenth and twelfth to the ninth and eighth centuries. The great epics were probably developed out of lays constantly retold and amplified. Old ballads were replaced by combinations of a number of episodes into a unity of action. The epic was characterized by extreme complexity and unity. In the early stages epic songs accompanied the dance. Singing was accompanied by the lyre and the melody helped to fix the metre which was always the same. A highly specialized skill meant that epic poetry was in the hands of those with excellent memories and poetical and linguistic abilities. The art of singing was attached to certain families, members of which learned the poetical art. The singer improvised to meet the demands of epic technique and while language became archaic it was rejuvenated by poets using the language of the age. In the *Odyssey* court minstrels were more conspicuous than in the *Iliad* and a profession probably developed with an interest in fixed chants. Professional story-tellers probably built up a system of signs, which were privately owned and carefully guarded for purposes of recitation. The disciple was required to show a capacity to handle and to use his master's book. Nilsson suggests that a great poet probably formed a school which brought the Greek epics to a point excelling all others.[10]

The Homeridae[e] became a profession of minstrels who, to please an audience, were required constantly to reshape the Homeric poems to suit the needs of new generations.

Restrictions incidental to the adaptability of archaic language to versification and the concern of a profession with limited changes made the poems less responsive to the demands of ordinary speech.[11] Generations of poets intensified the imagination of the *Iliad*[12] and had a profound influence on the literature of Greece and Europe. Under the influence of a profession the *Odyssey* reflected a changed, decentralized society with restrictions on royal prerogatives.

The Homeric poems of the Heroic age were produced in a society in which the ties of kindred were weakening and the bond of allegiance was growing. An irresponsible kingship resting on military prestige held together kingdoms with no national basis. Tribal cults were subordinated to the worship of a number of universally recognized and anthropomorphic deities. Society was largely free of restraint. Tribal law had ceased to maintain its force and the individual was free from obligations to kindred and community. Over a long period the courts had appropriated the culture, wealth, and luxury of earlier civilizations and the influence of a civilized people was stamped on a semi-civilized people.[13] An aristocratic civilization assumed a fixed residence, ownership of land, respect for "good breeding," and a high social position for women. Justice and right dealing were the all-important principles by which prince and peasant were equally bound.[14]

The epic had grown and declined with monarchy. The place of the epic in an aristocratic society assumed that mastery of words meant intellectual sovereignty. But the limited size of the epics, determined by the demands of an oral tradition, while permitting constant adaptation and improvement, assumed relative inflexibility and compelled the emergence of completely new content to describe conditions of marked change. In contrast with Hebrew books in which old and new elements were pieced together by scribes and in which the large size of the scriptures and their sacred and holy character checked the possibility of new developments, the oral tradition under the control of minstrels necessitated new developments. Popular poetry appeared in the form and style of language of the Homeric poems. Before the end of the eighth century Hesiod produced poetry in the heroic hexameter which in content was in sharp contrast with the Homeric poems. The adaptability of the oral tradition was shown in a production by an individual who made no attempt to conceal his personality and in which no interest was shown in court life or in the avoidance of indelicate subjects. In contrast with the place of woman in the chivalry of Homer, she had become the root of all evil.

Following the break of the individual from the minstrel tradition evident in Hesiod, the oral tradition became more flexible, poems were shorter, and responses to new demands were more effective. The change from kingdoms to republics in the eighth and seventh centuries was reflected in the development of an original style of poetry in the elegaic and the iambic. The iambic poetry of Archilochos (about 740–670 BC) responded to the demands of a more important public opinion and contributed powerfully to the breaking down of the heroic code in the latter half of the seventh century. He used a literary language slightly different from the Asiatic Ionic and his influence was reflected in its acceptance in Athens in the seventh century.

Music was an integral part of the oral tradition and accentuated its flexibility. The lyre was used to accompany epic poetry and was the chief instrument of the Apollonian cult. Song was united to poetry. The Aeolians centring at Lesbos made important contributions in its improvement and gave it a prominent place in the development of lyric poetry. In lyrics the oral tradition was extended to express the feelings of women. Sappho, in the words of Jaeger, explored the last recesses of personal emotion.

The appearance of a large number of short personal lyrics in the late seventh and sixth centuries has been held to coincide with the spread of writing and an increase in the use of papyrus. The position of professional minstrels was weakened as literature was propagated and perpetuated by the increase in writing. Decline of Phoenicia had been followed by expansion of Greece. An increase in foreign and domestic trade, particularly

after the introduction of coined money from Lydia, accompanied the decline of an aristocratic society. Changes in social, economic, and political conditions demanded fresh response in
literature and provided material by which the response could be
made. In 670 BC Egyptian ports were opened to Greek trade and
after 660 BC Greeks were given permission to go anywhere in
Egypt in recognition of their services as mercenaries in the war
against Assyria. In about 650 BC a Greek settlement was founded at Naucratis. Greek expansion continued after the capture of
Tyre by Nebuchadnezzar in 574 BC but was checked by the
arrival of the Persians in Egypt in 525 BC. The availability of
papyrus favoured the spread of writing but difficulties in obtain-
ing it delayed encroachment on the oral tradition.

New types of literature reflected the efficiency of the oral
tradition in expressing the needs of social change. It permitted a
changing perspective as to the place of older types of literature.
In the Homeric poems the sacred myths were taken over from
earlier civilizations, humanized and incorporated in heroic
mythology. The gods became anthropomorphic deities. Magical
rites were adopted into a worship of gods but their magical
character with belief in power or mana which pervaded everything was pushed into the background. Migratory people had
left their local gods behind or subordinated them to the place of
retainers and followers in a hierarchical structure of great deities
in which Zeus held the first place. The old nature gods were
unable to meet new demands. Deities of universal significance
were built up to express the higher functions of life and myths
were transformed to influence the conduct of men.
Anthropomorphism and the absence of magic and limitations
on the power of the gods assumed rationalism and the necessity
of finding order and coherence in the world. "The Greek view
of the relation of men to the gods was mechanical." Decline of
belief in the supernatural led to the explanation of nature in
terms of natural causes. With the independent search for truth,
science was separated from myth. "By his religion man has been
made at home in the world." The minstrels were followed by the

rhapsodists and in turn by the Ionian philosopher. The latter built up where the former pulled down.[15]

In contrast with the Hebrew phrase[16] "and God said" repeated at every new creative act of Jahweh and implying the creative word or *Logos* standing at the head of a series of creative acts, the Greeks placed Eros at the head of the procreative series.

> The Logos[g] is a substantialization of an intellectual property or power of God, the creator, who is stationed outside the world and brings the world into existence by his own personal fiat. The Greek gods are stationed inside the world; they are descended from Heaven and Earth, the two greatest and most exalted parts of the universe; and they are generated acts by the mighty power of Eros, who likewise belongs within the world as an all-engendering primitive force.[17]

In the expansion of maritime trade Ionian cities, notably Miletus, occupied an important place. A common language emerged to meet the demands of merchants and navigators. The Ionians were the first to create a literary language not peculiar to the city. The epic poems as creations of the Panhellenic spirit gave a consciousness of nationality and the epic language became a common bond overriding numerous dialects and preparing the way for the acceptance of the Ionic alphabet and the Attic dialect. With a written language differences in dialects were further weakened.

Navigation implied an intensive concern with nature in sea, air, and land. Thales of Miletus (640–546 BC) as a merchant and probably interested in architecture and agriculture seized on the possibilities of mathematics. He is said to have discovered trigonometry by measuring the distances of ships at sea from land. An interest in geometry followed acquaintance with land measurement in Egypt. Study of astronomy with its importance to navigation enabled him to master Babylonian contributions and to predict an eclipse of 28 May 585 BC. But whereas in

Egypt mathematics like ethics and medicine had been developed empirically and stopped short of philosophy, it became to Thales a means of discarding allegory and myth and advancing universal generalizations. He concluded that the nature of things is water, and that the all is alive and full of daemons or gods. Opposition was evoked in Anaximander[h] (about 611–547 BC), a cartographer, who sought for a more general conception unlimited by qualities. Geometry was used to develop a conception of the earth and of the universe. An idea of the cosmos implied a break with current religious beliefs and a revelation that Being was divine. Only in eternal Being could eternal Becoming have its origin. By abstraction Anaximander drew a line of distinction between supersensible soul substance and sensible embodiments. Primary *physis* was distinguished from visible elements. It is significant that he was the first to write down his thoughts in prose[18] and to publish them, thus definitely addressing the public and giving up the privacy of his thought. The use of prose reflected a revolutionary break, an appeal to rational authority and the influence of the logic of writing.

Milesian philosophers began by clearing away the overgrowth to discover a fundamental conceptual framework. They attacked problems which had been emphasized in religious and popular representation. Social custom, structure, and institutions lay behind religion and religion behind philosophy. The Olympian tradition drew a fast line between men and gods, and human society and the rest of nature. The notion of a system of *moira* each filled by a specific living force, shaping itself into spirits, gods, and human souls with clearness of conception and imagery left its stamp on philosophy. In philosophy influenced by *moira* the world was pluralistic, rationalistic, fatalistic, opposed to other-worldliness,[19] and distributed into spatial provinces. Nature was a substance which was also soul and god and the living stuff from which daemons, gods, and souls took shape. Philosophers speculated about the nature of things or *physis*, an animate and divine substance, and emphasized likeness, kinship, material continuity with the result that their notion of causality was static, simultaneous, and spatial. Under the shadow of *moira* and geometry the science of nature became concerned with the thing in itself and its internal properties rather than its behaviour towards other things. Science found its ideal in geometry, the science of space measurement, and was concerned with the static aspect of structure, arrangement, and order.

The discovery of nature has been described as one of the greatest achievements of the human mind since it was the basis of the idea of universal law. It assumed the detachment of self from the external object, the concern of intelligence with the practical needs of action in dealing with the object, and a belief in unseen supernatural powers behind or within the object. Separated from theology, science denied the distinction between experience and revelation, the natural and the supernatural.

The strength of the oral tradition and the relative simplicity of the alphabet checked the possible development of a highly specialized profession of scribes and the growth of a monopoly of the priesthood over education. A military aristocracy restricted the influence of a priestly class and poets imposed control over public opinion. The Greeks had no Bible with a sacred literature attempting to give reasons and coherence to the scheme of things, making dogmatic assertions and strangling science in infancy. Without a sacred book and a powerful priesthood the ties of religion were weakened and rational philosophy was developed by the ablest minds to answer the demand for generalizations acceptable to everyone. "The Hebrews made philosophy the handmaid of religion and the Greeks subordinated religion to philosophy." The oral tradition facilitated and encouraged the introduction of a new medium such as mathematics. Humanizing of the gods and absence of a belief in a divine creator freed thought from dogmatic prejudice and the terrors of religion.[20] It permitted a gradual transition in which philosophy with its coherent structures could develop in undisturbed freedom and appeal to the lay mind. In turn "it was not so much the absence of a priesthood as the existence of the scientific schools that saved Greece" (Burnet). No energy was lost in learning a second language and the freshness and elasticity of an oral tradition left their stamp on thought and literature.

As an alternative to trade, colonization flourished from about 750 BC to 550 BC and was accompanied by the establishment of new city-states. Colonial activity has been described as the highest political achievement of the Greeks. The Delphic oracle became a centre of advice for colonizers and new city-states grew up under the protection of Apollo. Difficulties of land subdivision in a system of property which excluded individual members from a share in the common estate were evaded by colonization. The example of personal land ownership in the colonies probably weakened the family system in the mother country. "Freedom flourishes in colonies. Ancient usages cannot be preserved ... as at home ... Where every man lives on the labour of his hands, equality arises, even where it did not originally exist" (Heeren).[21]

The city-state was founded for purposes of security and emerged in a period of violent dissolution of public order. "It is significant that it was from the common bond of mutual defence and the maintenance of a common camp of refuge, in an age of violence, that the Greek city-state and its citizens took their eventual nomenclature."[22] Consequently the Greeks were not obsessed like the Phoenicians with the "unquiet spirit of gain."[23] Athletic and musical competitions at festivals of the gods created a sense of community in the city-state. An interest in a common literature strengthened the bond of language which was reinforced by the initiation of the Olympic games in 776 BC. "Political science, ignored by the Phoenicians, became to the Greeks the highest of the practical sciences, the science of man, not as a trader but as a man, fulfilling his function as a member of the social organism and living with the fullness of life."[24]

The shift from the heroic kingship to an aristocratic form of government was apparently accompanied by a change from the voluntary to the obligatory. In the early aristocracy magistrates administered the unwritten customary law. "In the absence of a written code, those who declare and interpret laws may be properly said to make them" (Thirlwall). Supervision over the laws was exercised by the hearing of formal complaints against the judges. About the middle of the seventh century individuals were appointed in Athens to manage the judicial system, to keep official copies of pubic enactments, and to review legislation annually. Three pairs of two recorders each made up the first collegiate magistracy to have custody over public records and to revise the laws. Recorders were appointed in pairs to secure an accurate copy. In Solon's time nine archons, including the recorders and three principal officers, had the general initiative in legislation. With the use of writing the judicial order became a public document, definite and ascertainable. Records were not published at first, but with an interest in writing for publication the number of those who could read increased rapidly.[25] The laws of Draco and Solon were written on *stelae* of wood or stone and laws were regularly recorded on the walls of a public building or on separate *stelae* in a public place. Immediate publication was probably well established in the generation after Draco.

The demand for codes of law which appeared first in the colonies in south Italy, Sicily, and parts of Greece in the seventh century followed the complexities of different systems of customary law introduced by colonists from various city-states and the spread of writing. The influence of Delphi and its sanctions of compilations of law reinforced the emphasis of writing on uniformity.[26] The example of written laws in the colonies was probably followed by demands for written laws in the mother country, but here they became a compromise with a strong oral tradition. In his code of 621 BC Draco, a Eupatrid, modified and developed existing law in reducing it to writing. Dictated by "implacable religion" it was very severe regarding debtors, although the severity was checked by a constitutional change which guaranteed an individual the right to appear before the Areopagus and to prosecute the magistrate who had wronged him.

The strength of the oral tradition in Athens was evident in the slow development of codes, in the position of magistrates who continued to exercise judicial functions, in a constitutional system which permitted protests against grievances, and in the powers granted to individual law makers in periods of difficulty. In about 594 BC Solon,[i] a Eupatrid by birth and a member of the trading class, was given extraordinary powers to introduce reforms suited to a community in which industry and commerce had become important. Following the pattern of Ionian scientific ideas, he developed the universal truth that violation of justice meant disruption of the life of the community. "*Any* act of injustice, impairing the *common* security, threatens everyone's *individual* security — and family solidarity can interpose no effective protection."[27] Every citizen was allowed to act for the community as a protection to the community. Individual vengeance was being replaced by social retribution. There emerged the idea of individual responsibility for one's own fault which struck at the root of authority and pointed to the idea of the necessity of compromise and order.

The family was weakened by various changes. Asiatic pomp with women's lamentations at funerals of the Ionian nobility was prohibited. Introduction of the will enabled the head to name an heir outside the family. Brothers could share in the patrimony and women could enjoy rights of inheritance though they were inferior to those of men. The legal inalienability of the family estate had led to the invention of a special type of pledge involving a sale with the option of redemption. *Horoi* or ward stones were specially engraved and erected on the property to indicate the control of the creditor and the rights of the occupant. The difficulties of a primitive law of debt resting on personal security were enhanced by an aristocracy that controlled wealth and the administration of justice. Solon abrogated the institution of personal security and destroyed the *horoi* or ward stones. The oral tradition effectively resisted the encroachments of the word engraved on stone. Prohibition of the practice of pledging the person for debt prevented enslavement of labour becoming a disruptive force and became the salvation of political freedom. The religion of property was weakened by wresting the earth from religion and facilitating ownership by labour. An attempt was made to reconcile the liberty of the labourer with the drudgery of labour. Commerce was adapted to politics and pursued with a new ideal and more worthy ends than with Phoenicians. The principle of personal freedom was established as the inalienable birthright of the Athenian citizen.[28] "These things I wrought by main strength, fashioning that blend of force and justice that is law" (Solon).

The power of the oral tradition was reflected in the institution of machinery designed to permit continuous adjustment. "The constitution of the judicial courts out of the whole people was the secret of democracy which Solon discovered. It is his title to fame in the history of the growth of popular government in Europe."[29] The council of Areopagus surrendered its claims of right of birth and membership in it was fixed in terms of landed property. The Eupatrids no longer dominated and archons could even be elected outside the priestly class. While the working class was excluded from the Areopagus the popular assembly was revised to give it a voice in the government. The constitution was designed to preserve a balance by preventing either party from securing control. The people were given enough power to maintain their rights and to uphold the reign of law. Freedom of prosecution and appeals from magisterial decisions to the popular assembly were given to all citizens. Anyone could intervene on behalf of those being wronged by appeal to the populace. A record of all decisions in both public and private suits was made and a body of case law built up. Regular written records were produced by the men of initiative.

Solon's economic reforms favoured the position of the Greek merchant by hastening the transition from a barter to a money economy and by encouraging the "long future" production of wine and olives rather than the "short future" production of cereals of special interest to the nobles. In order to build up industry, exports of natural products other than olive oil were prohibited and training in crafts made almost compulsory. Exports of olive oil and pottery supported an aristocracy of wealth. Family estates were broken up into private domains and labour migrated to the cities. The increased use of coinage enabled merchants of Phrygia and Lydia to exploit gold- and silver-mines. With greater opportunity to manage their own affairs individuals became more independent. Money permeated social relations and encouraged political and economic freedom. Sales, bequests, keeping of accounts and registrations of contracts and treaties followed the spread of writing. A commercial class opposed landowners and the nobility and supported individualism and the rise of tyrants. "In every Greek there was a hidden tyrant" (Burckhardt). Party struggles broke out as early as the fifth year after the archonship of Solon, and in 561–560 BC Peisistratos, who had become wealthy as a result of his organization of the mining population, seized the government of Athens. With no religious functions the tyrants could not be kings, but they exploited antagonism to the nobles and the rich. To offset the position of religion as a support to the political privileges of the old nobility, the Peisistratids gave official recognition to the worship of Dionysus. In 537 BC they assembled a collection of oracles in opposition to the influence of the temple of Delphi. The importance of the arts as a basis of popularity was recognized, the temple of Athena Polias[k] was completed, and the Panathenaia was reorganized as a great national festival and public recitals of Homeric poems given by Ionian minstrels. "Their court was the source of the inexhaustible stream of poetry and art which flowed for centuries through the symposia of Athens."[30] Through the intervention of Sparta the tyrants were overthrown in 510 BC.

The limitations of Ionian philosophy as a basis of political science were evident in the success of the tyrants. Destruction of the authority of tradition and myth and release of the individual left Ionians without the constructive political energy to form a permanent and historically active state (Jaeger). Political impotence paralleled the work of the natural philosophers. Olympian theology dominated by *moira* and the scientific tradition dominated by the concept of spatial externality reflected an interest in land, land measurement, and geometry. Expansion of trade implied an increasing interest in arithmetic rather than geometry. As a result the mystery religions and the mystical tradition of philosophy emerged to redress the balance. *Moira* was replaced by Time and number (the measure of time) and by righteousness (*Dike*). As a typical mystery god, Dionysus was fundamentally a human daemon. As a wandering deity he was not a fixed part of an official state religion but had a church of trans-social organization. Outside the Olympian polity he became the god of his church defined precisely by a unique relation to the daemon soul. His worshippers would have only one god. The characteristic rite was sacramental — an act of communion and reunion with the daemon, whereas that of worshippers of the Olympian god was commercial in the form of a gift or a bribe. Olympian theology and the philosophy of spatial externality emphasized discontinuity and discreteness, whereas the mystic religion held out a prospect of union with God. As a religion of the life of earth and man, of the life which dies but is perpetually reborn, Dionysian worship had a secret of vitality which offset Olympianism with its divine jealousies and the impassable gulf of *moira*.

The new religion was compelled to make compromises with the old, which eventually left it stereotyped and sterile. It was reformed and modified by the Orphic revival which was probably influenced by Mithraism and spread from the country to the city in response to the demands of those who had been forced off the land. Belief that the soul came from God and did not perish implied that it must be kept pure during its earthly existence. The Orphic was concerned with salvation by the purifying rites of his individual soul. Religious observances were designed to secure by purifications the ransom of the soul from the punishment of imprisonment in successive bodies. Belief in the transmigration of souls assumed the corollary of abstinence from animal flesh and disappearance of the blood sacrifice. Barriers between gods and men were overcome by a mysterious means of purification which removed defilements of the soul, raised mankind to the level of the divine, and assured an immortality of bliss. In its demand for justice for the individual it included the fatal conception of a lower world as a place of punishment for the prosperous and unjust. Orphism had the "incontestable originality" of combining religions into a system and making the individual in relation to guilt and retribution the centre of its teaching. It offset the influence of the temples of the seventh century by an emphasis on sacred literature, but it was weakened by the absence of a church.

Pythagoreanism attempted to intellectualize the content of Orphism. A native of Samos, Pythagoras migrated to southern Italy about 530 BC. From a commercial centre he became familiar with the importance of a theory of numbers in calculating sums of money. In contrast with the rigid geometrical symmetry of the cosmos developed by Anaximander in the east, number was the principle of all things. "Things are numbers." A background of geometry and land was replaced by one of arithmetic and money. Pythagoras saw the importance of number as an aid to the reconstruction of any representation of the conditions involved in the order of nature.[31] He gave absolute forms a substantial reality separate from things that embody them in one world. An interest in mathematics was reinforced by the discovery that musical intervals corresponded to certain arithmetical ratios between lengths of string at the same tension, the relation between the four fixed notes[j] of the octave 6–8–9–12. A music philosophy was substituted for the mere ritual washing away of sin of Orphism. Purity was extended from a ritual notion to the moral sphere. Pythagoreanism became the basis for a cult of the *élite* rather than the masses, and communities appeared in southern Italy and Sicily.

As a result of Orphism and Pythagoreanism a reconciliation of Dionysian religion with Apollo became possible. The form of ecstasies which centred around Dionysus was regulated and orgies were restricted to official communities. The cult was brought into line with ancestral customs. The Delphic oracle had no sacred book and with its maxims "know thyself" and "nothing overmuch" has been compared to a serious newspaper managed by a cautious editorial committee with no principles in particular. With a powerful oral tradition it overpowered the dangers of extreme organized religious frenzies. Ritual purification became a support to the state by giving definite form to the fear of a dead man's vengeance, heightening respect for human life, and discouraging the practice of vendetta.

The influence of Apollo on the mystic religions paralleled the decline and fall of the tyrants. Cleisthenes became engaged over an extended period in the task of restoring popular government and in developing a constitution which would facilitate adaptation of law to social change. To temper the bitterness of party strife ostracism was introduced in 508–507 BC. Opposition leaders were eliminated for a limited period without dishonour or the loss of privileges of citizenship and property, and government was protected against party struggle and betrayal. It became possible for Cleisthenes[32] in his fight against his fellow nobles to introduce reforms in 503–502 BC which gave more direct means of self-expression and control of government to the people. The tyrants and Dionysian religion had pointed to the weakness of Solon's reforms as they reflected the influence of Ionian philosophy. The patriarchal system and the idea of consanguinity gave the great families of the nobility a privileged position in the cult and religion through their interpretation of sacral laws. The calendar of sacrifices and festivals of the religious cult based on the lunar year led to difficulties of cyclical regulation and to demands for the emancipation of time reckoning. Cleisthenes's reforms replaced the lunar calendar[33] by a solar calendar of 10 months of 36 or 37 days each arranged by secular authorities and linked to constitutional adjustments in which the number of tribes was increased to 10, from each of which 50 were elected by lot to serve in rotation on a monthly basis as a standing committee in a council of 500. Election by lot maintained a respect for the belief in the divine will as the basis of laws, and was a safeguard of equality of civic rights and equality before the law. The essential governing bodies became the council of 500 and the courts with their large popularly chosen juries. Divisive issues were transferred to a new forum and settled by reliance on public opinion rather than on force. A concept of the people in a democratic electoral system based on the territorial principle became the basis of the constitution. Aristocratic power was weakened by control over the measurement of time. The family state was broken down and its political and religious claims inherited by the new state. The Greeks seized on the spatial concept as developed by Ionian philosophers and on the temporal concept emphasized by mystical religions to construct a political society which stood the test of resistance to the Persian empire. The Greeks opposed the raising of gods and religion to an independent position dominating the state and brought to an end the threat of a theocratical and monarchical order. Miletus was captured by the Persians in 494 BC and Themistocles, as leader of the radical democrats and elected to the archonship in 493 BC, determined upon an increase in the size of the fleet. Commercial and maritime interests were attached to the cause of democracy. In contrast to the *hoplite* in the army who was in a position of relative wealth, the sailor was drawn from the poorer classes. Aristotle held that naval power was followed by mob rule. The Persians were defeated in 478 BC and a sense of common nationality was reinforced by security of access to new markets and to new sources of food and raw materials.

The reforms of Cleisthenes in weakening the influence of religion made it possible for citizens of other cities to be accepted in Athens. The bar to mixed marriages was removed with possible implications[34] in the advantages of new blood and a maximum of ability. The migration of Ionians of intelligence and daring, and representing a culture "in many ways the most wonderful phenomenon of Greek history" (Gilbert Murray), brought a profound stimulus to Athenian life. Ionian thinkers opposed the uncritical acceptance of popular ideologies and attempts were made to reconcile the static concepts of order and space with the dynamic concepts based on mythical religions. Heraclitus (about 540–475 BC) emphasized the latter with its principle of *Dike* or righteousness and contributed to the break-up of concepts of state absolutism. He denied being altogether and regarded all becoming as originating in a war of opposites. "I contemplate the becoming." The whole essence of actuality was activity and fire was introduced as a world-shaping force. Mind was introduced as a metaphysical fact beyond all differentiation and movement. Man was given a place as a completely cosmic being and the claim of wisdom to supremacy was justified by saying that it taught men in speech and action to follow the truth of nature and its divine law. True wisdom was found in language since it was an expression of common wisdom which is in all men and only partly obscured by false private opinions. The structure of man's speech was an embodiment of the structure of the world. *Logos* was recorded in speech and *physis* was a representation of social consciousness. "Do not listen to me but to the word and confess that all things are one." Philosophy was humanized. "I sought for myself." "Great learning does not teach insight."

Parmenides,[m] born about 539 BC, wrote in verse presumably to reach a wide audience. He used the didactic epic to show that thought reduced everything to a single uniform essence. Even the intellect itself was demolished and logic became a basic form for the separation of the world of truth from the world of opinion. Empedocles[n] (490–430 BC), a citizen of a Dorian state, as founder of the Sicilian school of medicine attempted to combine the mystic tradition with Ionian science by emphasizing complexity. He revived the elements of fire, air, earth, and water, and added two soul substances, love and strife, to develop the idea of being and the theory of a primal source of all becoming. Denial of monism strengthened the position of Anaxagoras (500–428 BC) who assumed chaos and mind with free will dependent only on itself for escape from chaos. From this he aimed at the principle of selfhood or personality. Leucippus and Democritus held that the universe was impenetrable and eternal but not continuous; a primary substance with a diversity of forms and infinite arrangement. In atomism *physis* lost its associations of growth and life. It provided for the concepts of staticism and change and became the background of cosmopolitan individualism.

Philosophy had its impact on larger numbers of the population. The work of Anaxagoras was in prose and made available in an inexpensive and widely read book.[35] Xenophanes used poetry and developed the *silloi* which was satirical in character. Poetry was recited and the rhapsode was held in high esteem. He attacked Homer as a source of errors and denied that gods had human forms.

> But if cattle and horses had hands and were able
> To paint with their hands and to fashion such pictures
>   as men do,
> Then horses would pattern the forms of the gods
>   after horses
> and cows after cattle, giving them just such a shape
> as those which they find in themselves

"Men imagine not only the forms of gods but their ways of life to be like their own" (Aristotle). In the words of Jaeger,[36] by his influence in the dissemination of philosophy he transfused philosophical ideas into the intellectual blood-stream of Greece. Xenophanes was the first to formulate religious universalism.

The Dionysian tradition had retreated in the face of restraints imposed by Delphi, legal reforms, and advance in philosophy, but it advanced from the courts of the tyrants to the artistic outburst of the fifth century. Stonecutting had been used in the publication of laws° and in the making of records as Greek epigraphy attests. Sculpture escaped from the traditions of imperialism in the East. Polytheism and the art of statuary based on it checked the development of a divine unity as a dogma. "The cause of myth and plastic art are really one" (Dill). After the defeat of the Persians, when the festival and the worship of Zeus became stronger bonds among the Greeks, Olympian victors became heroes of the first rank and were celebrated in statues. Sculpture ceased to be exclusively the handmaid of religion and emancipated itself from architecture. Pindar the Theban[p] (502–452 BC) wrote hymns celebrating the greatest moments in the lives of athletes and pointed to the advantages of the wide diffusion of the poem in contrast with the immobility of the statue. He has been called "the Homer of the Pythagorean school and captivated by the doctrine of migrations of the soul and its ordeal and chastisement in preparation for a future life emphasized the possibility of elevation to lofty spiritual rank in the form of a hero" (Dill). With Theognis, the Megarian, he was repelled by the social revolution inspired by Ionian cities and addressed his work to nobles by whom he was sponsored. Simonides went further and wrote odes for a fixed price and made independent sales of his work to the public. The price system had been extended and adapted to new demands.

The choral lyric as perfected by Pindar became a link between the epic and the drama. It has been described as the art form of the Dorian aristocracy as the drama became the expression of Athenian democracy. Tragedy, like the Dionysian ritual, had the essential function "through pity and fear to effect the purgation of such emotions" (Aristotle). Performances as a purge or purification renewed life. Tragedy was a rebirth of the myth. In development of the drama from the primitive chorus dancing around the altar of Dionysus, the dithyramb,[q] "a community of unconscious actors who mutually regard themselves as transformed among one another" (Nietzsche), was split. The mimetic element in which music dominated the words was suppressed. The reed pipe or aulos,[r] apparently taken over from earlier civilizations by the Ionians, became the chief instrument of the Dionysian cult and "the only and exclusive instrument of the theatre."[37] As the epics abandoned musical accompaniment, the style of dancing songs was liberated, so the freeing of the dithyramb from music enabled the leader who varied the drama and song of the chorus by recitations centring around the adventures of Dionysus, to become the actor.[38] The reciter became a separate person from the dancers. Not later than 472 BC Aeschylus added a second actor[s] and made possible dramatic action. The complete circle with the actor in the centre was changed to allow the spectators to occupy a half circle and the actor to turn towards a quarter circle. A third actor was added in the latter part of Aeschylus's career.ᵗ The epic spirit was combined to the dramatic form and since the whole story could not be treated in a single tragedy, three tragedies linked by a fable were used. Sophocles subordinated the choral to the dramatic element, employed three actors, and increased the chorus from twelve to fifteen. The trilogy became separate plays without a link.ᵘ

Aeschylus attempted a reconciliation between the old and the new gods of justice and followed the ideal of justifying God's ways to man. A hero could be "born in the new spirit of freedom." In the heroes of Sophocles the divine was blended with human character. To know oneself was to know man's powerlessness and to know the indestructible and conquering majesty of suffering humanity. Tragedy restored the power of embracing all human interests to Greek poetry.[39] It claimed the interest and participation of the entire people. The power of the oral tradition was at its height.

Euripides has been described by Nietzsche[40] as the destroyer of myth and the genius of music. He brought the spectator from the benches to the stage. In contrast with Sophoclean man, the man of Euripides triumphed over the fiercest onslaughts of faith. The collectivism of Aeschylus was replaced by individualism. Tragedy ceased to be the most expressive form and to reflect the profoundest significance of the myth. The audience had lost faith in social life and the power of the oral tradition began to wane. The rationalism of Euripides dominated the new comedy.[41] As the popular assembly became the constitutional organ of public opinion the dramatist became a sort of journalist influencing men by giving practical effect to their sentiments. Prepossessions were strengthened by being reflected in exaggerated form. The comedy of Aristophanesᵛ resembled vehement party journalism but was directed against persons or general principles and tendencies and not against measures.[42]

The impact of writing on the oral tradition became increasingly evident in the second half of the fifth century. Prose reflected the demands of the city-state and to some extent of philosophers. According to Jaeger the evolutionary expression of the ethos of the new state was prose. Written laws assumed the development of prose[w] in clear and universally valid sentences. Prose began with plain, accurate statements of public importance. Its development was hampered by the oral tradition in the Homeric epic pattern. In the sixth century it appeared in philosophy, genealogy, geography, and history, and its growth followed an interest in individuals and a concern with characters and stories. Literature was treated before history. Ionian writers treated the annals of cities and of peoples separately. At the beginning of the fifth century "Hecateus[x] of Miletus thus speaks, I write as I deem true, for the traditions of the Greeks seem to me manifold and laughable." An individual could use the "sacred majesty" of a book to express his views. Writing was beginning to destroy the bond of Greek life. In 470 BC Athens had no reading public, but by 430 BC Herodotus found it convenient to turn his recitations into book form. In the Athens of Pericles "reading was universally diffused" (Curtius), but prose literature developed largely after the beginning of the Peloponnesian War. In his talent for conversation and his concern in arousing the interest of an audience, Herodotus[y] stood at the fountain-head of European prose literature.

Intense literary creativeness on the highest scale and the culminating point in Greek literature in the fifth century corresponded with a very limited book production. Rhapsodies had been written down and circulated on manuscripts in the seventh century. Lyrics in the form of dialogue and action had grown out of the choral song and were followed by dramatic poetry. In the fifth century the *Iliad* and the *Odyssey* were given a separate privileged position in the public recitations of the Panathenaia. The earliest book trade was a result of the popularity of the Attic tragedy as was the first public library in 330 BC. By the time of Euripides[43] plays were widely read after the performance and it is significant that he was said to have been the first Greek to own a library. The demand for more efficient writing was probably evident in the change in writing. Following the Semites the Greeks began by writing from right to left, but they continued in a *boustrophedon* style and finally, by the end of the fifth century, wrote from left to right and generally reversed individual Semitic letters. The oral tradition left its impress in a demand for truthfulness and economy of words. Starting with facts they could not easily become victims of words.[44] The Attic dialect, a variety of Ionic, gradually replaced Ionic and became the dominant language.

The power of the oral tradition was reflected in political as in artistic developments. After the Persian wars national enthusiasm and strengthening of political authority led to the suppression of mysticism and individualistic religious cults and an emphasis on city and new cults. The city-state and religion became a unity. In Athens the prestige of the Areopagus had increased during the Persian wars, but its supremacy came to an end in 462 BC. In 450 BC[z] the citizen roll was drastically revised and large numbers were excluded and in 449 BC Pericles deprived the Areopagus still further of important powers. The state paid a small amount to citizens for each day's attendance as a juror or at meetings of the public assembly and an amount to permit every citizen to attend the theatre at public festivals. The courts were empanelled from a list of jurymen selected by lot and Athenians became interested in keeping down the number of those receiving payment. From one-half to one-third of the citizens were supported at public expense and became a class of rentiers living on returns from taxes on trade and resident aliens.

The effect of these changes was shown in the difficulties of the Athenian empire.[45] In 454 BC the centre of the Delian league was transferred from Delos to Athens, making the latter the treasury, mint, supreme court, and legal and commercial capital of eastern Hellas. Political and criminal cases were decided by regulations of general application laid down at Athens with the result that the courts suffered from congestion and juries were suspected of susceptibility to irrelevant pleas. The allies protested against oppressive features in judicial control and levying of tribute. Charges of

favouritism to democratic states were made by those less fortu-
nately placed. The peace of Callias (449 BC) recognized Athenian
claims to dominate the Aegean basin and Greek cities along the
coast as far as the eastern boundary of Lydia. The peace of 445 BC
reflected a vital need of inter-state co-operation and seemed to
mark the end of the principle of the autonomous self-sufficient
state. Following the great rebellion of 440 BC a general equilibrium existed between the surviving oligarchies supported by Sparta
and the democratic interests of the Athenian empire. But fourteen
years after a principle of conciliation had been adopted in 445 BC
an appeal was made to force.

The spread of writing contributed to the collapse of Greek
civilization by widening the gap between the city-states. In
Sparta the oral tradition and its emphasis on music persisted.
Only a few laws had been solemnly introduced and fixed in
writing and the legislation of Lycurgus persisted in the oral tradition. Citizens were subjected to an aristocratic military system.
Sparta[46] became the head and centre of oligarchy and Athens of
democracy. The institutions of Sparta carried the Greek capacity for law and discipline to its farthest point and those of Athens
the capacity for rich and spontaneous individual development.
The deeply rooted division between Ionian and Dorian Greeks
was reinforced by geography, dialect, and cultural development.
The long struggle of the Peloponnesian wars ended in the fall of
Athens in 404 BC. In turn Spartan supremacy declined after
defeat by the Thebans at Leuctra in 371 BC. Thebes declined after
362. Philip of Macedonia emphasized disunity by systematic
propaganda and after the battle of Chaeronea the Greek city-
states,[aa] with the exception of Rhodes, were subordinated to
him. Ancient empires had been absorbed in the problem of
international affairs, Greece in individual development.
Civilization was concerned with absorption of the two strands.

The powerful oral tradition of the Greeks and the flexibility
of the alphabet enabled them to resist the tendencies of empire
in the East towards absolute monarchism and theocracy. They
drove a wedge between the political empire concept with its

emphasis on space and the ecclesiastical empire concept with its emphasis on time and reduced them to the rational proportions of the city-state. The monopoly of complex systems of writing, which had been the basis of large-scale organizations of the East, was destroyed. The adaptability of the alphabet to language weakened the possibilities of uniformity and enhanced the problems of government with fatal results to large-scale political organization. But the destruction of concepts of absolutism assumed a new approach of rationalism, which was to change the concept of history in the West.

5 — THE WRITTEN TRADITION AND THE ROMAN EMPIRE

The achievements of a rich oral tradition in Greek civilization became the basis of Western culture. The power of Greek culture to awaken the special forces of each people by whom it was adopted and to lead them to develop shapes of their own has been described with particular reference to Rome.[1] The slumbering national forces were liberated to form a culture moulded by the interpenetration of native and Greek elements. Greek colonies in Italy and Sicily and Greek traders apparently introduced the alphabet in the early part of the seventh century, and it was developed into a Graeco-Etruscan script in the second half of the century.[2] In the sixth century the rule of tyrants in Greece was paralleled in Rome, and Greek gods were introduced by the Etruscans. The plastic cult image, the human representation of the deity, and the architecture of the cult-building reached Rome in their complete forms and took their place with equal rights with animal shapes set in nature. The Greek house of God in the Capitoline temple[a] was dedicated in 509 or 507 BC. The Sibylline books were introduced through the Etruscans, placed in the cella, and adopted in 499 BC. Authority was set up to guard them and at their bidding Greek cults, including Ceres,[b] Liber, and Libera, gods of the *plebs*, were introduced following a famine, and Demeter, Dionysios, and Kore introduced in 496 BC. Codification of the cults and a deliberate arrangement in the order of gods and festivals in the earliest calendar probably coincided with the spread of writing, and was carried out to mark the union of two separate settlements in the city of Rome under the direction of a king.

In the fifth and fourth centuries Rome took up a position of isolation in the face of Greek culture. The king was defeated and an aristocracy of patricians became the ruling class. The old principle that hereditary religion established the right of property was restored. Two annual officers, the praetors, later called consuls, replaced the king and the power of the Senate was increased. To meet the demands of the plebeians whose powers had been weakened by the defeat of the king a tribunate^c of two, later increased to ten, with immunity from arrest, was set up in 494 BC to protect them from the arbitrary authority of the consuls.

The *pontifices* assumed the sacred obligations of the king and as a privileged minority in a sacerdotal college monopolized the knowledge of unwritten laws. Equipped with trained memories a series of juristic oligarchies applied all the principles by which disputes were settled. The task of maintaining a body of law was met through the oral tradition by reference to rules of conduct, information, conclusions converted into slogans, axioms, and doggerel verse. Authority was strengthened by the association of members with religious offices, and the power of the priesthood was increased by the absence of a written body of law. Priests became the makers, expounders, and administrators of law hampered by no meddlesome legislators and capricious monarchs. The results of their work have been described as comparable to the philosophical ideas of the Greeks and the religious ideas of the Semites.

The tribunes developed deliberative assemblies and other institutions for the plebeians and demanded that laws should be reduced to writing and made public. The *pontifex maximus* had recorded the names of magistrates and important events on a wooden tablet and the practice was followed by requests for elaborate details partly to imitate the model of Greek codifications.[3] The decemvirs' code was worked out in 451 and 450 BC and became the Twelve Tables. In spite of this encroachment of the written tradition, interpretation remained in the hands of the college of pontiffs and law was developed by legal fictions. The code maintained the power of the father over the son but admitted that patrimony might be divided among brothers. Property belonged to the individual and not to the *gens*, and the right to transmit property by will was conceded. The fiction of a pretended sale made possible the selection of the one chosen as heir. Inability of plebeians to contract a sacred marriage was overcome by recognition of a fictitious sale of the wife to the husband. One year's cohabitation established the same legal ties as purchase or religious ceremony, but if in each year the wife interrupted cohabitation by no more than three nights the establishment of the husband's power could be prevented.

Plebeian powers were steadily conceded and extended. In 445 BC the law against marriage between the two orders was withdrawn. Encroachments on the position of the consul began in 444 BC and to isolate and protect its religious function the position of the censor was instituted in 443 BC. Two censors were chosen every four or five years to determine assessments for purposes of taxation and after about a century they were able to decide the composition of the Senate. The struggle was renewed after the sack of Rome by the Gauls in 396 BC, and the Licinian laws in 367 BC required that one consul must be plebeian. New offices, the praetorship, and the curule aedileship, in which the praetor officially administered justice, were created by the patricians in 366. Knowledge of the legal process, i.e., legislatures (content of civil law) was gradually made public after 312 BC, and the ascendancy of the patrician pontiffs came to an end in 304 BC. The *lex Ogulnia* admitted plebeians to the offices[d] of *pontifices* and *augures* in 300 BC. After 287 BC measures of the plebeian assembly had the force of laws. In 253 BC the first plebeian *pontifex maximus* was appointed and, significantly, he was the first to profess law publicly.

In spite of increasing power of the plebeians in the determination of law, the influence of the oral tradition persisted, partly because of its adaptability to new demands and partly because the *prudentes* or lawyers probably continued in their connections with the priestly class. Dominance of the Italian peninsula and expansion of territory was followed by an increase in trade with the Greeks and by the adoption of silver coinage

by the Senate in 268 BC.ᶜ To administer justice for aliens a second praetor, *peregrinus*, was added in 242 BC, in contrast with the
first praetor, *urbanus*. The number of praetors was increased to
four in 227 BC and to six in 198 BC. The peregrine court familiarized Romans with the standard practices of commercial peoples[4] and enhanced a respect for equity. Lawyers were trained in
the use of formula until even the urban court could abandon the
rigid *legis actiones*.

Under the *per legis actionem* procedure, the praetor and the
parties concerned had their roles fixed by law and new formu-
laries were composed to destroy its rigidity. Under the *per for-
mulam* procedure introduced about 150 BC the action was
divided and the issue was first defined before the magistrate. A
written instruction called the formula was sent to the *judex*
ordering him to condemn or dismiss the defendant according to
the answer to the question raised. The exact question in dispute
was therefore determined by trained lawyers and the actual facts
by laymen (*judex*) who settled the dispute according to the formula decided by the praetor, a trained legal expert. The older
spoken formulae were displaced by written formulae, but only
after the technique of the jurist had been fixed to a degree that
the innovation had little influence. Formulary procedure had an
important influence on a powerful and independent development of *jus praetorum* which accompanied the increased powers
of the praetor. The *lex Aebutia*, about 120 BC, established documentary procedure or the formulary system as an optional
process and avoided the excessive technicality and formalism of
the system of *legis actiones*. The praetors issued edicts stating the
rules of procedure to govern during their year of office, which
were placed in black letters with red captions on white wooden
tablets posted in the forum. The praetor generally adopted the
edict of his predecessor, but with modifications. Control over
procedure implied control over fundamental changes in law.[5]
The *lex Cornelia*, 67 BC, required the praetor to abide by his edict
during his year of office. The edicts gave flexibility and certain-
ty and became a source of equity.

Until the time of Cicero, laws and precedents were kept to a large extent in the memories of men and the results of the oral tradition were evident in the achievements of jurists. In the peregrine court the progressive character of law was evident in the development of almost the whole of the law of contract, "one of the greatest achievements of classical jurisprudence." Property was divided into movables and immovables, and contracts and conveyances between organized groups were ceremonious in the highest degree and required a number of witnesses and assistants. Contracts created obligations and were separated from conveyances which transferred property rights. Steps in ceremonial were dropped, simplified, or neglected until in specific contracts, on which "the activity and energy of social intercourse" depended, no form was used. A contract was a pact plus an obligation, "the most beautiful monument" of the sagacity of Roman juris-consults.[6] "The positive duty resulting from one man's reliance on the word of another is among the slowest conquests of advancing civilization."[7]

Contract replaced forms of reciprocity in rights and duties having their origin in the family held together by the *patria potestas*. Legal fictions permitted the creation of artificial relations and there has been "none to which I conceive mankind to be more deeply indebted."[8] The father's powers were limited as facilities for their voluntary surrender were multiplied. The perpetual guardianship of women died out and the Roman female attained a position of personal and proprietary independence. The greatest possible latitude was give to individual initiative and the right of ownership was as unrestricted as possible. "Property has nothing in common with possession."[9f] Possession was merely an outwork of ownership and an aid to its better protection. *Res publica* had its counterpart in *res privata*. The state became a creature of law to be discussed in terms of legal competence. The relations of the state to religious institutions and of political philosophy to philosophy, which had scarcely been problems in the unity of the Greek *polis*, were vital to the Romans.[10]

The achievements of civil law in the concepts of the family, property, and contract were not made by the state, though sanctioned by its protection, but by practising lawyers. *Lex*, used for the conclusion of treaties, the regulation of provinces and local areas, and ordinary matters under constitutional law, was sparingly used as a source of law.[11] Treaties were engraved on bronze or stone and stored in the Capitoline temple,[g] laws of the centuriate assembly in the Temple of Saturn, and important decrees of the Senate in the Temple of Ceres. The influence of the written tradition shown in the problems of *lex* was in striking contrast with the power of the oral tradition in civil law, a contrast that boded ill for the history of the republic and the empire.

The success of Roman arms in extending the territory of the republic created problems of government. Wars and alliances left Rome as mistress of Italy by 260 BC. War with Carthage from 265 to 241 BC was followed by the acquisition of Sicily and the Lipari Islands. From 236 to 219 BC Carthage extended her territory to include Spain, but conflict with Rome after 218 BC again brought defeat and the drastic reductions of the treaty of 202 BC. The third Punic war after 153 BC ended in the destruction of Carthage. War with Carthage involved conflict with Hellenistic kingdoms. Assisted by the fleets of Pergamum and Rhodes, and with the support of Greek cities, Rome declared war on Macedonia in 200 BC and compelled withdrawal from Greece, Thrace, and Asia Minor. After the outbreak of rebellion in 171 BC the Macedonian kingdom was extinguished in 168 BC, and the position of Rhodes was weakened in 166 BC when Rome in the interest of Athens declared Delos a free port. Opposition to Rome among the Greek cities was followed by drastic measures including the destruction of Corinth in 146 BC. The dominance of trading communities on the Mediterranean came to an end.

Rome became concerned with the task of Eastern empires. Philip and Alexander[h] had developed efficient instruments of war and rapidly overran the city-states and built a Macedonian empire with control over the sea, the Persian empire, and territory as far east as India. Through deification of the ruler,

Alexander had established cohesion in a single *cosmopolis* which joined the eastern Mediterranean with western Asia and transcended cities, tribes, and nations. "Man as a political animal, a fraction of the *polis* or self-governing city had ended with Aristotle, with Alexander begins man as an individual" (A.J. Carlyle). The problems of separatist tendencies in earlier empires immediately emerged and after Alexander's death four dynasties were established, the Seleucids controlling roughly the former Persian empire, the Ptolemies in Egypt, the Antigonids in Macedonia, and the Attalids in Pergamum.

The impact of Greek culture in these kingdoms varied with their respective traditions. The Seleucids inheriting the problems of the Persian empire attempted to dominate Persian, Babylonian, and Hebrew religions, but the concept of the Greek city-state made slight impression. The kingdom collapsed and left legacies of better memories of resistance to persecution. Monarchies without the cement of nationality and religion and depending on force and solution of dynastic problems were insecure.

The Ptolemies inherited the problems of empire in Egypt. To offset the influence of the powerful priestly class at Thebes a new capital was built and a new centre for a monopoly of knowledge was established at Alexandria. A new god Serapis, probably the only god successfully made by man, was deliberately created. The Serapeum became to the Egyptian cult what the temple had been to the religion of Israel.[12] Politics "changed the government of heaven when changing that of earth" (Cumont). The cursive style of Egyptian writing was abbreviated in business and private correspondence in a popular or demotic style. The crucial position of Egyptian script was destroyed. Introduction of Greek script was probably accompanied by displacement of the brush by the reed (*Phyragmites aegypteia*). Thicker than the brush, it was cut to a point and split to form a pen. Easy access to supplies of papyrus facilitated development of the Alexandrian library. By 285 BC the library established by Ptolemy I had 20,000 manuscripts, and by the middle of the first century 700,000, while a smaller library established by Ptolemy II in the Serapeum possibly for duplicates had 42,800.[13] The library was accompanied by the university. Scholars established texts and the authenticity of classical works.[14] The *Iliad* and the *Odyssey*[i] through the work of Aristarchus were made into a sort of vulgate by 150 BC, eventually to come under the "fatal glamour of false knowledge diffused by the printed text" (Gilbert Murray). The Hebrew scriptures were translated and edited, the Laws under Ptolemy II probably between 283 and 246 BC, Isaiah and Jeremiah between 170 and 132 BC, the Prophets and Psalms by the latter date, and Ecclesiastes about 100 BC. Alexandria brought the philosophical or religious ideas of East and West, of India, Palestine, Persia, and Greece to a focus. The Pythagorean system combined influences of philosophy and religion and supported the identification of Osiris and Dionysus. Personified reason or the *Logos*[j] as the rational part of the soul with an existence above the daemons had emerged as a second god by 350 BC. An idea of definite conversion or of abiding change in the individual mind had appeared. In the museum science became the spiritual continuation of the work of Aristotle. Ptolemaic systematization left its stamp on geography and astronomy. Geometry was developed by Euclid about 300 BC to the point that it probably hindered the invention of a system of numerical notation. Aristarchus of Samos (310–230 BC) discovered that the sun was far larger than the earth and regarded the geocentric theory as impossible. The power of the written tradition made the Alexandrine age one of "erudition and criticism,"[15] of specialists rather than poets and scholars. The Alexandrine man was "a librarian and corrector of proofs and who, pitiable wretch, goes blind from the dust of books and printers' errors" (Nietzsche). Collectomania and large libraries accompanied taste and respectability.[16] Aesthetic opinions were crystallized and the dilettante appeared. Literature was divorced from life, thought from action, poetry from philosophy. In the *Argonautica* Apollonius in his revolt against Callimachus protested that a great book was a great evil.[17] Astrology proved stronger than astronomy. Geography began in science and ended in literature. Strabo's geography has been described as the swan song of Hellenism, the last unified view of the universe.

The oral tradition of Greece as it had crystallized in the writings of Plato and Aristotle had profound significance for Alexandria. Plato opposed the naturalistic cosmogonies of poets and physical philosophers with the support of internationalized monotheism spreading from Babylonia and Egypt. It has been suggested that belief in the divinity of the stars and acquaintance with the technique of mental repression in Egypt led Plato to state that governments must be free to lie. The inscription over Plato's Academy, "Let none enter who knows not geometry," implied a neglect of *physis* and of the study of growth. Aristotle, a student of Plato probably from 367 to 347 BC, left the Academy after Plato's death and eventually set up his Lyceum in 325 BC. As an Ionian and the son of a doctor he became interested in biological sciences which implied a concern with observation rather than with system. Greek medicine had its significance in relation to ideals of health. It insisted on the principle that experience is the basis of all knowledge, emphasized exactness, and distinguished the real causes of illness and symptoms by taking them out of the sphere of moral law. "One must attend in medicine not primarily to plausible theories but to experience combined with reason."[18] The biological sciences emphasized classification, which, in the words of Whitehead, stood half-way between the immediate concreteness of the individual theory and the complete abstractions of mathematical notions and involved an emphasis on logic. His system was provisional and open, and pointed to a striving towards totality of problems rather than finished knowledge. As a biologist rather than a physicist, he leaned towards a final cause. The science of natural knowledge was built up and set beside astronomy in the realm of philosophy. The dethronement of mathematics as a formative element created a breach between philosophy and science. Metaphysics surrendered to special sciences.

Cheap subsidized supplies of papyrus became the basis for an extensive administrative system as well as large libraries. Ptolemy II built up a monopoly of papyrus following a decline in price from two drachmae for a roll in 333 BC to a drachma for several rolls in 296 BC, in spite of a general rise in prices incidental to the flow of treasure from the East. After 279 BC a roll cost nearly two drachmae. Prices in Delos were two or three times those in Egypt following a policy of increasing efficiency in production and lowering prices in home market by maintaining or increasing them in the foreign market by an export tax or a prohibition of exports.[19] The temple monopolies of the Pharaohs were continued in the monopoly system of the Ptolemies, who farmed their estates and filled their treasuries. "Compulsion always leads to oppression and compulsion was the only recourse of a government that regarded itself as the sole ruling power in economic life." "Cumulation of offices, nepotism, control by various means of many offices, are well known phenomena in any decaying bureaucratic régime" (Rostovtzeff). An Egyptian theocratic state compelled its conquerors to establish similar institutions designed to reduce its power.

The Attalids had shielded a number of cities from attacks by the Gauls and gradually increased the influence of Pergamum. To offset the influence of Alexandria, Eumenes II (197–159 BC) built up a library and encouraged a variety of scholarly studies in contrast with the verbal scholarship of Alexandria. Apollodorus probably left Egypt for Pergamum after the accession of Eurgetes II or about 146 BC. As a result of the prohibition of exports of papyrus to Pergamum, Eumenes II encouraged the use of parchment,[20] by the establishment of a monopoly and of royal factories employing large numbers of slaves.[21] Cattle and hides were imported through Cyzicus from the Euxine. Pergamum was "in all probability the source of that renewal of Atticism to which we owe in great part the preservation of the masterpieces of Attic prose" (Susemihl).[22] Its art reflected the influence of the meeting of civilization and barbarism, a conflict of good and evil, in the attempt at unfamiliar ways of expression.[23]

The Antigonids gradually transformed the small city-states of Greece into municipalities. They captured Athens in 261 BC and maintained a garrison in the city to 229 BC. They adopted an opportunistic policy towards the formulation of leagues of cities. A league of twelve cities was dissolved by Antigonus Gonatas, but after 280 BC the Achaean league was formed and rapidly extended under Aratus. Antigonus Doson checked aggression from the Spartans by defeating them at Sellasia in 222 BC. The Aetolian league expanded during a period of Macedonian weakness from about 311 to 245 BC. The Achaean league was destroyed by Rome in 168 BC.

In spite of particularism, common interests were developed throughout the Hellenistic period. "There are many cities but they are one Hellas." Hellenistic Greek as a common speech was developed from Attic. With supplies[24] of papyrus and parchment and the employment of educated slaves, books were produced on an unprecedented scale. Hellenistic capitals provided a large reading public. In the words of Tarn, a world empty of machines and full of slaves demanded easy material for reading. The great bulk of writing was represented by third-hand compendia of snippets and textbooks, short cuts to knowledge, quantities of tragedies, and an active comedy of manners in Athens. Literary men wrote books about other books and became bibliophiles. Though rhetoric had emerged to serve the democracy of Sicily and was introduced at Acragas in 472 BC and at Syracuse in 466 BC, it was brought to Athens by Gorgias only in 427 BC. Probably in 378–377 BC[k] laws were enacted requiring pleadings before the Athenian courts to be presented in writing, partly to save time and jury fees and partly to meet the demands of professional speech-writers. By the second century everything had been swamped by the growth of rhetoric. In philosophy in the schools of Athens constructive system building was replaced by elementary pedagogy. In the third century alien influences on staff and in student body increased. Detachment of the individual from politics after 300 BC necessitated a concern in philosophy with happiness, conduct, and ethics. Classical Greek philosophy became crystallized in writing and was superseded by philosophy, which emphasized teaching. Zeno, the founder of Stoicism, was a hellenized Phoenician from Citium in Cyprus and came to Athens about 320 BC. Free from the prepossessions and prejudices of Greek political thought, Stoicism became a collection of doctrines and a religion to take the place of polytheism. They returned to Heraclitus in an emphasis on a single principle of life. "Right reason is the law of nature, the standard everywhere of what is just and right, unchangeable in its principles, binding on all men whether ruler or subjects, the law of God."[25] Stoicism was over and above all cults authorized by the state. "It made man at home in the universe" (Edwyn Bevan). All human beings had reason and a fundamental equality. "Before the law of nature all men have an equal status." Dogmatism followed the conclusion that power governing the universe was rational. The Cynics protested against the idealization of institutions of the city-state and poured contempt on popular religion and worship of material images of the Divine. "They were probably the purest monotheists that classical antiquity produced."[26] Epicurus established a school, based on atomism and the writings of Democritus, at Athens in 307 BC. He emphasized experience and natural philosophy in contrast with Plato's concern with mathematics and the priority of reason. He refused to recognize the gods of popular belief and denied the validity of popular superstition. To him the very fear of death, of which the great ones claimed to be free, lay at the root of civic ambition.

The Olympian religion and the city-state were replaced by philosophy and science for the educated and by Eastern religions for the common man. Communication between those under the influence of philosophy and those under the influence of religions became increasingly difficult. Cultural division facilitated the development of a class structure. Division between Athens and Alexandria and Pergamum followed the increasing emphasis on the written tradition, weakened science and philosophy, and opened the way to religions from the East and force from Rome in the West.

Following success in the East, Rome came under the direct influence of Hellenism. "Captive Greece took captive her proud conqueror" (Horace). About 272 BC Livius Andronicus[27] came to

Rome. He translated the *Odyssey* and as the first Greek to write Latin became the founder of Latin literature. In 240 BC he introduced the drama[l] to Rome following demands of soldiers returned from Greek settlements in the south for tragedies and comedies at Roman festivals. In 249 BC a choir of virgins introduced the Greek choral lyric. The Greek new comedy of the fourth century was adapted to audiences accustomed to the dramatic technique of the tragic stage. By 200 BC Greek plays could be presented without serious alterations. Opposition to Greek culture favoured an emphasis on Latin prose which had been confined to blunt sentences adapted to the economy of stone writing in laws, treaties, and official records. Cato protested that Greek literature would be the ruin of Rome and in his polemics helped to lay the foundations for a dignified versatile language. In 161 BC the Senate empowered the praetor to expel all teachers of rhetoric and philosophy and in 154 BC expelled two disciples of Epicurus. The spread of Greek metaphysics and psychology was probably checked, but Greek teachers and grammarians enhanced the popularity of Hellenistic ideals in literature in the second half of the second century. In about 168 BC Crates of Mallos,[m] the most distinguished scholar of the Pergamese school,[28] established the first school of grammar in Rome and reflected the erudition and discernment of Hellenistic literary criticism.

Prose gained fresh power in attempts to meet problems of the Republic which followed a marked increase in wealth. Direct taxation was abolished by the Senate after 167 BC. Large-scale farming and absentee ownership brought protests against the increased power of the Senate, particularly after revolt of the slaves in 139 BC. The Gracchi were among the first to use the weapon of Greek rhetoric on behalf of the democratic cause. Gaius Gracchus increased the range of forensic prose and made it "vivid, clear, versatile and vibrant" (Tenney Frank). Large numbers entered the political arena and speeches were given wider publicity through an enlarged circle of readers. Public speech moulded prose style. Over the long period from 500 to

100 BC harsh sounds had been eliminated and the Latin language reached maturity. In an edict of the censors of 92 BC Licinius Crassus attempted to discourage Latin schools of rhetoric, but its influence was evident in the development of prose as a finished product to its climax under Cicero. Broken speech was converted into a literary instrument with "concentration and surcharge, magnificent sonority and architectonic sentence building." Written speech became almost the equal of oral speech. Following the models of Isocrates, Cicero dominated the history of belles-lettres in Europe. Latin became a philosophical language and his widely read books and compilations were vehicles for the spread of Stoicism.

Epicureanism and Stoicism with a common ideal, "the complete emancipation of the soul from the yoke of passion and superstition" (Asquith), were spread by living teachers and the spoken word to the disadvantage of Platonism and Aristotelianism. Lucretius, following Epicurus in the didactic verse of *De rerum natura*, attacked the spirit of cringing before the gods, the enslavement of the soul incidental to the belief in the beyond and the fear of death, the cruelties of sacrifice, signs and wonders, the mystification of seers and the interpreters of dreams. Stoicism proved more acceptable. It spread from Rhodes through the teachings of Chrysippus and Poseidonius, who taught Panaetius. The latter restated Stoic philosophy for assimilation by Romans of the aristocratic class and with Polybius in the third quarter of the second century introduced it to the circle of Scipio Amelianus. Through Cicero, who wrote that "a single copy of the Twelve Tables has greater weight and authority than all the philosophies of the world" (*De oratore*), Stoicism received fresh support in its influence on Roman law. Stoic philosophy brought the ideas of world state, natural justice, and universal citizenship in an ethical sense, which were independent and superior to the enactment of kings. The conception of natural law brought enlightened criticism to bear on custom, helped to destroy the religious and ceremonial character of law, promoted equality before the law, emphasized the factor of intent, and mitigated unreasoning harshness. It was "an ultimate principle of fitness with regard to the nature of man as a rational and social being, which is, or ought to be, the justification of every form of positive law" (Pollock). The *jus gentium* began to be conceived as a law common to all mankind and equivalent to the law of nature. "We are servants of the law in order that we may be free" (Cicero).

The spread of writing reinforced Greek influence. Books and readers probably emerged in the third century to meet the needs of the state and the demands of agriculture and law. In the second century books were securely established but circulated in a very limited educated class. After the defeat of Perseus of Macedonia (168 BC), the consul Aemilius Paulus brought the library of the king to Rome. Sulla brought the library of Apollion of Teus, including works of Aristotle and Theophrastus, from Athens to Rome. New biographies and contemporary histories were brought out and larger numbers of writers demanded more compendious and reliable reference works. Dominance of Egypt gave access to papyrus, which was more convenient than bark, the name of which persisted in the word *liber*, meaning book.[29] Under the Ptolemies papyrus production increased and the quality was improved through domestic cultivation which made it possible to harvest it all the year round. Sale was regulated under royal monopoly but private individuals cultivated and prepared it in factories. The best papyrus was purchased by the state at a fixed price chiefly for the use of notaries and poorer grades were sold outside the monopoly.

The character of the book trade is illustrated in the interests of Atticus, a friend of Cicero's, who accumulated a large library from books collected in Greece and became a publisher. In 61 BC he was criticizing a collection of Cicero's orations which had been put in book form and by 56 BC apparently controlled Cicero's publications. Slaves were trained as copyists, readers, and librarians, and in 55 BC he had a copying establishment.[30] The *strihoi*, a measurement of fifteen or sixteen syllables, was apparently used as a device for paying copyists as well as in making citations and in protecting purchasers. Stichometry facilitated counting of the number of lines and establishing of market prices for manuscripts. The average rate of production for copyists was 250 strihoi per hour. Private libraries emerged and Vitruvius advised that "the sleeping rooms and libraries should face towards the east; for their utilization demands the morning light; also the books in the library will not decay."

The effect of writing was evident in every phase of cultural life. Manuscripts written by Plautus for a single performance were resurrected from the state archives by the aediles. After Terence old plays glutted the market and new writers were discouraged. The conflict of the Greek method of scansion with Roman pronunciation by stress accent weakened the drama and demands for cheaper amusement reduced the mimes to low levels and drove the intelligent from the theatre. In law Greek influence favoured the abstract formulation of legal doctrines demanded by codes. Literal interpretation led to neglect of the nature of the matter itself. "The reasons underlying the legal system should not be inquired into, otherwise much that is certain would collapse" (Neratius).[31] In 198 BC Sextus Aelius had compiled the *Tripertita*, the earliest systematic treatise, and in 95 BC Quintus Mercius Scaevola, consul, made the first digest of civil law in twenty-eight books. A treatise of Saevius Sulpicius Rufus, consul, in 51 BC, provided systematic comment on the edicts of the urban praetor. Julius Caesar proposed the establishment of a library under Marcus Terentius Varro to reduce "all existing codes of civil law to a more simplified form by extracting only the essential features and combining them in a select series of legal documents," and to make works in Greek and Latin available to the public.[32] As the written tradition was extended shorthand was introduced to bridge the gap with the oral tradition. Cicero dictated to Tiro, a freedman who used shorthand. In 63 BC stenographers were apparently introduced in the Senate and in 59 BC an official gazette *acta diurna* and the *acta senatus* including minutes of the Senate were started by Julius Caesar as consul. Publication of proceedings compelled speakers to consider the outside public. In 52 BC the triumvirs[n] severely limited the time for pleas in court, which reinforced the demand for matter-of-fact style in the Senate and brought disaster to the style of Cicero.

The problem of government over large areas compelled an emphasis on bureaucratic administration. Models were available in the large secretarial departments of Hellenistic kingdoms. Concentration of control weakened the power of the Senate. As early as 327 BC the practice of extending the power of the consul by lengthening the time of his appointment to enable him to conduct campaigns over longer periods was introduced. In 149 BC judicial procedure was extended to cover cases of magisterial extortion in the provinces, including bribery and treason, but its effects were more than offset by the effects of reforms in the army introduced by Marius and Sulla and severance from the civil authorities. Nominally the provinces were protected by regulations of the Senate, but Roman governors returned with wealth, ambitions, and an experience of absolute power disastrous to the Republic. A fixed tribute was imposed on conquered nations in the West and following the practice of monarchies, revenues were farmed in the East. The system meant "government by the unpaid aristocrat and exploitation by the irresponsible profiteer" (H. Stuart Jones). In the third and second centuries BC "the Senate governed but did not reign whilst the people reigned but did not govern" (H. Stuart Jones), and dissension between the Senate and the people became the opportunity of Caesarism backed by an army.

The spread of writing contributed to the downfall of the Republic and the emergence of the empire. With the growth of administration the power of the emperor was enhanced and in turn used to secure new support. Eastern religions were mobilized in the interest of the empire. Following a severe pestilence the Greek god Asklepios was brought from *Epidaurus*[o] to Rome in 293 BC and a temple dedicated to him in 291 BC. The migration of deities in the second half of the third century compelled the Senate to attempt to check the spread of sacred writings in 213

BC. The *Magna Mater*,[33] a pre-Phrygian goddess, was, however, of special interest to the nobility and in 204 BC her transfer to Rome was advised by the Sybils. Attalus who had helped the Romans against Philip assisted in her migration. Official recognition assumed a privileged position. "A breach had been made in the cracked wall of old Roman principles, through which the entire Orient finally gained ingress" (Cumont), although the authorities had isolated the religion to prevent contagion at the expense of Roman customs. Junius Brutus, *praetor urbanus*, celebrated dedication of the temple in the Palatinate in 191 BC. In the last days of the second Punic war the mystic cult of Bacchus[p] was introduced from Tarentum and in the early years of the second century BC the Dionysiac orgies "descended on Rome like a pestilence." In 139 BC an edict attempted to check the spread of astrology. The spread of worship of Isis and Serapis from Egypt was followed by orders for the destruction of its altars and statues in 59, 58, 53, and 48 BC. Under Julius Caesar an Alexandrian astronomer had reformed the calendar and the dates of the festivals of Isis were marked by Alexandrian priests. When Octavian accepted the title of Augustus in 27 BC he revived Roman religion. Ruined temples were restored and the temple of Apollo, his mother, and sister was dedicated and in 17 BC, at his secular celebration, Augustus made them the equal of old deities. Apollo became the chief divinity and the rites were placed under the jurisdiction of fifteen men. After a fire in 83 BC additions had been made to the sacred collection of Sibylline books and Augustus ordered the destruction of over 2,000 copies of pseudo-books of unlicensed divination and prohibited books on magic. The remainder were transferred from the temple of the Capitoline Jupiter to a new house closely associated with the imperial residence. Deliberate emphasis was given to cults related to the Julian *gens*. In 12 BC Augustus became *Pontifex Maximus* and the colleges came under his control. The oath of officials and soldiers was associated with the *genius* of the emperor and the *divi Caesares* of the past.

Emperor worship was steadily reinforced from the East. Pompey had been greeted as a god and after his defeat in 48 BC his place was taken by Julius Caesar. After the death of the latter his deification was fixed by law on 1 January 42 BC. Octavian had discredited Antony in his alliance with Cleopatra, the one living representative of the divine monarchies in the East, but as a successor to the Ptolemies he himself necessarily became a god and by 9 BC was worshipped in the East as a saviour. The cult of the living ruler spread rapidly in the provinces after the long and prosperous rule of Augustus, and Caligula (AD 37–41) was probably declared a god before the Senate. Eastern religions were held in check, although a bloody persecution of the priests of the cult of Isis and Serapis by Tiberius in AD 19 was followed by the erection of a temple of Isis Campensis by Caligula in AD 38. Claudius gave new importance to the *Magna Mater* by establishing a complete cycle of events for an annual celebration on 15–17 March to mark the beginning of spring. The cult was especially attractive to women and under Trajan spread to the provinces. After the death of Nero (34–68), the last of the line of Caesars, the Flavian dynasty attempted to prove its legitimacy by assuming a divinity similar to that of its predecessor. Under Trajan the imperial cult gained in importance and the emperor became the vice-regent of God. Hadrian revived the religious attitude of Augustus in the classicism of art and architecture. Distrust of a divinized sovereign led to the avoidance of titles suggesting kingly authority, but deified Caesars were worshipped as symbols of continuity and legitimacy.

After Marcus Aurelius, his son Commodus (180–93) probably claimed sacrifices and images and weakened the two pillars of the empire, namely, rejection of oriental cults and postponement of the apotheosis of the emperor until after death. He was initiated to the mysteries of Mithra and recognition was followed by rapid advance. Deification of living emperors assumed public worship of them. In the following century of war the emperors relied to an increasing extent on force. Septimius Severus (193–211) was an African by birth and the Severi gave fresh support to foreign cults.

Elagabalus made his own god, Baal of Emesa, the proper lord of Rome but was murdered by his troops in AD 222. Caracalla

Alexander (222–35) erected a temple to Serapis and in his name he reflected the interest of Alexander in the idea of a world empire rather than the Roman attitude of maintaining distinctions between the ruler and his subjects. In AD 273[q] Aurelian defeated Queen Zenobia, who had formed a large state, at Palmyra, and in AD 274 he proclaimed the dethronement of Roman idolatry and dedicated a shrine to the god *Sol Invictus*. The twenty-fifth of December, marking the sun's entrance on a new course of triumph, became the great festival of Mithra's sacred year. Diocletian (284–305) completed the work begun by Aurelian, though he was not worshipped as *dominus et deus*,[r] and an oriental cult became the religion of the empire bringing a new conception of the emperor and the empire. The disappearance of formal privileges of the Senate and the dyarchy weakened constitutionalism and strengthened an autocracy in an intricate bureaucratic state. Mithraism had spread with the army in the West and particularly in Germany and the Danubian provinces. After reaching its peak about AD 250, it suffered a severe blow in the loss of Dacia in AD 275. Hellenism never surrendered to the gods of hereditary enemies and Mithra was excluded from the Hellenic world. Diocletian, in establishing a system of tetrarchy, recognized the growing division between the Latin West and the Greek East.

The rise of absolutism in a bureaucratic state reflected the influence of writing and was supported by an increase in the production of papyrus. Under Augustus cultivation, manufacture, and sale were placed in private hands. An embarkation tax was probably substituted for an export tax since Rome was the chief importer.[34] Manufacture shifted from small villages to more important towns. The *ouvrier-fabricant* became a workman in a factory. The swamps of the Nile delta supplied a convenient, reasonably priced material for an administrative organization covering territory from Britain to Mesopotamia.

Augustus overcame the distrust of experts and government without paid officials inherited by the Romans from the Greek city-state and created a civil service. He became his own chancellor of the Exchequer and introduced a trained personnel for the collection of taxes. Systems of account were devised to provide a guarantee of efficiency. Freedmen[35] who had probably been Hellenic slaves and had acquired literary and linguistic skill had been used by Julius Caesar as officers of the mint, and in the first century they were generally in control of correspondence with all parts of the empire. Augustus, following Persian example, organized a state post with the use of relays. Later a messenger was sent to travel the whole distance and to supplement written with verbal instructions. After the death of Nero, Vitellius, who represented the army on the Rhine, began to assign officers in the imperial bureaux to the knights. While freedmen continued as efficient administrators Vespasian recruited the governing class from the whole empire and Hadrian gave greater importance to the knights in the civil service at the expense of the power of the Senate. Bureaucratic interference began to sap the freedom and independence of municipal life.[36] *Equites* as secretaries introduced a new epoch in the development of a bureacracy. Severus created the *res privata principis* which became a central treasury and openly claimed it as his own. Procuratorships were treated as rewards for services and as pensioning posts for discharged officers. Gallienus excluded the senatorial order from imperial administration and gave control of the legions and of the more important provinces to the imperial *praefecti*. By about AD 250 the fiction of dualism of emperor and Senate had collapsed. Diocletian separated control of the military arm from the civil authority and left provincial governors only with judicial and administrative functions. The large provinces were divided into small units and were subject to a vast bureaucracy.

The effects of bureaucracy were evident in the codification of law. Under the empire the urban edict which had been an important instrument in the advance of law ceased to be a living source of law. "While the Roman state was alive and developing no code was constituted or even proposed" (Savigny). The praetor became dependent and lost initiative and, under Hadrian, Salvus Julianus codified the edict in a final and fixed form about

AD 130. A limited number of privileged jurists gave answers by the emperor's authority and under seal. These replies reached high authority by the time of Gaius who prepared the Institutes about AD 161. By the end of the third century the formulary system had been displaced by magisterial procedure which became legally inquisitorial and actually accusatorial. After Tiberius torture was applied to free-born accused persons and after Severus to free-born citizens. In the third century capital punishment became ordinary for serious and even comparatively trivial crimes. The decline of legal science at the end of the third century when the calamity of legal insecurity overtook the empire was accompanied by private and official collections. The un-Roman state legislation was extended to the domain of civil law. The empire was accompanied by statute law. The letter of the law became supreme and decrees were inexorably and unalterably fixed. The living growth was replaced by the dead letter.

Attempts were made in the empire to build up the prestige of Rome to offset that of Alexandria by establishing libraries. Libraries were associated with temples as the most magnificent, accessible, and secure of public edicifices.' Augustus built two libraries, including the Palatine in which books were divided into Greek and Latin sections. Tiberius, Vespasian, Trajan, and Hadrian continued the imperial practice. By the fourth century Rome possessed at least 28 libraries with perhaps 20,000 rolls each divided into Greek and Roman sections. Municipal libraries were scattered throughout the empire.[37] Private libraries had become indications of conspicuous consumption.[38] Pliny gave an estimated £9,000 to establish a library at Como and an endowment of over £800 to maintain it.

The growth of libraries supported a trade chiefly in Latin books, since Alexandria continued as an important centre in the publication of Greek books. A single bookselling firm with 100 slaves trained as scribes could produce through the use of dictation a thousand copies of Martial (Book II) in ten hours, which, plainly bound, sold at an estimate of 6 to 8 pence and yielded a profit of 100 per cent. Large-scale production and moderate prices assumed a wide distribution. An important export business[39] followed extension of territory and improvement of roads, particularly in Spain and the western provinces. Native languages were displaced by Latin and by the end of Augustus's reign Spain was as Latin as Italy. Druidism in Gaul with its oral traditions and long poems (Caesar's *Gallic Wars*) disappeared in favour of a book trade in Lyons.

In the empire books became instruments of literary propaganda. Patronage was used by Augustus as it had been by the Ptolemies. Maecenas brought together a literary group, chiefly Italians, and encouraged writers such as Virgil and Horace to achievements of the highest craftsmanship in a golden literary age. An artificial delicate literature which accompanied a profession of letters diverged increasingly with popular taste, and the death of Augustus was followed by almost immediate collapse. Suppression of public life in the empire, punishment, and confiscation of work reflecting on the emperor brought hypocritical silence, subterfuge, and servility. Vespasian took an active part in controlling education as a means of directing the influence of professors and rhetoricians who controlled the views of the upper classes. A system of higher schools of grammar and rhetoric was established and fixed endowments given to professors of the liberal arts. Quintilian became the first professor of Latin rhetoric in Rome in AD 71. "Declamation is the most modern of all exercises and also by far the most useful" (Quintilian). In the silver age, roughly from AD 14 to 128, the strongest voices such as Tacitus and Juvenal were those of protest. Writers turned to the compilation of facts. The elder Pliny, who held a high place in the councils of Vespasian, wrote thirty-seven books in his *Natural History*, for which 2,000 volumes were consulted. The younger Pliny's panegyric on Trajan "became the parent and model of the prostituted rhetoric of the Gallic renaissance in the fourth century."[40] Hadrian opened the Athenaeum as the first school for higher education and supported Athenian schools. "After a long eclipse, the rhetorical culture of Greece vigorously addressed itself in the reign of

Hadrian to the conquest of the West."[41] Marcus Aurelius established four professorships in Athens with a salary of 10,000 denarii each to support the teaching of Stoic, Platonic, Peripatetic, and Epicurean philosophers.

The written tradition dependent on papyrus and the roll supported an emphasis on centralized bureaucratic administration. Rome became dependent on the army, territorial expansion, and law at the expense of trade and an international economy. Trade with India increased following the discovery about AD 50 that the monsoons provided a reliable means of transit for sailing-vessels, and by the fourth century Rome had probably lost two-thirds of her gold and one-half of her silver to the East. The inflation under Commodus was marked by decline of the value of the denarius by two-thirds.[42]

As a result of the decline of trade Roman religion escaped from the demands made upon Greek religion for adjustment in relation to time. Altheim describes the revelation of the gods to Romans in single historical acts and not in actions beyond time. The single day or hour had a unique position. Continuity was a sequence of single moments in a close series. Everything represented the completion of that spoken by the gods or *fatum* and the results were evident in various aspects of Roman culture. The sculpture of historical situations differed from that of the Greeks in making distinct differentiation between the main and subsidiary figures in a group. The number of figures was restricted by insistence on a separate figure as the basis of composition. A concern with concrete and individual representation rather than the universal and the ideal was stressed in the epic documentary[43] tradition of columns of Trajan and Marcus Aurelius. Continuous epic narrative technique was adapted to the uninterrupted continuity of surface of the book scroll, but the illustration of rolled manuscripts in continuous band forms was cut into pieces of the same size as the column width of single pages — each piece normally with one single scene depicting the hardships of the emperor and the troops in the field on great spiral columns. These types of representation and those of emperors after Vespasian[t] on coins were effectively propagandist. Architecture characterized by solidity of construction and magnificence of conception reflected the demands of the imperial state. The discovery of cement[u] about 180 BC enabled the Romans to develop on a large scale the arch, the vault, and the dome. Vaulted architecture became an expression of equilibrium, stability, and permanence, monuments which persisted through centuries of neglect.

The individual with demands on religion for "the most positive and realistic assurances of his own personal salvation" was neglected in the process of political unification. After Augustus the combination of creative forces in the *princeps* and the poet was followed by a settlement of religious forms and social stratification. A prescribed and formal collective demonstration replaced the free revelation of personality. To meet a widespread demand for individual salvation to be procured primarily by the aid of a deity, redemptive religions were developed with great energy. They appealed to the lowest strata of society, developed in regions less exposed to the full impact of imperial expansion, and used a medium such as parchment designed to offset the centralizing tendencies of papyrus.

The limitations of papyrus were shown in the use of smaller rolls to preserve a fragile medium and to enhance convenience for reference. Codices of papyrus were introduced in Egypt possibly following the gift of 200,000 volumes of the library of Pergamum from Antony to Cleopatra. These were probably in parchment and possibly in codices. In the codex a number of sheets twice the size of a required page were folded once in the middle to make two leaves of four pages each. It could be increased in size and was more convenient than the roll for reference. On the other hand, in a small quire of eight to ten leaves sewn together inside a cover, the papyrus tended to tear away from the stitching with use and age, and in a quire of over fifty sheets the papyrus became too bulky. Parchment offset these inconveniences. The untanned hides of calves or sheep were put into limewater and thoroughly soaked, the hair scraped off, and the skin stretched to dry on a frame. It was then rubbed with chalk and pumice-stone until it was even and smooth, and the finished product cut into pieces about the size of the thin pieces of wood covered with wax and written on with a stylus used for writing in Greece and Rome.[44] The pieces were arranged in quires with the hair side facing the hair side and fastened together in a codex. Used on both sides parchment was economical, durable, convenient, easy to transport, to write on, to read, and to consult. Ink could be removed and the parchment used again as in palimpsests. A sharp-pointed split pen could be used in place of the reed. Light and heavy strokes led to the development of uncials. The influence of waxed tablets on Roman cursive writing in the first three centuries declined and an enlarged and flowing hand of a rounder type suggested the importance of parchment. Demands for durability in school books and in small popular editions used by travellers were followed by an increase in the use of the parchment codex.

Use of the parchment codex gave Christians an enormous advantage over other religions. Christianity began as a ferment within Judaism and a protest against the increasing rigidity of the theocracy following the gap between Hebrew as a sacred language and Aramaic as the vernacular and accentuated by the persecutions of Antiochus. Its position was strengthened by the influence of Judaism as it had been assimilated to Hellenism in Egypt. Withdrawal of Christians from Jerusalem to Pella during the war against Rome severed bonds of sympathy between the two religions. Destruction of the Temple by Titus in AD 70 hastened the break between the orthodox Rabbinism of the Talmud and Mishna and Hellenistic Judaism of the dispersion. In AD 50 Jerusalem and Antioch were important Christian centres, but fifty years later they had been replaced by Ephesus and Rome. The Jewish scriptures which had been translated into Greek at Alexandria were used as a Bible by Christians, but its cumbersome forty rolls proved inconvenient in comparison with the parchment codex. An interest in publishing Christian letters was developed at Antioch, beginning with those written by Paul between AD 50 and 62, and published in two papyrus rolls about AD 90, and continuing with Luke and Acts published as two volumes about the end of the century. Mark was written and published as a popular book at Rome about AD 70. The four gospels were published as a collection not later than AD 125, and by AD 140 publishers were using the codex and a book-reading public of the Greek vernacular was assumed. Christianity continued as a Greek movement almost to the end of the second century, by which date codices capable of containing four-fifths of the New Testament were being used in North Africa. Early in the third century the codex was divided into quires and these were bound in a book. The codex was used to an increasing extent for Christian works, but the roll continued to be used chiefly for pagan works. The oral tradition of Christianity was crystallized in books which became sacred. The break with Judaism compelled reliance on an effective appeal to Gentiles of other religions with important results for Christianity.[45] "It is the irony of every religion that the most popular parts of it are those which do not belong to it but have been brought into it from those beliefs which it tried to supersede."[46]

The position of Christianity was strengthened by the work of scholars in attempts to establish a synthesis between Hebraic religion and Greek philosophy and the organization of the Church.[47] St. Clement was followed by Origen, his pupil, who brought together Jewish revised versions of the Old Testament in the *Hexapla*,[v] and after having being driven from Alexandria in AD 231 established a centre of study at Caesarea. Pamphilus founded a local library of his works which became a nucleus of Christian writings. Harnack has described the adherence of Christian learning at Alexandria and Caesarea to the Church as a decisive factor. It offset the powerful influence[48] of a learned Babylonian priesthood emphasizing cuneiform writing, which had been encouraged by the Seleucids in opposition to Persian religions. But the power of local cults in the East was evident in translations of the Bible into Syriac, Coptic, and later Armenian, and imposed serious strains on unity of organization. The primacy of the Roman

Church had been established by the end of the first century and a Catholic confederation emerged about AD 180. After the middle of the third century Christianity became a syncretist religion. "The Christian religion is a synthesis and only those who have dim eyes can assert that the intellectual empires of Babylonia and Persia have fallen" (Cheyne).[49] "The triumph of the church will ... appear more and more as the culmination of a long evolution of beliefs" (Cumont).

In the East, Christianity was checked by the religion of Iran and in turn its position was consolidated in Hellenism. After Alexander, prayers and canticles of the religion of Iran which had been transmitted orally were committed to writing through fear of their destruction. Religious autonomy contributed to the defeat of the Seleucids, to expansion of the Parthian empire, and to the fall of Babylon in 125 BC. Syncretism brought reconciliation between Babylonian and Persian religions, which became a support to the Sassanid dynasty established in AD 228. A new capital at Ctesiphon was chosen and a ruling priesthood placed in charge of a reconstituted Mazdaism. The *Avesta* became a sacred book and the priests assumed responsibility for the teaching of reading, writing, and reckoning in the complex Pahlavi, a mixture of Aryan and Semitic. In the indecisive struggle with the Sassanids, Rome imitated Persian customs and religion, and Diocletian established an oriental court. Diocletian was the last emperor to celebrate a triumph and the last to be deified. The opposition of Hellenism compelled Constantine to choose a religion suited to its demands. Diocletian attempted to exterminate Christianity, but persecution brought prominence and the victory of Constantine in 312 was regarded as a victory of Christianity over Mithraism. In 313 the so-called edict of Milan secured the privileges of a licensed cult for Christianity, recognized the Church as a corporation by authorizing it to hold property, and dethroned paganism as a state religion. The Lord's Day Act of 321 suggested that the divorce between religion and politics could not be maintained. The Council of Nicaea in 325 called by Constantine denounced the dogma of Arius that the son of God was a created being and therefore not eternal and accepted that of Athanasius that Christ was the son of God, unbegotten and consubstantial (of one essence) with his Father. In the selection of a new capital at Constantinople,[50] dedicated on 11 May 330, Constantine was concerned with its possibilities of military defence and with the prospect of support from the large Christian population of Asia Minor and from proximity to the most important centres of Hellenistic culture. He emphasized a strong centralized authority and joined a powerful ecclesiastical interest to a military bureaucracy. Caesaropapism implied authority of the emperor over the Church.[w] Christianity became a religion of conquerors and Constantine rather than Christ was to christianize Europe.

The Nicene decisions proved unacceptable to the East and by 335 Constantine began to favour Arianism, and in 337 he died in the "odour of Arian sanctity." Wulfilas, a Goth, became an active Arian missionary in Dacia about AD 340. He invented a Gothic alphabet, in part from Greek letters and in part from runes of the northmen, and translated part of the scriptures into the Gothic language. The Council of Rimini in 359 was a return to Arianism, but the death of Valens in 378 and the Council of Constantinople called by Theodosius in 381 brought it to an end.

The Goths were driven back from Constantinople and pressed westward to create problems for the Western empire. Theodosius, as emperor of the East, was compelled to give assistance to the West and after his death in 395 left the empire to his two sons. Theodosianism regarded Trinitarian Christianity as a principle of political cohesion and paganism was ruthlessly exterminated. The Delphic oracle was officially closed in 390 and the temple of Serapis in Alexandria was destroyed in 391. Closing of the temples of pagan cults in 392, following a decree that every sacrifice was an act of treason against the emperor, meant the closing of pagan libraries. Later Stilicho ordered the burning of the Sibylline books. Ammanius Marcellinus could write "the libraries like tombs are closed forever." In 396 pagan worship was prohibited. The pagan calendar and pagan festivals were replaced by the Christian calendar and Christian festivals.

As the power of the empire was weakened in the West that of the Church at Rome increased and difficulties with heresies in the East became more acute. In 390 Theodosius was refused admission to worship by Ambrose at Milan until he had done public penance for the massacre at Antioch. After the sack of Rome in 410, Eastern heresies became more vocal. Attempts of Alexandrian patriarchs to establish a papacy were defeated by Leo the Great (440–61), who founded the pontifical monarchy of the West. Pelagius and his disciple Coelestius rejected the doctrines of predestination and original sin, and were excommunicated in 417. At the Œcumenical Council at Ephesus 431 Pelagianism and the dogma of Nestorius, patriarch of Constantinople, that Jesus was only a man become God and that the virgin was not the mother of God, were condemned. The Council of Ephesus in 431 assured a temporary triumph for Monophysitism, the doctrine of Cyril that human nature was absorbed by the divine substance in Christ, but its rejection by the Council of Chalcedon in 451 enabled the Roman papacy to establish authority over the Eastern Church. Rejection of the doctrine alienated Christians in Syria and Egypt. After the fall of the Western empire in 476 an attempt was made by Zeno (474–91) to restore harmony with the Monophysites by an edict in 482, but in turn it brought division between Constantinople and Rome.[x] Justinian attempted to reconcile Rome, Syria, and Egypt, but in 551 the patriarch of Alexandria left the episcopal city and the Coptic liturgy was given its final form.

Justinian attempted to strengthen the prestige of the Eastern empire by strengthening the resources of Constantinople.[y] In 529 he closed the schools of Athens. Constantine had started a library by ordering Eusebius to procure fifty copies of the sacred scriptures written on prepared parchment. The great manuscripts of Christian literature were produced in the first half of the fourth century. About 300 Gregorius and Hermanogenianus attempted to bring order into Roman law. In 425 Theodosius II established a university with thirty-one professors. The codex of Theodosianes completed in 438 included decrees issued by

Christian emperors since Constantine, and was used in abridgement by the Visigoths. By the fifth century the imperial library was estimated at 120,000 volumes, and while it was destroyed in 477 it was restored under Zeno. Justinian's great achievements have been described as the code of civil law[51] and the cathedral of St. Sophia. A commission appointed in 528 published imperial constitutions promulgated since Hadrian. A second commission appointed in 530 published the decisions of the great jurisconsults in 533 in the *Digest*. Decrees from 534 to 565 were published as the *Novellae leges*. The principles of the new code were summarized in the *Institutes*, a single manual for students. Written in Latin the *Corpus juris civilis* was followed by Greek commentaries and summaries. Latin, which had been the official language for all imperial decrees and edicts, was replaced by Greek in 627. The *Digest*, as the final development of Roman law, was a complete renunciation of systematic continuity. "The laws of Rome were never reduced to a system till its virtue and taste had perished." The codes exercised a powerful influence on the legal systems of Europe. The work of the classical Roman jurists and the vitality of their influence are "among the most remarkable proofs in history that the indestructibility of matter is as nothing compared with the indestructibility of mind."[52] Justinian's law influence European life more than it has been affected by any other work except the Bible.[53]

Justinian purchased his success in the West with large concessions to the king of Persia in 532. After his death and the beginning of the Heraclian dynasty in 610 the disaffection of the Monophysitic populations of Egypt, Syria, and Palestine facilitated the capture of Palestine in 614 and Egypt by the Persians in 618 or 619. Although territory was recaptured by Heraclius it was lost again to the Arabs, who captured Jerusalem in 637 or 638, Cyprus in 650, and by the close of the seventh century had conquered the eastern and southern provinces of the Byzantine empire, North Africa, and Spain. But the hard core of the empire was to persist until 1453. "In some sense the walls of Constantinople represented for the East the gun and gunpowder for lack of which the Empire in the West had perished" (N.H. Baynes), but its continuity was a reflection of the success with which the concept of empire had been grasped.

The Byzantine empire developed on the basis of a compromise between organization reflecting the bias of different media: that of papyrus in the development of an imperial bureaucracy in relation to a vast area and that of parchment in the development of an ecclesiastical hierarchy in relation to time. It persisted with a success paralleled by that of the compromise between monarchical elements based on stone and religious elements based on clay, which characterized the long period of the Kassite dynasty in the Babylonian empire.

6 — PARCHMENT
AND PAPER

The spread of Mohammedanism reduced exports of papyrus from Egypt. It had been imported at Bordeaux and Marseilles for use in schools and in the bureaucratic administration, but between 659 and 679 was replaced by parchment in the Merovingian court and after 716[1] practically disappeared. The change roughly coincided with the rise of the Carolingian dynasty. In contrast with papyrus, which was produced in a restricted area under centralized control to meet the demands of a centralized bureaucratic administration and which was largely limited by its fragile character to water navigation, parchment was the product of a widely scattered agricultural economy suited to the demands of a decentralized administration and to land transportation.

An appraisal of a civilization based on a medium of communication demands a recognition of the significance of peculiarities of the medium. Papyrus largely disappeared but parchment could be preserved. Historical writing is distorted by over-emphasizing periods and regions in which durable materials prevail and under-emphasizing periods and regions in which impermanent or unknown materials prevail. The parchment codex was adapted to large books in emphasizing facility of reference and consequently lent itself to religion and law in the scriptures and the codes. A permanent medium suited to use over wide areas facilitated the establishment of libraries, and the production of a limited number of large books which could be copied. Since the material of an earlier culture must be recopied, an extensive censorship emerged in which material suited to religion and law was given enormous emphasis. The size of the scriptures and of the writings of the Fathers made heavy demands on the energies available for copying. With the breakdown of the Roman empire in the West and the increasing importance of the Church, law was largely neglected. We have described the implications of papyrus to the rise and fall of bureaucratic administration in the Roman empire and the tendency of each medium of communication to create monopolies of knowledge to the point that the human spirit breaks through at new levels of society and on the outer fringes, and can now turn to the implications of parchment to the civilization of the West in the growth of a monopoly of knowledge and to its breakdown following the introduction of paper.

The peculiarities of parchment gave an important impetus to the power of monastic organization. In Egypt retreat from the ubiquitous demands of the state favoured the establishment of monasteries. Buddhism, probably introduced into Egypt after the Persian occupation in 525 BC, provided a model. Pachomios, formerly a pagan monk of Serapis, started the first monastic community at Tabennisi in AD 322. St. Basil the Great worked out the elements of Christian *moralia*, and as a law-giver drafted a scheme of communal organization to provide appropriate means for its realization, and became the founder of Greek monasticism. Athanasius carried a knowledge of monasticism to Rome in 340. Jerome visited Egyptian monasteries in 386 and introduced a Latin version of the rules of Pachomios.[a] Monasticism spread with rapidity as a protest against the worldliness of Christianity under Caesaropapism and against the sacramental sacerdotal basis of the Church established by St. Cyprian (about 200–58), who held that no one could remain permanently without sin after baptism, and that sins must be expunged by exceptional works of merit, notably alms-giving.[2] Recognition of its power was evident in an edict of 361 in which Constantius exempted monks from public obligations. Between 420 and 430 St. John Cassian completed the classics of monasticism in the *Institutes* and the *Collations*. Monasticism spread with great rapidity in Gaul, but in spite of its independence it was gradually brought under control and in the Council of Chalcedon in 451 establishment of a monastery was made conditional to the bishop's permission. The Council of Orleans in 511 subordinated monks and abbots to episcopal authority. Monasticism probably strengthened the independence of the Gallic bishop who succeeded to the dignity of the Augustan cult[b] in the municipal community and followed the lines of demarcation of the Roman administrative system. Gallican organization defeated Arianism and became largely independent of the papacy.

Eastern Monasticism was gradually adapted to the demands of the West. St. Benedict followed St. Basil but differed in the "elimination of austerity and in the sinking of the individual in the community." He founded a monastery at Monte Cassino about 520 and published his rule about 526. It required each monk to spend a specified amount of time each day in reading and assumed a library and provision for copying books. In 531 Cassiodorus, a[c] minister under Theodoric, established a monastery at Vivarium and with his successors "completed the work of St. Benedict by making the writing of books, the preservation of authors, a sacred duty and an act of piety" (Lowe). He was the first librarian of the Latin West and collected manuscripts of ancient writings on a large scale. His *Institutiones divinarum lectionum* outlined a scheme of study for monks and included an account of the methods and technique of transcription. Organization of a *scriptorium* in which books were copied provided a model for Benedictine monasteries. He "gave a scholarly bent to Western monasticism and played a major role in the preservation and transmission of classical culture"[3] and exercised an important influence on literature of the West.[4]

Western monasticism was securely established over a wide area under Gregory the Great (596–604). He disapproved of the "idle vanities of secular learning." "For the same mouth cannot sing the praises of Jupiter and the praises of Christ." "There is no merit in a faith whereof reason provides the proof." Monasticism was given a higher religious status and the Benedictine order gained enormously from his support. At the same time he encouraged extension of the Church.

Since Ireland had never been a part of the Roman empire, monasticism lacked the discipline of Roman order. Independent and self-governing monasteries were established through the work of St. Patrick after about 432. Absence of a fixed endowment favoured the abbot rather than the bishop. Columba[d] crossed over to the isle of Iona about 565 and developed the practice of establishing religious houses in relation to the central body. With great missionary zeal Columbanus monks migrated to the Continent and established monasteries at Gallus about 613 and at Bobbio in 614. Conflict with the Roman Church led to the calling of a synod at Whitby in 664 by King Oswin and ultimately to acceptance of the Roman system.[e] Iona recognized the Roman Easter in 714. Benedict Biscop brought from Rome "many books[f] of all subjects of divine learning"[5] (Bede), and from the resources of his monastery established at Wearmouth in 674 Bede prepared his Ecclesiastical History. Libraries increased rapidly in England from 670 to 735 and fresh impetus was given to Irish and English influence on the Continent. Wynfrith, renamed Boniface (680–754), was sent to Germany by Gregory II and with his successor Lull drew on English libraries to meet the needs of new monasteries, particularly at Fulda. York had superseded Yarrow as the chief educational centre of England, indeed of medieval Europe, and from here Alcuin, "a man of wide reading rather than original thought," was brought by Charlemagne to the palace school at Aachen after 781. Transcriptions were made from English codices, and after Danish raids, from Roman codices and a large collection of books built up at Aachen to supply the monasteries of France and Germany. Alcuin "marks the beginning of the period ... described as the Benedictine age ... extending ... to the rise of the University of Paris."[6]

The position of the Church was profoundly affected by the success of Mohammedanism in the East and in the West, and by the problems of political organization which accompanied it. In the Byzantine empire Constantine IV administered the first check to Islam in a treaty of 678, but the menace persisted until Leo III, who was crowned emperor in 717, defeated the Moslems at Constantinople in 717–18. An attempt had been made to restore religious unity between the Patriarch of Constantinople and the papacy in the Œcumenical Council of Constantinople (680–81), but such attempts alienated Monophysite influence and it became necessary to take effective steps to weaken its support to the Mohammedans and to check Mohammedan aggression. Mohammedanism developed its strength in relation to various peoples who came under its control by emphasizing the sacred position of the written word. "Images are an abomination of the work of Satan" (Koran). The Caliph Iezid II (720–24) ordered the destruction of all pictures in the Christian churches within his dominion. In AD 730 Leo III issued a decree, sanctioned by the signature of the patriarch, against images and a decree of Constantine V in 753–54 solemnly condemned image worship.[7] Proscription of images was not only designed to strengthen the empire externally but also internally, since it was aimed at the monks "who found in the images and in their cult the most powerful sanction for their acts,"[8] and who had come into possession of large landed properties through exemption from taxes and had become competitors of the state for labour. The Isaurian emperors secularized large monastic properties, restricted the number of monks, and through persecution, particularly after the martyrdom of Stephen in 764, drove large numbers to Italy.

In the West, Pope Gregory I had regarded images as useful for the illiterate "who could at least read by looking at the walls what they cannot read in books." In a letter to the bishop of Marseilles in 599 he wrote "in forbidding the adoration of pictures, you deserve commendation, but in destroying them you are to blame."[9] Pope Gregory III was the last pope to be confirmed by the Byzantine emperor. In 731 the iconoclasts were anathematized and excluded from the Church. In 732 defeat of the Arabs by Charles Martel brought Mohammedan expansion in the West to an end. "Without Islam the Frankish empire would probably never have existed and Charlemagne without Mahomet would be inconceivable" (Pirenne). The aristocracy of the Merovingian line had been weakened by the increasing power of the Church. Boniface brought the tradition of an organized Church under the authority of the pope from England to Germany and his consecration[g] of Pepin in 751 provided a precedent for the later crowning of Charlemagne. Pope Zacharias[h] 741–52 recognized in the person of Pepin the succession of the family of mayors of the palace. In 754 Pepin presented territories formerly belonging to the Byzantine empire to Stephen II. The election of Paul was announced to Pepin and not to the emperor, and after 772 the papacy no longer dated documents by the years of the reign of the Eastern emperor. The Synod of Gentilly summoned in 767 by Pepin approved the practice of image worship and the Lateran Council of 769 decided that images were subject to veneration by all Christians.

In order to recapture the sympathy of the West, Leo IV abandoned the antimonastic policy in 775. At the Œcumenical Council of Nicaea in 787 images were allowed "due salutation and honourable reverence but not the worship which pertains alone to the divine nature,"[10] and the decrees were approved by Pope Hadrian. Charlemagne, on the other hand, in the *Caroline Books* (790) and the Synod of Frankfort in 794, attacked the decrees of the Council of Nicaea and forbade the worship or veneration of images. These views were tolerated by the pope since Constantinople refused to recognize his territorial claims. With the accession of Irene, a woman, to the Byzantine throne in 797, Charlemagne and the Papacy, following Salic law, regarded the position as vacant and Charlemagne was crowned emperor[11] in 800. The humiliation of the Byzantine empire was confirmed in the treaty of 812 in which two emperors were recognized and Italy, except for Venice and districts in the south part, was lost to the Eastern empire. Leo V was crowned in 813 and a local council in Constantinople in 815 revived the decrees of 753 and proscribed images.

The Carolingian dynasty recruited its secretaries and notaries from the educational institutions controlled by the Church and Charlemagne demanded higher educational qualifications for the clergy. In capitularies of 787 he established schools in connection with every abbey. An *armarium* for the teaching of writing was added to the *scriptorium*. He insisted on uniform obedience in the monasteries to the rule of St. Benedict and was active in securing a uniform liturgy[i] and ritual in church services. The texts, including a revised Vulgate, were written in the Caroline minuscule which was apparently developed at Corbie and which gradually prevailed over other scripts. It marked the triumph of control by the Church over education. Writing "being in itself an instrument of conservatism, it was in the nature of things extremely conservative" (Lowe). The use of abbreviations and suspensions made reading and writing highly skilled crafts.

The Visigothic miniscule, which had wide circulation in the *Etymologica* and the *Chronicle* of Isidore, archbishop of Seville, and which had spread with the migration of Spanish scholars after the Saracen invasion, had been finally suppressed by an ecclesiastical council in favour of the Gallic minuscule, which in turn was superseded by the Caroline minuscule. The uncial and the half-uncial which had probably been used by scribes writing on parchment reached their highest developments in the fifth and sixth centuries respectively. Demands for more rapid writing and the necessity of economy in the use of parchment had favoured the half-uncial. In Ireland scant supplies of parchment led to a crowded half-uncial script and extensive use of a system of abbreviation. It was followed by English script probably in the seventh century which was "less bizarre, clearer and less crowded" (Lowe). Both English and Irish scripts spread to the Continent, the influence of the latter being evident in the large number of palimpsests at St. Gall and Bobbio. The demands of public and private notaries for a more efficient script led after the fourth century to a new cursive of curved strokes and a new type of ligature which became the base for a book script and the minuscule. From this the Caroline minuscule was apparently developed and eventually won its way, even in Rome, against the uncial script or *littera Romana*, and finally against the entrenched position of Beneventan script[12] in southern Italy. The clear, precise, and simple Carolingian miniscule replaced a diversity of script and became the basis for more efficient communication.

The achievements of Charlemagne were disastrously impaired by the Teutonic principle of equal division among the heirs, which was accepted by the sons of Louis the Pious after the battle of Fontenoy in 841. An empire extending from Hamburg to Barcelona was permanently split into independent and national kingdoms. Attacks from the Danes and the Magyars accentuated local organizations of force and separatist tendencies. Defeat of the Danes at Paris in 886 marked the beginnings of a new kingdom in France. In the East, defeat of the Magyars in 933 and in 955 laid the foundations of royal power in Henry the Fowler and his son Otto[j] the Great, who was crowned by John XII in Rome as emperor in 962. Power was extended in a marriage arranged between Otto II and Theophano, a Byzantine princess. Otto III (983–1002) began the Teutonic reforms by nominating Germans to the papacy. These encroachments on the Church brought resistance from monastic organizations notably by the Order of Cluni.[k] In 1059, under the influence of Hildebrand, Nicholas II fixed a definite body to choose the supreme pontiff and to evade control by the emperor. With Hildebrand's succession to the papacy reforms of a drastic nature were introduced. The Church was to be freed from ties binding it to the state. It became a sin for an ecclesiastic to receive a benefice from laymen. Condemnation of feudal investitures of land to the clergy struck a deadly blow at the authority of the secular arm. Within the Church, celibacy was enforced as a means of exercising control over men's consciences, preventing the establishment of ecclesiastical dynasties, and guaranteeing the supremacy of Rome. He attempted to extinguish simony and to make the clergy a caste and a pattern of purity to the laity.

Parchment as adapted to the demands of monasticism had contributed to the development of a powerful ecclesiastical organization in western Europe. The monopoly of knowledge that had been built up invited competition from a new medium of communication, which appeared on the fringes of western European culture and was available to meet the demands of lower strata of society. The impact of Mohammedanism, which followed its abhorrence of images, was enormously strengthened by a new medium in which the written word became a more potent force. The significance of paper and the brush had been evident in China and the Far East, and its influence was enhanced by substitution of the pen in western Asia and Europe.

In China[13] writing began with the use of silk and the hair brush, invented in the third century BC for painting, and bamboo, but the inconveniences of these media led to the development of paper about AD 105. Textiles were broken down into fibres which, placed in a solution of water to secure uniformity, could be matted into paper and dried. Rags could be used and gradually flax fibres in linen were found to be more satisfactory. Use of the brush implied that writing developed from painting to pictographs. "A picture is worth a thousand words" (Confucius). Ink[14] made from lamp black was gradually improved between AD 220 and 419 to produce indelible writing. Since the pictograph was never exposed to conventionalization, which came with successive conquests in the West, each character represented a single word and about 1,500 came into general use.

Attempts had been made to preserve the oral tradition by an edict against books in 213 BC, but this had been revoked in 191 BC. Paper was used to establish Confucianism in classical literature and to supplement the oral tradition in the development of an examination system after AD 124 for the selection of talent for administrative purposes. The governing official class was made up of scholars. The empire was organized in districts connected by roads and post relays over which official reports, news-letters, and official gazettes were sent from and to the central administration. Imperial organization was designed to check independent thought. The polished essay was introduced as "a clever contrivance adopted by a former dynasty to prevent the literate from thinking too much." Protests of public opinion were largely reflected in songs and ballads reflecting on the dangers of maladministration which had befallen previous governments. The Chinese were "consistently and thoroughly cynical about most of their officials all the time" (Lin Yutang). Student movements, developed in relation to the civil service, grew up in opposition to empresses and eunuchs, but with little notion of personal civil rights were rigorously suppressed.[15]

The wide gap between the governing and the lower classes facilitated the spread of Buddhism from India. Monopoly of knowledge of the Veda by the Brahmans invited the introduction of a medium from the periphery that would appeal to the lower classes. The power of the oral tradition as controlled by a priestly class in India had resisted the spread of Buddhism and writing, but after Alexander they spread rapidly with the encouragement of Asoka.[16l] But weakening of Macedonian power was followed by the decline of Buddhism and its migration to central and further Asia. Again the monopoly of the Brahmans invited the inroads of Mohammedanism and success accompanied its alphabet and access to supplies of paper. In China Buddhism[m] found an efficient medium of communication in paper and emphasis on the importance of a knowledge of writing. Characters were cut in reverse on wooden blocks, reproduced on paper in large quantities, and sold as charms. With this advance in printing, attempts were made to reproduce the classics cut in stone by making ink rubbings on very thin transparent paper for impressions on wood. The enormous labour involved in cutting large numbers of woodcuts for single pages implied state support on a generous scale.

Communication in China was handicapped in the oral tradition and large numbers of dialects, but it was facilitated by a relatively simple script which was understood throughout the empire and bridged enormous gaps. The emphasis on space concepts in imperial organization implied a neglect of time concepts[17] and inability to solve dynastic problems. Domination of the Mongols from 1280 to 1368 suggested the limitations of political organization, but also the advantages of a tenacious language.

Paper was probably introduced to the West from China by the reign of the Persian king Chosroes II, but the technique of manufacture was learned by the Mohammedans. Chinese workmen had been brought to Tibet to manufacture paper in 648. After the capture of Samarkand in 704 and of Turkestan in 751 manufacturing began in the West. Expansion of Mohammedan territory to the east created problems of government that became acute with dynastic difficulties incidental to polygamy, which had been extremely effective in conquest but was less suited to periods of order. Omayyah at Damascus established his government on the Arab tribal system and came into conflict with the new Moslems, who had been subjects of the Persian kingdom. Abassid capitalized Persian antagonism and the last Omayyad caliph was slain in 750. The Abassids started a new capital at Bagdad[18] and completed it in 763. A member of the Omayyah family escaped to Spain and established the Caliphate of Cordova which declared its independence in 756. At Bagdad, located at considerable distance from supplies of papyrus in Egypt and prohibited from using pig skins for parchment and reluctant to use other animal skins because of difficulties of detection, the Mohammedans concentrated on paper production. The introduction of paper coincided with the splendour and prosperity of Haroun al Raschid (787–809).

Persia had been a repository of Greek philosophy. Followers of Nestorius at Edessa,[n] founded in 428, and other colleges in Berytus and Antioch translated Greek and Latin works into Syriac. After the closing of Edessa by Zeno in 489 scholars migrated to Nisibis and then to Jundeshapur. Scholars fled from Athens, following the closing down of the schools by Justinian in 529, to Persia. After the capture of Alexandria in 642 the university was spared, but in 718–20 moved to Antioch. The tradition of learning was continued under the Abassids. The Caliph Al-Mamun (813–33) founded a school to translate Greek, Syriac, and Persian works into Arabic. Hunayn ibn Ishaq headed a group of translators who made large numbers of works in medicine available in Syriac and Arabic.

Increase in the prestige of Bagdad following the interest in scholarship stimulated an interest in learning in Constantinople. The iconoclastic party established supremacy after the death of Leo in 820 and a vigorous edict of 832 was followed by persecution of painters[19] who were chiefly monks. With the accession of Michael, however, a council in 843 restored the sacred images to the veneration that had formerly been shown to them. Settlement of the controversy was followed by intellectual revival. Caesar Bardas established a university presided over by Leo the mathematician. Basil I, the founder of a Macedonian dynasty, and his son Leo VI compiled the legal code in sixty books and as the *Basilica* (887–93) it became "the most complete monument of Graeco-Roman law" (Vasiliev). Photius, a prodigious scholar with a belief in the universality of knowledge, became the patriarch of Constantinople in 858 and gave a tremendous stimulus to learning. The prestige of Constantinople in turn invoked the hostility of Rome. The attack of Photius on Latin influence and his opposition to the *filioque* addition to the Latin creed led to his excommunication by Pope Nicholas I in 863. In turn the pope was anathematized and denounced for his illegal interference in the Eastern Church in 867. Union with Rome was restored in 869 but again broken from 879 to 893. During this period of difficulty the influence of the Eastern Church was extended by missionary activity in competition with Rome. In 864 King Boris of Bulgaria was baptized and, soon after, his people became Christians.[20] St. Cyril and St. Methodius translated the scriptures into Slavic and invented the Glagolithic alphabet. The offices were celebrated in the Slavic tongue and a Slavic clergy was organized with the sanction of the patriarch of Constantinople. The university was closed in 959 but reopened in 1045 under Constantine IX Monomachus. The intelligentsia became a ruling element in the state. As head of the faculty of philosophy Psellus gave a powerful impetus to Platonism and brought the encyclopedic phase of Byzantine scholarship to an end.[21] The emphasis on secular learning that characterized Byzantine education widened the breach with Rome and in 1054 the Churches of the East and the West finally separated.

In the eleventh century the energy of the Abassids was replaced by that of the Seljuk Turks. In 1070 Atzig, the Seljuk Turkish general, captured Jerusalem and in 1071 Byzantine forces were defeated at Manzikert. The Byzantine emperors were compelled to turn to the papacy for assistance, but the latter turned to the idea of the crusades. The fratricidal abuses of private war in a feudal society incidental to feudal over-population were checked by concentrating attention on the sanctity of battle against the infidel. Division in the leadership of the crusades and in the objectives of the papacy, the German emperor, and the Byzantine emperor limited the possibilities of success. The kingdom of Jerusalem was established between 1100 and 1131, but in 1187 Jerusalem was lost. Attention was directed towards Byzantium and in 1204 Constantinople was captured and the Latin states set up in the East. Holy relics were transferred to west European churches. In the Lateran Council of 1215 the pope was proclaimed head of all Eastern Latin patriarchs. The Greeks retreated to Nicaea and began an intensive reorganization of political and religious life. A council in 1234 intended to bring union between the East and the West ended by the Greeks stating: "'You are heretics. As we have found you heretics and excommunicated so we leave you now as heretics and excommunicated,' to which the Catholics replied 'You also are heretics.'"[22] Constantinople was recaptured by the Greeks in 1261 and the dream of the papacy brought to an end. But Byzantium was irrecoverably weakened during the crusades by the rise of Venice, Genoa, and Pisa and the shift of commercial activity from Constantinople to the West. Large territorial organizations were ground down with advantage to the commercial city-state.

The commercial revolution beginning about 1275 was marked by the spread in the manufacture of paper to Europe.[23] Paper facilitated the growth of credit in the use of documents for insurance and bills of exchange. With Arabic numerals it enormously enhanced the efficiency of commerce. Production had increased in Bagdad and by 1226 it was celebrated for its manufacture of an excellent grade of paper. Over one hundred booksellers and paper-sellers were located on the chief street. Damascus became an important export centre. The sack of Bagdad in 1227 and its capture by the Mongols in 1258 brought this activity to an end. Apparently its use began to supersede papyrus even in Egypt, since in the eleventh century mummies were being disinterred for supplies of cloth for paper-making. The unsatisfactory character of the Arabian paper led Roger of Sicily in 1145 to order the recopying of acts written on it and Frederick II in 1221 to prohibit its use for public acts. It was claimed that Fez had 400 paper-mills in the twelfth century. The manufacture moved to Xativa at least by 1173 but again its poor quality involved limited use. Attempts were made in Italy to improve the quality of paper by the introduction of stamps run by water power to produce a finer pulp, the use of metallic forms, and the introduction of glue for sizing. The production of a better quality was marked by the use of *filigraines* or watermarks about 1282. A paper-mill existed at Fabriano before 1268 and at least seven paper-makers were located at that centre in 1283. The superior quality of paper was accompanied by a rapid extension of markets. Towards the end of the second third of the thirteenth century the more primitive Arab processes were gradually abolished. Marked increase in production in Italy after 1300 was evident in exports to the French Midi. By the latter part of the fourteenth century Italian paper-makers had migrated to France, the art of paper-making was still further improved, and paper production had moved to the north. Linen production beginning in Flanders spread to other areas after the eleventh century, particularly as it brought a decline in cutaneous diseases. Linen rags were available in larger quantities and paper manufacture became established near large centres such as Paris and Languedoc to meet the demands of governments, universities, and schools. The long apprenticeship and training necessary for paper-makers meant that skilled labour had a monopoly. Numerous attempts were made to check the migration of paper-makers, but the cost of moving labour to take advantage of such geographic factors as power and water proved less than that of moving the raw material and the finished product. Monopoly positions of various sites were gradually broken down. In contrast with parchment, which could be produced over wide areas, paper was essentially a product of the cities in terms of cheap supplies of rags and of markets. The control of monasteries in rural districts over education was replaced by the growth of cathedral schools and universities in cities. The religious prejudice against a product of Judeo-Arabic origin was gradually broken as the demands of trade and of government increased.

The impact of Moslem civilization[24] on the West was most powerful through Sicily and Spain. After the Mohammedans had been expelled in 1090 enlightened rulers in Sicily encouraged the translation of Arabic works on a large scale. Under Frederick II (1194–1250) Greek, Latin, and Arabic were recognized for legal purposes. About 1228 Michael Scot translated the biological works of Aristotle. Farrachius translated the enormous medical treatise of Rhazes of Khorasan (865–925). In Spain the Caliph Hakin II established at Cordova the largest library of over 400,000 volumes in a total of at least seventy libraries. After the fall of Toledo in 1085, Cordova in 1236, and Seville in 1248, the resources of the Moslem world were thrown open to the West. Adelard of Bath translated the trigonometrical tables of al-Khwarizmi in 1126 and Evendeath (1090–1165) made available the system of Arabic numerical notation which slowly gained ground throughout Europe. The work of Averroes (1126–98), the greatest of Moslem philosophers, in his commentaries on Aristotle was made available by Michael Scot in Toledo after 1217. Jews[25] were active in the transmission of Greek learning from Spain to Christian Europe. Maimonides (1153–1204) contributed to the accommodation of Aristotelian teaching to biblical doctrine. As these works became available to the West the Church attempted to offset them and to adapt them to Christian teaching. Albertus Magnus and other schoolmen made prodigious compilations of knowledge. St. Thomas Aquinas, influenced by Maimonides and Averroes, attempted to give reason a proper place between skeptical mysticism and rationalism divorced from the belief in the possibility of a revealed religion. He was assisted by direct translations from the Greek following the fall of Constantinople, which placed the work of Aristotle in a clearer light. From the Latin translations of Aristotle's work at Toledo to the translation from the Greek of Constantinople about 1260 meant that knowledge passed from "a phase of almost total darkness to one of nearly perfect light."[26]

The effect of the spread in the use of paper was evident in the increasing importance of the vernacular. An emphasis on Latin in the monastery and the church widened the gap between the oral and the written tradition. Bilingualism implied lack of "clearness of speech and therefore of thought."[27] "One language blunts the other." Learned literature was written in a complex script and "in the inmost thoughts even of the most learned men, the mother tongue seems always, or nearly always, to have remained uppermost."[28] Latin was hampered as a medium by the widening gap with the vernacular and its limitations were more severe as it reflected a celibate type of thought. Scholars were concerned with letters rather than sounds and linguistic instruction emphasized eye philology rather than ear philology.[29] The position of Latin had been entrenched as a result of the conflict with the Eastern Church since encouragement of the Slavic liturgy in the East was followed by insistence on Latin in the West.[30] At Toulouse in 1229 the synod decreed that "lay people shall not have books of scripture, except the psalter and the divine office; and they shall not have these in the vulgar tongue." In spite of the policy of the Church, translations were made of portions of the Gospel, and to avoid persecution and to spread its influence, large portions were memorized notably by members of the lower classes unable to read. The Waldensians, followers of Peter Waldo of Lyons, after 1150 were particularly concerned as they were inspired by lay reading of the New Testament and were declared heretics by the papal edict of Verona in 1184 and ordered to be delivered to the secular arm. Innocent III declared in a letter in 1199 "in this matter certain laymen appear to be justly accused; because they hold secret conventicles, usurp to themselves the office of preaching, elude the simplicity of priests and scorn the company of those who cling not to these things ... the secret mysteries of the faith ought not therefore to be explained to all men in all places."[31] Feudal courts became increasingly centres of literary activity in the vernacular, particularly with the prominent position occupied by women and the importance of patronage.[32] Charlemagne ordered the preservation of vernacular literature which had been transmitted orally.[33] Alfred the Great wrote in his translation of Gregory's *Pastoral Rule*:

> Therefore it seems better to me, if it seems likewise to you, that we turn some books which are most needful for all persons into the tongue which we can all understand; and that you act ... to the end that all the youth now in England of free men who have the wealth to be able to apply themselves to it, be set to learning so long as they are no use for anything else, until the time when they can read English writing well: let those afterwards be instructed further in the Latin language.

In Provence patronage supported a rich troubadour literature in the twelfth century. Vernacular literature favoured the growth of heretical writings[34] and led to the Albigensian crusade° beginning in 1209 and ending with the destruction of the civilization of southern France in the Treaty of Paris in 1229. The Dominican (1215) and the Franciscan (1210) preaching orders were established to bridge the widening gap between the older monasticism and the vernacular. "An age of friars succeeded an age of monks" (Rashdall). In turn the Inquisition[35] was developed to detect heresy with greater facility. The papal bull *Ad Extirpanda* in 1252 established the Inquisition which had been worked out between 1227 and 1241.

The interest in the Byzantine empire in law was[36] transmitted to Italy as the Church increased in power and the emperor in the West realized its possibilities in resisting the aggression of the papacy. The early teachers in law at Bologna were supported by the patronage of emperors. The teaching of Irnerius (1100–30) led to a systematic study of the *Corpus Juris Civilis*. The glossators followed and the study of law in Italy made substantial advance at the expense of theology. Study of the jurisprudence of the *Digest* facilitated the development of law in relation to the demands of trade and commerce and urban communities. As Roman law was developed in the interest of the emperors the Church followed with canon law based on the *Decretum* of Gratian completed in 1142 and accepted as a code by Gregory IX in 1234. After the breakdown of the German kingdom under the weight of the Roman empire with the death of Frederick II,[37] the Germanic and imperial crown to check the power of the papacy became elective. The Emperor Louis IV resisted the demands of the papacy and was excommunicated, but with the assistance of Marsilius and William of Occam he deposed John XXII and elected a Franciscan pope. The diets of Frankfort in 1338 and 1339 insisted that the empire was held from God alone. Marsilius held that the ultimate source of power was in the people and that the Church consisted of all Christians in contrast with the claims of the papacy.

Roman law was in a sense a continuation of tradition in Italy. Paris became the great centre of theology. The influence of classical civilization[38] shown in the writings of John Scotus Erigena became more powerful following acquaintance with the work of Aristotle and led to the development of scholasticism centring in the University of Paris.[39] The Latin language was made subtle and flexible and became the basis of the rich possibilities of the French vernacular. The Dominicans, notably Albertus Magnus (1193–1280) and Thomas Aquinas (1227–74), pressed "the whole Aristotelian philosophy into the service of the church." Located at the capital of a great state the University of Paris dominated the theology of the Church even to the extent of overawing the papacy. In turn the prestige of Paris gave the king of France an important weapon in resisting the claims of the papacy as expressed in the *Unam Sanctam* of Boniface VIII in 1302 "that it is altogether necessary for salvation for all human creatures, that they should be subject to the Roman pontiff." Attempts to build up financial strength were resisted by France and became more onerous for England. The French monarchy under Philip the Fair was supported by French lawyers. "From a broad political and social point of view one of the most important results of the university was the creation, or at least the enormously increased power and importance of the lawyer class" (Rashdall). "Lawyers, that powerful profession of which historians and politicians do not recognize the permeating influence. No inconsiderable part of history is the record of the illusions of statesmen" (Morley). In opposition to the papacy and the emperor there emerged a central principle of French law, "the King is Emperor within his own realm." Every power that made supremacy effective was transferred to the king, and the emperor was left in theoretical supremacy. "Writing is a witness very hard to corrupt; the customs were therefore reduced to writing."[40] "They were made more general, and they received the stamp of royal authority."[41] The power of France over the papacy became evident in the "Babylonian captivity" (1308–78) of Avignon, the great schism from 1378 to 1417, repression of the Inquisition, and the hostility of England.

Roman law strengthened the position of the monarchy in France, but it had limited importance in England where the oral tradition was more strongly entrenched. The common law was developed from customs which had emerged over a long period and which, as in the case of the formative period of Roman law, were carried in the memories of men.[42] "While, however, they use *leges* and a written law in almost all lands, in England alone there has been used within its boundaries an unwritten law and custom. In England legal right is based on an unwritten law which usage has approved ... For the English hold many things by customary law which they do not hold by *lex*" (Bracton).[43] "To reduce in every instance the law (*leges*) and rights (*jura*) of the Realm into writing would be, in our times, absolutely impossible, as well on account of the ignorance of writers, as of the confused multiplicity of the laws" (Glanvill).[44] As late as 1628 Sir John Davis wrote: "So the *customary law* of England, which we doe likewise call *jus commune* as comming neerest to the lawe of nature, which is the root and touchstone of all good lawes, and which is also *jus non scriptum* and written onely in the memory of man ... doth far excell our written lawes, namely our statutes or Acts or Parliament."[45] G.B. Adams has emphasized the necessity of calling men together to give a true account of customs and events under conditions in which writing did not exist. "The law was not made, it was only proved" (McIlwain). From this emerged the strength of the jury system and the growth of parliament. Representatives of smaller communities before the county court were followed by representatives of boroughs and counties in parliament which provided a knowledge of men, customs, and opinions. "A foundation of common law was indispensable to a house of common politics" (Pollard). Common law escaped the powerful influence of lawyers such as had isolated property in Roman law and retained the complex concept of ownership with far-reaching significance to the growth of trade and politics.

As the court in France strengthened the position of French in contrast with Latin, the court in England, particularly as a result of the war with France, strengthened the position of English in contrast with French.[46] In 1362 a statute ordered all pleading at law courts to be in English and in the same year the Lord Chancellor first opened parliament in English. The influence of the vernacular was evident in literature, and in its struggle against Latin in religion. Wycliffe believed that Dominion is founded in grace and that all human authority is conditioned by the worthiness of the person exercising it, and advocated withdrawal of allegiance to such unworthiness as was evident in monastic foundations and the papacy. Since the immediate responsibility of every Christian was to follow the life of Christ, the Bible must be made available in the vernacular. Under his influence a first version was produced in 1382, and a later version completed by 1395 provided the unlearned with scriptures which could be memorized. Though the unlicensed possession of books in English dealing with theology was prohibited in 1408[47] the influence of the translation persisted in England and spread to Prague. The popular preaching of the friars was checked by a direct appeal to the scriptures.

A civilization dominated by parchment as a medium developed its monopoly of knowledge through monasticism. The power of the Church was reflected in its success in the struggle with Frederick II, in the development of the Gothic cathedral[p] from 1040 to 1245, and in the work of Albertus Magnus and Thomas Aquinas. Its monopoly position had been weakened by the introduction and spread of paper,[48] but reorganizations and counter-attacks, notably in the Inquisition, delayed its collapse. Paper supported the growth of trade and of cities and of education beyond the control of the monasteries and, in turn, of the Church and the cathedrals. The rise of the vernacular was reflected in the patronage of literature by the courts and in the increasing role of lawyers. The Dominicans and the Franciscans attempted on the one hand to dominate the universities and on the other to reach large numbers by preaching in the vernacular.[49] Institutions were designed to bridge the widening gap between the Church, which emphasized Latin, and the demands of increasing literacy in the vernacular reflected in the spread of heresy. The problems were evident in the increasing division between the old monastic orders and the new and between the new orders. The influence of the Dominicans in Paris was offset by that of the Franciscans in Oxford. Emphasis on vows of poverty brought division in the Church which was exploited by monarchies and political writers. Literature supported by the patronage of the courts reinforced the position of the vernacular in the poetry of the troubadours, and in that of such writers as Dante, Petrarch, Boccaccio, and Chaucer. In contrast with the significance of celibacy in the Church, the importance of women in the courts favoured a vernacular literature.[50] "A man's proper vernacular is nearest unto him in as much as it is more closely united to him, for it is singly and alone in his mind before any other" (Dante).

The rise of vernacular literature hastened and was hastened by the growth of nationalism. The Church had broken the German empire and in turn had been dominated by the French king.[51] Opposition to French supremacy was evident in the resistance of English nationalism to pleas of the papacy for financial support[52] and in the encouragement of universities to offset the influence of Paris. Opposition of the papacy to French control led on the one hand to the establishment of universities in Spain and in Germany and on the other to the growth of a Gallican Church under the control of the French crown. The papacy triumphed over the Council as representative of the Church through the support of canon lawyers in 1448, but its success led to the Reformation. "The worst corruption of the Middle Ages lay in the transformation of the sacerdotal hierarchy into a hierarchy of lawyers" (Rashdall).

The growth of bureaucracy in the Roman empire had followed dependence on the papyrus roll, but stability assumed a fusion with religious organization based on the parchment codex. Bureaucracy in terms of the state implied an emphasis on space and a neglect of the problems of time and in terms of religion an emphasis on time and a neglect of the problems of space. The tenacity of the Byzantine empire assumed the achievement of a balance which recognized the role of space and time. The dominance of parchment in the West involved an exaggeration of the significance of time. A monopoly of knowledge based on parchment invited competition from a new medium such as paper which emphasized the significance of space as reflected in the growth of nationalist monarchies. A fusion between a monopoly of knowledge developed by ecclesiastical organization with emphasis on parchment and a rural monasticism, and a monopoly of knowledge developed by political organization with emphasis on paper and urban industry and trade gave power and influence to the French empire.

In its struggle to maintain the supremacy of Latin the Church was concerned not only with opposition to the vernaculars but also with opposition to other learned languages, notably Greek and Hebrew. The iconoclastic controversies had been accompanied by the migration of monks to Italy, and the weakening of the Byzantine empire was marked by the transmission of manuscripts of classical writings. In 1395 Emmanuel Chrysoloras became a teacher of Greek in Florence and manuscripts were brought in large numbers to Italy in the fifteenth century. Scholars from the East introduced a new respect for Plato and the overwhelming influence of Aristotle in the West came to an end.

Paper "permitted the old costly material by which thought was transmitted to be superseded by an economical substance, which was to facilitate the diffusion of the works of human intelligence."[53] It brought a revolution ... of high importance without which the art of writing would have been much less practised, and the invention of printing less serviceable to mankind."[54] The spread of writing was accompanied by improvement in instruments. In the sixth century reed pens were being displaced by quills. Iron pens were perfected in the fourteenth century. The demands of trade in the thirteenth century were met by increasing supplies of paper and the rise of clerks skilled in cursive writing and accounting.

Parchment was slowly displaced by paper in the universities, churches, and monasteries. The Greeks began to use paper in manuscripts in the twelfth century and Italians in the thirteenth century, but it was sparingly used, in spite of the very high cost of parchment notably in the thirteenth century, until the fifteenth century. Monasteries continued to support the slow and costly production of parchment manuscripts. Writing on parchment required strength and effort. "Their fingers hold the pen but the whole body toils." Working six hours a day the scribe produced from two to four pages and required from ten months to a year and a quarter to copy a Bible. The size of the scriptures absorbed the energies of monasteries. Libraries were slowly built up and uniform rules in the care of books were generally adopted in the thirteenth century. Demands for space led to the standing of books upright on the shelves in the fourteenth and fifteenth centuries and to the rush of library construction in the fifteenth century.[55]

Universities demanded textbooks on a large scale and by the end of the thirteenth century monastic began to be replaced by lay scribes. In 1275 the University of Paris made provision for a group of copyists and calligraphy became the concern of a corporation of copyists. Dialectical discussion in class characteristic of a bookless age declined with the increasing importance of the authority of the textbook. The universities favoured dictation and the preparation of a number of copies in a short period. The effect of textbooks on lectures was evident in a statute of the University of Paris in 1355 against the abuses of dictating word for word. The University of Paris controlled the sale of parchment, fixed the number of booksellers and copyists, and regulated their activities in making, renting, and selling books. The demands of universities and lawyers were met by the development of a book trade in theology, medicine, and law. It was estimated that Paris had 10,000 copyists by the middle of the fifteenth century

In cities without the restrictions of university regulations an important market was built up. In Florence and Venice an important trade in manuscripts was developed in the early part of the fifteenth century, and at Frankfort and Nordlingen manuscripts in the German vernacular were manifolded and sold on a large scale. In Florence Vespasiano di Bisticci[q] had a staff of copyists producing manuscripts in Latin, Greek, and Hebrew. The manuscript trade assumed the development of a large number of private libraries built up by wealthy merchants and noblemen of Church and state. Such demands were accompanied by the rapid advance of illumination in Italy in the fourteenth and fifteenth centuries. The example was followed in France where illumination reached its peak in the first half of the fifteenth century. "The production of illuminated manuscripts had become in France almost a staple industry. Books of Hours in particular were produced in vast numbers not only to the order of wealthy patrons but also for booksellers."[56] In the latter part of the fifteenth century Flemish illuminators surpassed French and Italian craftsmen especially in "the delicacy of their handling of landscape and portraiture."[57]

Guild regulations restricted the use of engraving for the illumination of manuscripts, but the demands of monks for the production of religious pictures as a device for propaganda of the faith and as an exchange for penance following the organization of indulgences by Clement VI and Boniface IX led to the use of wood engravings. As in China the demands of religion in Buddhism had led to the wide-scale production of block prints, so in Europe block prints possibly introduced from China during the Mongolian supremacy began to appear in the latter part of the fourteenth century. Large numbers of prints could be produced cheaply and distributed widely. The objection of copyists' guilds to engraving of a text on the same block as the picture were overcome and block books began to appear as early as 1409.[58] As in China paper and block printing were adapted to the large-scale demands of religion, but in the West the sale of indulgences to offset the decline in revenue from the nation-states brought protests ending in the Reformation. Revenue from penance encouraged deeds for which penance was required and proved an unhappy support for ecclesiastical finance.

The monopoly of knowledge built up under ecclesiastical control in relation to time and based on the medium of parchment was undermined by the competition of paper. The bias of paper as a medium was evident in China with its bureaucratic administration developed in relation to the demands of space. A bureaucratic administration supported by a complex alphabetical script written with a brush implied limited possibilities of linking an oral and written tradition and facilitated the spread of Buddhism, with its emphasis on the production of charms and statues among the lower classes. Limited supplies of satisfactory writing material in India strengthened the monopoly of the oral tradition held by the Brahmans, emphasized the importance of the concept of time, and invited competition from the invaders during the period of expansion of the Macedonian empire. India had no god of writing but a goddess of knowledge, learning, and eloquence. The exclusive right of teaching was bestowed by God on hereditary priests. Invasion was accompanied by the spread of Buddhism and writing, but not to the extent of supporting a bureaucratic administration. The culture of Buddhist India became a civilizing and humanizing factor responsible for an empire based on spiritual and not on political and military unity.[59] The limited possibilities of political bureaucratic development with an emphasis on space in India accentuated an emphasis on religious development in contrast with the political bureaucratic development of China.[60] Hence Buddhism spread with great rapidity in China but eventually, failing to overwhelm the political bureaucracy, spread to Japan.

The spread of Buddhism and writing and printing in China was accompanied by an expansion of the paper industry and by its migration to the West through the Mohammedans. Paper responded to the invitation of the monopoly of knowledge based on parchment and reflected in monasticism with its emphasis on the concept of time and through competition hastened the development of political bureaucracy with its emphasis on the concept of space.

7 — PAPER AND
THE PRINTING PRESS

The monopoly built up by guilds of copyists and others concerned with the making of manuscripts had its effects in high prices which in turn invited attempts to produce at lower costs. It was significant that these attempts were made in territory marginal to France in which copyists' guilds held a strong monopoly, and that they were concerned with the production of an imitation of manuscripts such as Bibles, i.e., Latin Vulgate, which commanded, partly as a result of size, very high prices. In 1470 it was estimated in Paris that a printed Bible cost about one-fifth that of a manuscript Bible. The size of the scriptures had an important effect in hastening the introduction of the parchment codex and in turn the introduction of printing. The feudal divisions of Germany provided an escape from the more rigid central control of France.

Profits were dependent on exact reproductions of expensive manuscripts. It was necessary to develop arrangements by which type could be cast resembling exactly the letters of the manuscript and in sufficient quantity to facilitate setting up pages for printing. The alphabet, which had been conventionalized to a limited number of letters used in innumerable combinations in words, lent itself to adaptation to mechanical production of large numbers of the same letters which could be put together in the required combinations. In contrast with China, where the character of the script involved large-scale undertakings supported by governments, the alphabet permitted small-scale undertakings manageable by private enterprise.

The problem of producing quantities of letters with speed was solved through the resources of a highly technical metal industry. Letters were cut on punches, which were hardened and driven into softer metal to provide a cast for the letter. For arrangement on a page each letter must be of the same height and of the same length, though the sizes of letters and in turn the breadths varied. An adjustable mould suited to varying breadths and in which various punched letters could be inserted at the bottom was basic to efficient production of type. In addition it became important to secure a metal which had a low melting-point and which did not contract and expand in response to temperature. An alloy including lead and antimony, of which one expanded and the other contracted with increased temperature, gave satisfactory results. Solution of the problems of metal type production was accompanied by a solution of the problem of ink. Engraved wooden blocks used indelible ink which was not suited to metal. Painters had developed oil as a base for paint and linseed oil and lamp-black were adapted to ink for metal type. Finally, arrangements for pressing parchment and paper firmly on the inked type and releasing them quickly were worked out on a screw press. Rapid manipulation in raising and lowering the press was essential to low-cost printing. In the production of a large book capital investment in equipment and raw materials was substantial. A single press could employ at least two typesetters and two printers. Six presses were used to print the Gutenberg Bible. Early printers used an alphabet of over 150 characters, including ligatures and devices which had been introduced by copyists.

An increase in the number of trained printers, particularly after the sack of Mainz in 1462, was followed by migration to other centres in Germany and in Europe. Supplies of paper and a market for books attracted printers to Italy. Paper-makers became concerned with printing as a means of expanding the market. Imitation of manuscripts compelled printers to produce type corresponding to the various writing hands developed in different regions. In Germany gothic writing and gothic type prevailed, and in Italy the roman characters developed during the classical revival of the Renaissance predominated. Venice as a centre of trade in Greek manuscripts became a centre under the influence of Aldus for the production of Greek type. As the market for large, costly, and cumbersome folios was met, convenient crown octavos at moderate prices were produced. In turn italic as a more compact type based on the Vatican chancery script was used. The influence of copyists and illuminators delayed the introduction of printing in Paris until 1469, but the delay and the control exercised by the University favoured the introduction of roman type,[1] early in the sixteenth century. Printing spread to the Low countries and from there Caxton introduced it to England. Since Italy and France had concentrated on ecclesiastical and classical works, Caxton was compelled to emphasize books in English, and he printed translations and English works, notably those of Chaucer.

By the end of the fifteenth century presses had been established in the larger centres of Europe. They had been concerned with the reproduction of manuscripts for the use of the Church, law, medicine, and trade. They had reproduced manuscripts in Latin and in Greek and in the vernaculars notably in Germany and England. With these developments a book trade had been built up and the size of printing establishments increased. The task of making available the manuscripts which had accumulated over centuries had been well begun. Printing accentuated a commercial interest in the selection of books and the publisher concerned with markets began to displace the printer concerned with production. The monopoly of monasticism was further undermined. The authority of the written word declined. "The age of cathedrals had passed. The age of the printing press had begun."[2]

In Germany the vernacular became increasingly important after the fall of the Hohenstaufens in 1368. German music protected by the Hohenstaufens resisted encroachments from the Church. The large number of Dominican nunneries brought a demand for German words to explain scholastic terms and phrases and to adapt abstract thought to the minds of pious, imperfectly educated women. Mystical teaching was popularized in vernacular sermons and writings in opposition to scholasticism. Gerard Groote (1340–84), the founder of the Brotherhood of Common Life, set up schools in which translations of the vernacular were taught as a protest against the formalism of the Church. Lay people were instructed and German books and pamphlets circulated. At Deventer printing presses were set up and large numbers of works published in German. As a result of this background large numbers of German bibles were printed before the end of the fifteenth century in spite of the statement of the Archbishop of Mainz "that the poverty of our mother tongue is quite insufficient and that it would be necessary for translators to invent unknown names for things out of their head."[3]

An interest in vernacular scriptures, particularly after the rise of universities, led to conflicts between scholars and the Church.[4] John Reuchlin, a Hebrew scholar at Cologne, was bitterly attacked because of a pamphlet he had written in 1510. Erasmus continued the work of collating and translating manuscripts for publication and achieved notable success in collections of extracts from the classics. With the co-operation of John Froben, a printer at Basle, he published his Greek Testament in March 1516 which "contributed more to the liberation of the human mind from the thraldom of the clergy than all the uproar and rage of Luther's many pamphlets" (Mark Pattison). It became the basis of Luther's German translation printed in 1522, of Tyndale's English translation printed in 1526, and of Estienne's work printed in France in 1550. In his protests against the sale of indulgences by the church and the drain of money to Rome, Luther was led to emphasize the Pauline doctrine of justification by faith[a] and to attack the doctrine of the sacraments, the bondage of ecclesiastical enactments, and the self-glorification of the priesthood. He took full advantage of an established book trade and large numbers of copies of the New and later the Old Testament were widely distributed at low prices. Polemical literature implied the printing of pamphlets which were quickly produced on small presses, profitably sold, and capable of wide circulation in the hands of pedlars. High German became the

basis of modern German literature. The number of titles printed in Germany increased from 90 in 1513 to 146 in 1518 and 944
in 1523. In the struggle between the folios of ecclesiasticism and
the pamphlets and sheets of reformers, the Frankfort Fair
declined in importance, particularly after the establishment of a
press censorship in 1579, and Leipzig gained enormously as a
centre of the book trade. Large firms such as that of Koberger,
who concentrated on Catholic works, felt the effects of competition from firms concentrating on Protestant writings.

The outbreak of the Reformation in Germany was paralleled by repression in France and in regions dominated by the
Church and the emperor. In Italy Greek declined in importance
in the first quarter of the sixteenth century. The fall of Florence
in 1512, the sack of Rome in 1527, and the crowning of Charles
V at Bologna in 1530 were followed by an extension of Spanish
influence. But the decline of learning was marked by the
increasing effectiveness of the vernacular shown in the writings
of Machiavelli. In France the University of Paris and the monarchy offset the influence of the Frankfort Book Fair and introduced severe repressive measures against Lutheran publications
in 1534. Increased efficiency of the printing press, in which production had increased from 20 to 200 leaves per hour, and
restrictions on markets contributed to acute labour difficulties at
Lyons and Paris after 1538 and to the migration of such printers
as Estienne to Switzerland. The printing industry was encouraged, but regulations and suppression of attacks on royalty, religion, and public order led to the publication of books beyond
French borders for import to France, particularly after 1570. The
influence of the Jesuit Order established in 1540 and the bitter
struggle against Protestantism culminating in St. Bartholomew's
massacre in 1572 implied the decline of learning. "The women
and the ignorant — both very important conquests — had been
recovered through the confessional and the pulpit."[5] The position of Greek as an heretical language declined. "Philology is
eminently the Protestant science."[6] "From 1593, the date of
Scaliger's removal to Leyden, the supremacy in the republic of

learning was possessed by the Dutch."[7] "The deterioration of learning in the University of Paris circa 1600 is a striking fact in the literary history of Europe."[8]

Decline in learning in France was paralleled by an improvement of the position of the vernacular. As the contents of written manuscripts were made available through printing, the demand for writings of contemporary authors increased. The writings of Rabelais were designed to meet the demands of printers in Lyons, a centre less exposed to interference from the Sorbonne. Montaigne made "the first attempt to treat in a modern language and in a popular form, questions of great importance to human character and conduct."[9] He drove out "the servile pedantry of the schools" (Hallam). Printers such as Geoffrey Tory and Dolet supported the importance of the vernacular. "As to the ancients, as well Greeks as Romans, they have never taken any other instrument for their eloquence than their mother tongue" (Dolet). After the publication of Calvin's *Institution de la religion chrétienne* in 1540 Protestants[10] continuing their interest in translations of the scriptures made full use of the vernacular and their opponents were compelled to use it in reply. The monarchy recognized the importance of the vernacular in enhancing its prestige and unifying the realm. In 1539 an edict of Francis I brought to an end the use of Latin on the judicial bench and recognition of French as the official language. The Edict of Nantes (1597) was in part a recognition of the influence of Protestantism and the vernacular. By the end of the century the victory of French over Latin was decisive.

Restriction of publications in France was paralleled by encouragement of the production of paper. Mercantilist policies favoured the export of paper. In the words of the Rector of the University of Paris in 1554: *"par le moyen de la papeterie plus que autre trafic de marchandises qui ne passe en France, tire l'or estranger."* By the end of the century France dominated the export market for paper and supplied adjacent countries with raw material at low prices for the production of books which were smuggled into France. Such regions as the Netherlands and Switzerland, capable of resisting censorship, exploited the advantages of cheap paper by an emphasis on freedom of the press. Printers migrated from Lyons and Paris to Geneva and other centres.[11] In opposition to imports French printers supported censorship and accentuated the bitterness of the religious struggle between Huguenots and Catholics. "The Lyonnese printers availed themselves of the brand of "heretic" to get the Genevan books confiscated at the frontier and thus secure at least the French market. Protestant countries had no index and the Genevan printers could not retaliate in kind. They therefore endeavoured — more irritating still — to undersell."

In spite of censorship regulations in the Empire, Plantin built up an extensive publishing business in Antwerp after 1550. With the support of the Church and monarchs he completed a polyglot Bible in 1568. After the sack of Antwerp in 1576 he moved in 1583 to the University of Leyden which had been established as a Protestant centre of learning by William of Orange in 1575. He was the first publisher to associate typography with the work of the engraver on a large scale and produced a great series of illustrated works of enormous advantage to science, particularly botany. With his assistance Leyden became a centre of scholarship and learning, attracting notable scholars and scientists such as Clusius and Scaliger. Expansion of printing in the Netherlands was accompanied by the development of a large-scale type-founding industry which produced types of great variety.

An increase in printing in Europe was accompanied by the expansion of news services. News-letters were used by the Fuggers after 1554 and printed sheets developed with improvements in postal services organized by monarchies. Calendars were published in large quantities and by the end of the sixteenth century periodical publications were introduced at Cologne. Accessibility of information favoured the growth of new centres of finance. The success of Spanish arms supported by the Fugger mining interests of south Germany in Italy led to the rise of Genoa at the expense of Florence and the migration of

Florentine financiers to Lyons in France. "Discovery of Cape Good Hope and America meant that Lisbon superseded Venice and Netherland merchants shifted from fishing to the carrying trade between Spain and Antwerp."[12] By 1554 the Antwerp[13] money market had become largely dependent on Spanish-American silver. A daily bourse at Antwerp required a permanent news service to provide information on the rating of business houses of different nationalities. Loans were floated in Antwerp by the governments of the Netherlands, Spain, Portugal, and England. Antwerp and Lyons displaced the fairs and became the international clearing houses of Europe. Threats of the Inquisition were followed by the emigration of financiers from Antwerp and its destruction in 1576 was followed by the rise of Amsterdam and Holland. The Union of Utrecht in 1579 became the basis of a bourgeois republic. Calvinism was embraced and the privileged position of the priesthood destroyed.

In England suppression of printing was perhaps more effective than on the Continent, but the tendency towards absolutism under the Tudors hastened the influence of the Renaissance and facilitated the introduction of the Reformation. Henry VIII encouraged scholars, became an active founder of schools, and abolished the monasteries. The Renaissance stifled on the Continent blossomed in England. Under monasticism territory and wealth had been monopolized and celibacy became a drain on the resources of education. Abolition of the monasteries was followed by the disappearance of clerical celibacy and development of a wide range of interests. "Henry VIII with Thomas Wolsey, Thomas Cranmer, and Thomas Cromwell cleared the field and sowed the seed for Spenser, Sidney, Bacon and Shakespeare."[14] The accession of Queen Elizabeth permitted by absence of the Salic law which prevailed in France and dominance of a woman over the court were accompanied by patronage of literature. Since England, with its interest in wool rather than linen, was dependent on the Continent for supplies of paper, restrictions on publications were in the interests of mercantilism and maintenance of royal power. Influx of silver from

Potosi to Europe after 1545, rising prices, and defeat of the Armada provided the basis of Elizabethan prosperity. Restrictions on publications[15] accentuated an interest in the drama and enabled Shakespeare to exploit and expand the capacities of a language that had not been repressed by print. "Perhaps the greatest event in the literary history of England" was the success of Marlowe's *Tamburlaine* about 1587. "It naturalised tragedy ... and put an end ... to all the futilities of the theorists. Shakespeare appeared before academies when the processes of popular and literary education had not multiplied definitions and hardened usages. He enjoyed a freedom of invention unknown to his successors."[16] In Athens, tragedy flourished before writing was firmly established and in England before printing had developed its overwhelming power.

The flexibility of the alphabet and its adaptability to mechanization facilitated an approximation of the printed word to the oral tradition. The written tradition dependent on parchment had been inflexible. Paper had expanded in part in relation to the gap between the written tradition dependent on parchment and the oral tradition, and the printed word, at first strengthening the position of the written tradition by its emphasis on manuscripts, later in the sixteenth century bridged the gap with the oral tradition. By the end of that century the vernacular had become an effective basis of literature in the countries of Europe. The flexibility of the alphabet and printing introduced an overwhelmingly divisive influence in Western civilization by emphasizing the place of the vernaculars. The vitality of the vernaculars was strengthened by an emphasis on translations of the scriptures which gave them a sacred appeal.[17]

By the end of the sixteenth century the monopoly of knowledge built up in relation to parchment had been overwhelmed and a fusion achieved with a new monopoly of knowledge built up in relation to paper in the establishment of separate kingdoms in which the Church was dominated by the state as in Lutheranism and Anglicanism. In France the concordat of 1516 virtually separated the French Church from Rome and the importance of the scriptures in the vernacular was offset by the role of literature.[18] Jean Bodin furnished princes with an invincible weapon against religious claims. A common sovereign was the essential element of the political community. In countries in which scriptures in the vernacular were emphasized, the importance of interpretation supported scholarship and sects. "The prolific source of Protestant sectarianism was the notion that the scriptures speak unmistakably."[19] Demands for toleration were met in part in Calvinism. Geneva was a community, the first that modern times had seen "to combine individual and equal freedom with strict self imposed law to found society on the common endeavour after moral perfection." Self-control was the foundation of virtue and self-sacrifice the condition of common weal.[20]

In the seventeenth century France continued as a major source of exports of paper, but the results of a mercantilist policy favouring exports and restricting the publication of books led to collapse in the revocation of the Edict of Nantes in 1685 and the migration of large numbers of Huguenots including papermakers to important consuming countries such as Holland and England. Towards the end of the century Holland, with the use of wind power, introduced new methods of cutting rags which did away with the old process of rotting, shortened the length of the process, and produced a better quality of paper. About 1620 Blaeu introduced numerous improvements in the printing press which greatly increased output. Suppression of criticism under a despotic monarchy led to the printing of gazettes and publications in Holland to be smuggled into France. French refugees such as Pierre Bayle developed a critical literature which became the basis of the later criticism of Voltaire and the Encyclopaedists. Le Clerc was probably "the first person who understood the power which may be exercised over literature by a reviewer" (Hallam citing Bishop Monk). As a refugee Descartes worked out his philosophy and destroyed the influence of Aristotelianism. Dutch printers exploited their advantages in large-scale development of printing. The Elzivirs published a large number of works and distributed them throughout Europe. Paper was adapted to production of small formats. Type-founding[21] became a major activity and founts were sold to printers in England and Europe. It shifted from a handicraft undertaking to an industrial enterprise.

In England, as in France, suppression of printing was followed by imports of Dutch publications. Corantos were published in 1621 and were followed by newsbooks, but discussion of domestic news was prohibited. A star chamber decree[b] of 1637 restricted presses in London to twenty and type foundries to four. Such repression preceded the outbreak of civil war and insistence on freedom of the press such as Milton's *Areopagitica.* Abolition of the star chamber courts in 1641 was followed by intense activity in the publication of pamphlets and newsbooks supporting parliament or royalty.[c] "The slightest pamphlet is nowadays more vendable than the works of learnedest men." "Pamphlet-debate was the first great experiment in popular political education using the printing press as the organ of government of discussion."[22] Success of parliament was followed by suppression and the policy was continued after the Restoration. Roger L'Estrange introduced a rigorous censorship under the Licensing Act of 1662. Periods of suppression were accompanied by the rise of news-letters which evaded censorship. Restrictions on the press as a medium of political discussions were offset by the rise of coffee-houses in the second half of the century. The extreme difficulties of the press were met by the growth of advertising as a source of revenue, and it was significant that the first advertisements included books or products of the press, quack medicines, tea, and chocolate.

Suppression of the printing of certain types of literature released facilities for other types of literature of which the Bible, especially after the King James Version (1611), occupied a foremost place. It became a centre of Puritanical interest and marked the ascendancy of prose over poetry and the drama. The theatre was suppressed by the Puritans in 1647 but revived by Charles II in the Restoration and adapted to the demands of royal patronage.[23] The effects of printing in the increasing use of prose accentuated an interest in science. Worship of the ancients, especially in Aristotelianism, emphasized a sense of decline and despair, which was attacked by Bacon as a representative of the grandeur of the Elizabethan age. The attack of the Reformation on authority and emphasis on the Bible were accompanied by an attack on Aristotelianism and the vigorous sponsorship of science. "We are the ancients and the ancients are the youth." Belief in the scriptures defeated attempts to merge the Hebrew and the classic tradition. Science emerged as a result of the break. A concern with nature rather than mind emphasized truth obtained from things rather than books. The discoveries of Copernicus and Galileo[d] in astronomy, of Columbus in geography, of William Gilbert in magnetism, and of Harvey of the circulation of the blood reinforced the significance of science and of nature in contrast with books. "Words are wise men's counters — they do but reckon by them; but they are the money of fools" (Hobbes). The profound shift in philosophical approach was accompanied as Whitehead has shown by an advance in mathematics associated with the names of Descartes and Newton. In 1660 the Royal Society was founded to encourage an interest in science. "It will bring philosophy from *words* to *action*, seeing that men of business had so great a share in their first foundation" (Robert Hooke). Observation of the becoming replaced contemplation of being. The rise of deism rescued nature from Satan and restored it to God. Nature and reason vindicated the rights of individual freedom and property as opposed to the feudal and ecclesiastical order. Hobbes's attack on the soul weakened a central bulwark of ecclesiastical control. "To seek our Divinity merely in Books and writings, is *to seek the living among the dead*" (John Smith). "Why do we not, I say, turn over the living book of the world instead of dead papers" (Comenius). Science favoured prose and Sprat claimed that the Royal Society was designed "to separate the knowledge of nature from the colours of Rhetorick, the devices of Fancy, or the delightful deceit of the Fables" and was concerned lest "the whole spirit and vigour of their design, had been soon eaten out by the luxury and redundancy of speech." Milton resolved to rescue poetry from the Devil and to raise the English vernacular to the level of Italian by writing an epic which used the Bible as a source. But the prose style of Locke was an index of the age and had the tone of well-bred conversation without "the uncouth and pedantic jargon of the schools."[24] It followed "English prose style ... written in the fear of death by heretics for whom it was a religious but also a revolutionary activity."[25]

The impact of printing was evident not only in the philosophy of the seventeenth century but also in the rise of parliament. It contributed to the efficient conduct of business in the parliamentary system.[26] Law escaped the influence of the concept of nature which had been significant in the rise of science. There was "nothing more repellent to Anglo-Saxon instinct than the corruption of law by political ideology."[27] The imprecise character of the English language that followed its exposure to continental influence in French and Latin was not adapted to the precision of codes.

Sir Edward Coke regarded the common law as the fundamental law of the realm and the embodiment of reason, which parliament could not change. "When an act of Parliament is against common right and reason, or repugnant, or impossible to be performed, the common law will controul it, and adjudge such act to be void" (*Bonham case*, 1610). But parliament, in opposition to the absolute demands of the monarchy, claimed and exercised a sovereign power. A theory of might was substituted for a theory of law. "Common law is living and human, statutes have neither humanity nor humour."[28] Hobbes developed the theory of sovereignty that completely subordinated the Church to the civil power, which had begun with Marsilius of Padua and laid the basis for the conflict between sovereignty in the colonies and sovereignty in Great Britain and broke the British Empire.[29] The Instrument of Government that set up the Protectorate in 1653 was the first and last attempt to limit the power of parliament by a written constitution. The Revolution in 1689 established the legal supremacy of parliament, but written constitutions with limitations on legislatures persisted in the colonies with the belief in fundamental law.

The supremacy of parliament was strengthened by the new financial devices which spread from Antwerp and Amsterdam to London and which accompanied improvements in communication incidental to the growth of newspapers. The concept of municipal credit had spread from Italian cities.[30] The Republic of the United Netherlands was the first to use state credit as an effective weapon in the war of independence. Amsterdam as the successor to Antwerp developed an exchange concerned with stock rather than government securities. The Dutch East India Company, formed in 1602 as the first of the large corporations, was followed by the Bank of Amsterdam in 1609. Dutch trade expanded in relation to Asia after the annexation of Portugal by Spain in 1580 and in relation to Europe during the Thirty Years War (1618–48). The Amsterdam exchange facilitated the building of an effective coalition against Louis XIV. In England the state followed the Dutch pattern in assuming the form of a corporation whose members were responsible for its engagements by which large funded loans were floated at a low rate of interest. The revolution of 1689 was followed by the creation of public debt. The funding system was introduced in 1693, the Bank of England in 1694, and Exchequer Bills in 1696. Supremacy of parliament enabled England to introduce the great fundamental principle of public debt. Efficient use of reserves for paper currency enabled England to meet the drain of specie to India and extend her trade. The concept of possession in common law in contrast with the concept of absolute ownership in Roman law facilitated the growth of trade.[31] "Toleration was the necessary outcome of the new finance as it was of the new political system"[32] "Trade is most vigorously carried on, in every state and government, by the heterodox part of the same, and such as profess opinions different from what are publickly established."[33] In England "neither an absolute king nor an absolute church would ever again impede economic progress."[34]

With the expansion of paper production in England follow-ing the establishment of paper factories by Huguenot immi-grants and the accession of William and Mary, restrictions on printing were relaxed. John Locke[35] pointed to the enormous advantages of freedom of printing to Holland and to the serious losses attending the monopoly of the Stationers' Company in England, and in 1695 the Licensing Act was allowed to lapse – a step which, according to Macaulay, did "more for liberty and for civilization than the great charter or the Bill of Rights."

Advance in Holland and England was paralleled by decline in France and Germany. The outbreak of savage religious warfare from 1618 to 1648 left Germany a number of despotic principal-ities in which princes determined the religion of their subjects. Rapid improvement in communication destroyed conventions even in warfare, and religion accentuated savagery.[36] After 1648 the influence of Grotius, who had returned to the concept of natural law in discussing relations between sovereign states, became more powerful and the balance of power became a definite consideration. Louis XIV attempted to crush the republi-can press of Holland in the war of 1672 and expelled the Huguenots in 1685. The Gallican Church, secure in its suprema-cy, displayed the worst attributes of the state Church. Centralization dried up the stream of national life. French finance collapsed in 1648, but the disappearance of Italian financiers had not been accompanied by the development of an effective exchange. After the death of Colbert in 1683 the budget was dis-organized. But under Louis XIV the growth of efficient adminis-tration gave government comprehensiveness, decision, and consistency. "The government of Louis XIV appeared to be the first that was engaged solely in managing its affairs like a power at once definitive and progressive, which was not afraid of mak-ing innovations because it reckoned upon the future."[37] But by 1712 monarchy was worn out as much as Louis XIV.

In the eighteenth century French industry and trade became increasingly exposed to the effects of suppression. The French paper industry was influenced in a belated and slight fashion by improvements such as the use of cylinders and of wooden glazing rolls (about 1720) developed by the Dutch. Attempts to compete with the Dutch product were evident in detailed regulations of production and restrictions and embargoes on exports of rags. Difficulties of the French industry were evident in family control and the emergence of organized labour[38] intent on improved working conditions. Expansion of the Dutch trade had been accompanied by increased domestic and export markets and increased imports of rags as raw material. In England paper production was given encouragement by protection and expanded throughout the century. Large quantities of rags were imported from the Continent. The pronounced movement towards self-sufficiency created an acute problem in raw materials by the end of the century.

The end of the Licensing Act in 1695 was followed by a large number of publications and the appearance of the first daily sheet in 1701. The limitations of the hand press in which 2,000 sheets could be printed by relays of press men on one side in eight hours checked the circulation of single newspapers, led to the appearance of a large number of small papers,[39] and favoured other media in which time was a less important consideration.[40] The limitations of newspapers accentuated the importance of pamphlets as weapons of party warfare[41] and assumed the enlistment of effective writers such as Swift, Defoe, Addison, and Steele. Of Harley, Swift wrote, "no other man of affairs has ever made such use of a man of letters." The imposition of stamp taxes in 1712 restricted expansion and facilitated control of the press after the accession of Walpole to power. Taxes were increased in 1725 and the printing of parliamentary debates prohibited in 1738. With these restrictions printers concentrated on weeklies and in turn on summaries provided by monthlies such as the *Gentleman's Magazine*, started in 1731. With the support of a Copyright Act,[e] effective 1 April 1710, printers undertook compendious works and rapidly became publishers largely concerned with markets rather than craftsmanship. In the period prior to the growth of literacy publishers employed armies of scribblers in abridging, compiling, writing notes, and using scissors and paste. Ephraim Chambers's *Universal Dictionary of Arts and Sciences* was published by subscriptions in 1728. By the end of Walpole's administration publishers had developed more varied publications. In 1740 Richardson's *Pamela*ᶠ was published and was followed by other novels. The circulating library widened the market for new types of literature. In 1744 John Newbery began the publication of illustrated children's books.[42]

Destruction of the monopoly position of publishers by a legal decision in 1774, which denied the right to perpetual copyright under common law, was followed by publication of cheap reprints by small booksellers. Large publishers turned to large and expensive publications such as those of Robertson, Adam Smith, and Gibbon. Scottish writers had not been hampered by the long period of drudgery which had characterized English writing and had been supported directly by the universities. A Roman law tradition fostered an interest in philosophical speculation reflected in Adam Smith and Hume. The *Encyclopaedia Britannica*, published in Edinburgh in 1771, was dependent on scholarly writing. Scottish printers and booksellers participated in the expansion of the market after 1774. Constable began the notable publishing venture with which Scott was associated. Constable, "perhaps, the greatest publisher in the history of English letters, first broke in upon the monopoly of the London trade, and made letters what they now are."[43] Scott superseded the "pursuit of old black letter literature."[44] *The Edinburgh Review* was begun in 1802. English writers were rescued from hackwork, and Johnson and Goldsmith, following Pope, established the profession of authorship.[45]

In the second half of the century newspapers gained in importance through the demand for news of wars and through the support of advertising, especially after restrictions were imposed on sign posters. After 1774, following the efforts of Junius and Wilkes, the right of publishing parliamentary debates was established. Improvement in communications widened the market for the daily press. But the significance of more severe restrictions in stamp and advertisement taxes, and threats of libel suits, was evident in the enormous sale of pamphlets. Popular literature[46] became enormously important after 1790. Women writers occupied a prominent place. By the turn of the century romantic literature had struck its roots in English reading. The essay created in the eighteenth century hardly survived it.[47] The emphasis on reason and nature had been changed through the influence of Hume to an emphasis on nature and feeling. "Reason is and ought only to be the slave of the passions and can never pretend to any other office than to serve and obey them" (Hume). "Everyone believed in immortality until they heard Boyle give a lecture to prove it." Destruction of reason and natural law, political restrictions, the weakening of deism, and the rusty ecclesiastical machinery provided the background for the growth of Methodism under the direction of Whitefield and Wesley. Discontent was driven from the political to the religious channel.

Developments in Great Britain had profound implications for the colonies. Restriction of the press[48] was paralleled, but the expansion of literary activity in Great Britain, which had served as an outlet to political repression, overwhelmed the colonies[49] and compelled concentration on newspapers. Books were imported from Holland and England. The dominance of the printer in relation to the publication of laws of the assemblies and the post office led to the development of newspapers[50] largely dependent on the writings in English newspapers. The controversies of the English press prior to their control by Walpole were reprinted in the colonies.[51] The agitation against restrictions was carried out with more success than in Great Britain, in part by revolutionary spirits who had emigrated to avoid repression. Peter Zenger, tried for sedition, was acquitted by a jury in 1735. The concern of the printer in governmental patronage involved constant agitation and the large number of colonies defeated attempts at uniform supervision. Printers such as Benjamin Franklin could migrate from one colony to another. The attempt of Great Britain to impose the stamp tax in 1765 touched American public opinion at its source and was followed by determined resistance. "Printers, when uninfluenced by government, have generally arrayed themselves on the side of liberty, nor are they less remarkable for attention to the profits of their profession. A stamp duty which openly invaded the first, and threatened a great diminution of the last, provoked their united zealous oppostion."[52] In the period preceding the outbreak of the Revolution, paper production had increased on a substantial scale and the colonies were able to produce their own presses and type. With the importance of advertising, the newspaper became "part of the machinery of economic distribution." The power of the newspaper was reflected in the success of the Revolution[53] and in the adoption of the Bill of Rights guaranteeing freedom of the press.

After the Revolution newspapers were more closely attached to political parties and concerned with influencing pubic opinion. The resulting bitterness led Fenno to write in 1799: "The American newspapers are the most base, false, servile, and venal publications that ever polluted the fountains of writing — their editors the most ignorant, mercenary and vulgar automatons that ever were moved by the continually rusty wires of sordid mercantile avarice."[54] Attempts at repression led to the defeat of John Adams and the Federalist party. "The printers can never leave us in a state of perfect rest and union of opinion" (Jefferson). The empire was broken in part through the distorted effects of the uneven development of printing, which reinforced division incidental to the legal supremacy of parliament based on force and the persistence of an element of Roman law. Inability to adapt English institutions to new circumstances lost the colonies in the Western hemisphere and imperilled the empire in the East. Theory was unable to mediate between absolute dependence and absolute independence in Ireland and, in turn, in the colonies.[55] Religion, which developed in the colonies beyond the influence of episcopalianism,[56] strengthened resistance to the demands of parliament.

In France the difficulties of the paper industry were accompanied by problems of copyright and suppression which favoured continued emigration of printers and the smuggling of French works from Holland and Geneva. "Holland was now the great printing press of France and ... it is just to remember the indispensable services rendered by freedom of the press in Holland to the dissemination of French thought in the eighteenth century, as well as the shelter it gave to French thinkers in the seventeenth, by including Descartes, the greatest of them all."[57] None of Rousseau's chief works was printed in France. "That universal circulation of intelligence, which in England transmits the least vibration of feeling or alarm, with electric sensibility, from one end of the kingdom to another, and which unites in bands of connection men of similar interests and situations has no existence in France."[58] Publication of a large work such as an encyclopaedia[59] evaded difficulties of copyright and dangers of smuggling, appealed to prestige, and offered possibilities of escaping censorship. An association of publishers undertook support of the project based on Chambers's work in England. After numerous difficulties it was completed over two decades. With its completion secular literature triumphed over old institutions and doctrines. Spiritual power was transferred from ecclesiastical hands to the profession of letters. Theology and metaphysics were dwarfed by the physical sciences. The influence of the encyclopaedia was supported by the press in its attempts to escape the influence of monopoly. Limitations on advertising led to the appearance of diverse clandestine sheets in which leaders waged the battles of the Revolution. *"L'imprimerie est l'artillerie de la pensée"* (Rivarol). "All the wrath and indignation and revolt among the people reverberated first through the newspapers."[60] The violence of the press was followed by attempts at suppression and with the death of Desmoulins in 1794 freedom disappeared. *"Si je lache la bride à la presse, je ne resterai pas trois mois au pouvoir"* (Napoleon).[61] The policy of France, which favoured exports of paper and suppression of publication and which increased printing in Holland and England, created a disequilibrium, which ended in the Revolution. But his policy resting on a fusion of Church and state became the basis of an empire which extended in North America from the St. Lawrence to the Mississippi in the south and to the Saskatchewan in the north, and after its loss to Great Britain, and in turn the collapse of the first British Empire, became a basis of the second British Empire sufficiently secure to permit the reorganization the lack of which had precipitated the crisis of the first British Empire.

With the beginning of the nineteenth century the manufacture of paper and of printed material came under the influence of the industrial revolution. During the Napoleonic wars international capital fled from Amsterdam and Paris to England. The paper machine (Fourdrinier) was invented in France and improved and adopted in England.[62] Production was restricted by supplies of rags in spite of an increase in population and textile production until the utilization of wood in the second half of the century gave access to vast new supplies. Total production of paper in the United Kingdom increased from about 11,000 tons of hand-made paper in 1800 to 100,000 tons in 1861, of which 96,000 tons were machine-made, and to 652,000 tons, of which 648,000 tons were machine-made, in 1900.[63] Including imports of paper, consumption reached over a million tons by 1900. Prices declined, roughly from 1s. 6d. a pound in 1800 to 10d. in 1836, 6½d. in 1859, and less than 1d. a pound in 1900. Steam power was applied to printing by *The Times* in 1814 and gave it a powerful monopoly position in the first half of the century.

Production of newspapers was increased from 250 to 1,000 copies an hour to 12,000 copies by 1853. Taxes on paper, advertisements, and newspapers accentuated the importance of *The Times* monopoly and by the middle of the century its circulation exceeded the total of all other London papers. Media such as periodicals and magazines concerned with material other than news carried lighter taxes and expanded rapidly. In the struggle for the elimination of "taxes on knowledge"[64] the tax on paper was reduced, and in 1840 the penny postage was established. The possibilities of cheap large-scale agitation were shown in the success of the attacks on the Corn Laws and in the removal of the stamp and advertisement taxes in the fifties and the paper tax in 1861. As a result newspapers were established to challenge the position of *The Times*, such as the *News* in 1846 and the *Daily Telegraph* in 1855. The height of the political influence of *The Times* was reached in the Crimean War through the effective correspondence of Russell. The telegraph was exploited by new competitors in London and by provincial newspapers whose demands brought government ownership. The deteriorating effects of monopoly on *The Times* were shown in the unfortunate dependence on the New York *Herald*[65] for American news and support of the Southern States. In the Franco-Prussian war cooperation between the *News* and the New York *Tribune* enabled them to dominate in news. Acceptance of the Pigott papers, which were proved to be forgeries, brought loss of prestige and, by 1890, *The Times* was practically bankrupt. The Education Act of 1870 created a new demand for reading material which led to publication of *Tit-Bits* and *Answers*, the predecessors of the new journalism in the *Daily Mail* and the *Daily Express*.

The effects of cheaper paper and of the Education Act were evident also in the publishing industry. The circulating libraries of Mudie and Smith designed to meet the demand of women for fiction supported the three-volume novel which sold at 31*s.* 6*d.* Competition in the sale of single volumes led to the issue of a circular on 27 June 1894 declaring that after six months they would pay only 4*s.* a volume for novels in sets. By 1897 only one-volume novels appeared on the market. Triumph of the 6*s.* novel compelled publishers to concentrate on fiction commanding a wide sale. In the twentieth century the dominance of the circulating library in its demands for cloth-bound volumes was weakened further by the large-scale production and sale of small paper volumes.

The monopoly position of *The Times*, which accentuated the importance of media not concerned with news, had important results for the United States with its absence of international copyright legislation. The literature[66] of periodicals, magazines, and books associated with the names of Ainsworth, Dickens,

Collins, Thackeray, Trollope, and others, was exported to the United States. American literature was restricted or confined to newspapers and media in which English competition was relatively ineffective. American authors found an outlet in journalism. "Freedom of the press" and the growth of large centres contributed to the growth of newspapers and to the rapid improvement of technique. The cylinder press, the stereotype, the web press, and the linotype brought increases from 2,400 copies of 12 pages each per hour to 48,000 copies of 8 pages per hour in 1887 and to 96,000 copies of 8 pages per hour in 1893. Completion of the Atlantic Cable increased the importance of European news but introduced a condensed form of writing, which enabled the American to develop independently of the English language. Copyright legislation in 1890 protected American authors and accentuated differences in literature.

The importance of advertising in large centres strengthened the financial position of large newspapers and intensified competition between newspapers and centres. The demand for news to increase circulation hastened the development of the telegraph and the organization of news services. Monopoly positions were quickly made and quickly destroyed by technical change. The disturbances were reflected in political change. The journalistic activities of J.G. Bennett, Sen., the penny press, and street sales weakened the monopoly of the subscription system of the large blanket sheets of the mercantile press and were accompanied by the political disturbances of the Jacksonian age. The metropolitan press destroyed the single authority of Congress and after 1840 the party machine shifted power from Washington.[67] Introduction of fast presses by the *Chicago Tribune* in the fifties coincided with the rise of the Republican party followed by the election of Abraham Lincoln as President. Commercial activity in the North accompanying expansion of newspapers led to increasing friction with the less active South and development of the Middle West introduced a decisive element which contributed to the Civil War. Success of the North was followed by the dominance of the Republican party until

Pulitzer, with experience in St. Louis, introduced a fast press in New York and contributed to the return of the Democratic party under Cleveland. In turn W.R. Hearst, with experience in San Francisco, entered the New York field, and with Pulitzer's desertion sponsored the Democratic party.

The manufacture of paper from wood pulp[68] brought a decline in price from 8½ cents a pound in 1875 to 1½ cents in 1897. Pulpwood, chiefly spruce, was ground into small fibres by pressure against a rapidly revolving stone to produce mechanical pulp, which was mixed with pulp produced by the use of chemicals in the ratio of 75 to 80 per cent and 25 to 20 per cent. The industry implied access to large spruce forests, cheap abundance of water power,[69] and cheap transportation for raw material and finished product. Plants were located near large hydro-electric power sites. Large paper companies emerged to supply the necessary capital and to exercise an influence on prices. Attempts to raise prices were met by determined opposition from newspapers. Proprietors attempted to enhance their prestige and to increase circulation of their papers by taking an active part in politics. W.R. Hearst, like Horace Greeley, aimed at the mayoralty of New York, the governorship of New York state, and the presidency of the United States. American presidents, notably Theodore Roosevelt, made effective use of newspapers and favoured means of lowering the price of newsprint. The Taft administration succeeded in lowering tariffs on newsprint from Canada and the low tariff policy of the Democratic party under Woodrow Wilson reflected newspaper demands even more effectively.[70] Pressure from Canadian governmental authorities compelling the establishment of newsprint plants in Canada involved a lumpy type of development determined largely by the capacity of power sites. Increased production of newsprint led to the growth in size of newspapers, an emphasis on Sunday newspapers, and to new devices for the increase of circulation. The tabloids in which photographs became a central feature exploited the possibilities of lower levels of sensationalism. The effects paralleled the boom period of the twenties with its emphasis on advertising, on types of marketing organization designed to provide rapid and wide distribution of goods of the type adapted to advertising, and on types of news favourable to wide circulation of newspapers.

The highly sensitive economy built up in relation to newsprint and its monopoly position in relation to advertising hastened an emphasis on a new medium, notably the radio, which in turn contributed to a large-scale depression. The radio was accompanied by political change in the return of the Democratic party to power and the election of F.D. Roosevelt who claimed that "nothing would help him more than to have the newspapers against him." Localization of metropolitan newspapers in the United States was accompanied by weeklies and digests which provided a common denominator from a national rather than a metropolitan point of view. Illustrated papers and the radio responded to the demands of advertising for national coverage. The radio emphasized a lowest common denominator with profound effects on music. The significance of mechanization in print, photographs including the cinema, phonographs including the talkies, and radio has been evident in literature, art, and music. The pressure of mechanization on words[71] has been reflected in simplified spelling and an interest in semantics. The limitations of words have led to resort to architecture and the rise of skyscrapers as an advertising medium. In North America, in contrast with Great Britain and Europe, the book was subordinated to the newspaper. Mechanization involved an emphasis on best-sellers and the creation of a gap of unintelligibility of more artistic literary works.[72] Literature and other fields of scholarship have become feudalized in a modern manorial system. Monopolies of knowledge have been built up by publishing firms to some extent in co-operation with universities and exploited in textbooks. A large textbook subject to revision at suitable intervals can be profitably exploited at the expense of works of scholarship. Monopolies are subject to competition from new media, but these in turn reflect the conditions under which they appear. Department stores that concentrate on sales of the Bible[73] and orthodox literature leave open a wide field to publishers exploiting "untouchable" subjects in small cheap booklets.[74] If civilization may be measured by the tolerance of unintelligibility, its capacities are weakened by monopolies of knowledge built up in the same political area using the same language.

The impact of large-scale mechanization in communication in North America on Great Britain and Europe became significant with the new journalism of the late nineteenth and early twentieth centuries. The intense rivalry between Hearst and Pulitzer in New York during the Spanish-American war was paralleled by the marked increase in circulation of the *Daily Mail* and the *Daily Express* during the Boer War. American influence penetrated through the establishment of editions of American papers and the migration of journalists such as Blumenfeld and Lord Beaverbrook to Great Britain. Technique developed in the United States was imported and adapted in Great Britain and Europe. The effects of the new journalism were conspicuous in the acquisition of *The Times* in 1908 by Lord Northcliffe. Political journalism such as that of the *Westminster Gazette* was weakened. The prestige of the new journalism was shown in the creation of a newspaper peerage. The instability of foreign policy, which characterized the dominance of the newspaper in the United States, was introduced in Great Britain with the new journalism.[75] The effects became apparent in the lack of stability in foreign policy leading to war in 1914. After the sensational telegram sent by the Kaiser to Kruger during the Boer War, opinion was turned from Germany towards France.[76] The power of the press during the war was shown in drastic reorganizations of the Cabinet. After the war, the death of Northcliffe, and new arrangements for control of *The Times*, the *Daily Express* under Lord Beaverbrook turned from an emphasis on continental politics to imperial preference with significant implications to the traditional free-trade policy of Great Britain. In Great Britain the influence of newspapers favoured government ownership of radio as a means of checking encroachments on advertising revenue. As in the United States radio as a new medium enabled politicians, notably Baldwin, to resist the pressure of newspapers. But the increasing importance of advertising to newspapers in the period from 1919 to 1939 was accompanied by a decline of intelligent interest in domestic and foreign affairs.[77]

On the Continent the impact of American journalism was less direct because of a more strongly entrenched position of the book and differences in language and legal systems. Throughout the nineteenth century the French press,[78] with less dependence on advertising than Anglo-Saxon countries, was continually exposed to suppression or threats of suppression. After an escape from the rigid control of Napoleon journalists began a long struggle for freedom of the press. They exercised a decisive influence in the revolution of 1830 but later came under the repressive policy of Louis Napoleon. Under the censorship of the second empire French journalism became "the only considerable journalism in history in which form has prevailed over matter" and France was again exposed to competition from the Netherlands. In answer to complaints of the emperor of attacks by French refugees it was held that the "constitution of Belgium was made by journalists and the unrestrained liberty of the press is so interwoven with the constitution that the legislature itself has no power to deal with the case, nor any power short of a constituent assembly."[79] Partly as a result of the intensity of the struggle, journalism in France avoided anonymity and journalists became active politicians.[80] A large number of small political newspapers left the press exposed to manipulation by direct subsidy from external and internal groups.[81]

In Germany political censorship in small principalities had a powerful influence with the result that talent was turned to literature, to the universities, and to music. After the Napoleonic period and the increasing influence of Prussia, censorship was replaced by manipulation. The traditions of manipulation developed by Bismarck continued in the twentieth century under Goebbels.[82] Discrepancy in the rate of expansion of influence of the newspaper from the United States and England and Germany contributed inevitably to misunderstanding. The political press of a bureaucratic Roman law state differed sharply from that of a common law state. The interview of the Kaiser with the *Daily Telegraph* in 1909 was incomprehensible to English readers since an interview by King Edward VII in a German paper would have been unthinkable. The clash between traditions based on the book and the newspaper contributed to the outbreak of war. The Treaty of Versailles emphasized self-determination as a governing principle and recognized the significance of language[83] in the printing press. Consequently, it rapidly became outdated with the mechanization of the spoken word in the radio. Governmental influence over the press was extended to the radio. The loud speaker had decisive significance for the election of the Nazis. Regions dominated by the German language responded to the appeal of the spoken word inviting them to join a larger German Reich. The Second World War became to an important extent the result of a clash between the newspaper and the radio. In the conduct of the war the power of the mechanized spoken word was capitalized in the English-speaking world, notably by Churchill and Roosevelt. Russia had an enormous advantage in the difficulties of language and its impermeability to German propaganda. The sudden extension of communication precipitated an outbreak of savagery paralleling that of printing and the religious wars of the seventeenth century, and again devastating the regions of Germany.

In the Near East mechanized communication has been less effective as a basis of nationality. In the East, Greek civilization successfully resisted encroachments from Latin. After the fall of the Byzantine empire in 1453 the dominance of the Turk was not accompanied by a uniform language. In areas dominated by Mohammedanism abhorrence of images delayed the introduction of printing. Nationality failed to correspond with language largely because of religion. National feeling based on language was registered in protests against political arrangements.[84] Organization of the Russian empire checked the devastations of nomads, which had threatened Western civilization over two millennia.[85] Byzantine influence persisted in Russia in the relations of the Greek Orthodox Church to the state. Developments in communication were restricted. Russia had no Renaissance and no eighteenth century. The late development of a vernacular literature was reflected in the works of great Russian realist writers in the nineteenth century. A fusion of Church and state resisted Western influence until the effects of the revolutionary tradition in England, the United States, and France were crystallized in communism and communist literature.[86] The defeat of revolutionary tendencies in Germany, notably in 1848, the growth of nationalism, especially in Italy, and the increasing centralization of the Church evident in the doctrine of the infallibility[g] of the papacy were followed by the systematic organization of communism by Karl Marx and others. Resistance of the West made communism attractive to Russia as a weapon against caesaropapism. The Russian revolution supported by an interest in communism eventually contributed to the breakdown of the state which had given birth to printing and had survived its influence without revolution.

Monopolies of knowledge had developed and declined partly in relation to the medium of communication on which they were built and tended to alternate as they emphasized religion, decentralization, and time, and force, centralization, and space. Sumerian culture based on the medium of clay was fused with Semitic culture based on the medium of stone to produce the Babylonian empires. Egyptian civilization based on a fusion of dependence on stone and of dependence on papyrus produced an unstable empire, which eventually succumbed to religion. The Assyrian and Persian empires attempted to combine Egyptian and Babylonian civilization and the latter succeeded with its appeal to toleration. Hebrew civilization emphasized the sacred character of writing in opposition to political organizations that emphasized the graven image. Greek civilization based on the oral tradition produced the powerful leaven that destroyed political empires. Rome assumed control over the medium on which Egyptian civilization had been based and built up an extensive bureaucracy, but the latter survived in a fusion in the Byzantine empire with Christianity based on the parchment codex. In the West the weapons of Christianity included the arguments of St. Augustine emphasizing original sin and the weakness of political rulers. Political power became more important with the introduction of another medium, namely, paper, and in turn Locke and Rousseau developed arguments against original sin in the psychological *tabula rasa* and the emphasis on experience as a basis of learning. "Men always seek for a general theory to justify their efforts and they almost invariably choose one that is intellectually untenable" (Randall). The monopolies of knowledge based on language reinforced by mechanized communication led in turn to nationalism and the growth of communism. "If he desires that all should look up to him, let him permit himself to be known but not to be understood" (Hallam).

The enormous expansion of the printing industry and an emphasis on freedom of the press, which favoured the growth of monopolies, have intensified nationalism. Toynbee has suggested that prior to 1875 industrialism and nationalism worked together to build up great powers and thereafter industrialism became world wide and nationalism narrow and small.[87] Henry Adams has regarded 1870 as "the close of the literary epoch, when quarterlies gave way to monthlies, letter-press to illustration, volumes to pages." The effects of printing on nationalism have been conspicuous in common-law countries. "Success of a representative system of government has been materially influenced by the invention of printing,"[88] but its limitations have again been largely a result of printing. The publication of debates implied an effective control over the manner and context of parliamentary speeches. Lord Somers "knew of no good law proposed and passed in his time to which the public papers had not directed his attention."[89] The vicious circle is described by Dicey "Laws foster law-making opinion." "The capital fact in the mechanism of modern states is the energy of legislation"[90] (Maine). "The present age appears to me to be approaching fast to a similar usurpation of the functions of religion by law" (Coleridge). The position of lawyers has been strengthened. "In England, the profession of the law is that which seems to hold out the strongest attraction to talent, from the circumstance, that in it ability, coupled with execution even though unaided by patronage, cannot fail of attaining reward. It is frequently chosen as an introduction to public life. It also presents great advantages, from its being a qualification for many situations more or less remotely connected with it, as well as from the circumstances that several of the highest officers of the state must necessarily have sprung from its ranks."[91] In the United States, "the profession of law is the only aristocratic element which can be amalgamated without violence with the natural elements of democracy, and be advantageously and permanently combined with them."[92] The influence of the press on law has been tempered by the persistence of the oral tradition in the "spirit of a rational freedom diffused and become national in the consequent influence and control of public opinion and in its most precious organ, the jury" (Coleridge). "In proportion as you introduce the jury into the business of the courts you are enabled to diminish the number of judges, which is a great advantage."[93] In whatever manner the jury be applied, it cannot fail to exercise a powerful influence upon the national character; but this influence is prodigiously increased when it is introduced into civil cases."[94] As to Roman law "the basic difference between the two systems of jurisprudence is that the one accords privileges; while the other prohibits rights."[95] "The English and American lawyers investigate what has been done; the French advocate inquires what should have been done; the former produce precedents; the latter, reasons."[96]

In common-law countries particularly adapted to trade and emphasizing freedom of the press, monopoly of communication accentuates monopolistic tendencies in the publication of newspapers, periodicals, and books. Publishers exploit well-known authors and readers to check the appearance of new authors.[97] In turn reprints of established books weaken the position of writers. "Give me dead authors — they never keep you waiting for copy" and it might be added, for copyright. "Originality is the greatest disadvantage to its possessor in the intellectual market."[98] It becomes no longer possible to insist, following Montesquieu, that "the liberal theory of politics is a recurrent product of commerce."[99]

These changes have profound implications for empire. The British Empire, which gained from a fusion of Roman law traditions and common-law traditions, has been exposed to the effects of increasing nationalization based on an important extent on language under the influence of mechanization of the printed and the spoken word as in the case of the French in Canada, the Dutch in South America, the languages of India and Pakistan, and the attempt to revive the Irish language in Eire. The common-law tradition tends to become more powerful and to reflect the influence of elements which have been decentralizing in character. "Under the democratic control England must abandon all idea of influence upon the world's affairs" (Lord Salisbury).

The United States, with systems of mechanized communication and organized force, has sponsored a new type of imperialism imposed on common law in which sovereignty is preserved *de jure* and used to expand imperialism *de facto*.[100] It has been able to exploit the tendencies towards imperialism which have emerged in members of the British Commonwealth. Canada has been used as a means of penetrating the British Commonwealth. Resistance to this influence can be made effective by adherence to common-law traditions and notably to the cultural heritage of Europe. The state and the Church have lost control in large areas of Europe as a result of successive periods of occupation, and survival in the West depends on their continual subordination and on a recognition of the cultural leadership and supremacy of Europe. States are destroyed by lack of culture[101] (Jaeger), and so too are empires and civilizations. Mass production and standardization are the enemies of the West. The limitations of mechanization of the printed and the spoken word must be emphasized and determined efforts to recapture the vitality of the oral tradition must be made.[102]

Large-scale political organization implies a solution of problems of space in terms of administrative efficiency and of problems of time in terms of continuity. Elasticity of structure involves a persistent interest in the search for ability and persistent attacks on monopolies of knowledge. Stability involves a concern with the limitations of instruments of government as well as with their possibilities.

Concentration on a medium of communication implies a bias in the cultural development of the civilization concerned either towards an emphasis on space and political organization or towards an emphasis on time and religious organization. Introduction of a second medium tends to check the bias of the first and to create conditions suited to the growth of the empire. The Byzantine empire emerged from a fusion of a bias incidental to papyrus in relation to political organization and of parchment in relation to ecclesiastical organization. The dominance of parchment in the West gave a bias towards ecclesiastical organization which led to the introduction of paper with its bias towards political organization. With printing, paper facilitated an effective development of the vernaculars and gave expression to their vitality in the growth of nationalism. The adaptability of the alphabet to large-scale machine industry became the basis of literacy, advertising, and trade. The book as a specialized product of printing and, in turn, the newspaper strengthened the position of language as a basis of nationalism. In the United States the dominance of the newspaper led to large-scale development of monopolies of communication in terms of space and implied a neglect of problems of time. Regional monopolies of metropolitan newspapers have been strengthened by monopolies of press associations. The bias of paper towards an emphasis on space and its monopolies of knowledge has been checked by the development of a new medium,[103] the radio. The results have been evident in an increasing concern with problems of time reflected in the growth of planning and the socialized state. The instability involved in dependence on the newspaper in the United

States[104] and the Western world has facilitated an appeal to force as a possible stabilizing factor. The ability to develop a system of government in which the bias of communication can be checked and an appraisal of the significance of space and time can be reached remains a problem of empire and of the Western world.

NOTES

1 Introduction

1. *Essays by the Late Mark Pattison*, collected and arranged by Henry Nettleship (Oxford, 1889), vol. II, 400–01.

2. Francis Edward Mineka, *The Dissidence of Dissent* (Chapel Hill, 1944), 278.

3. *Monthly Repository*, 1834, 320. Cited ibid., 278–79.

4. Thomas Constable, *Archibald Constable and His Literary Correspondents* (London, 1873), 270.

5. James Bryce, *Studies in History and Jurisprudence* (London, 1901), 254–55.

6. For a discussion of the background of political organization see F.J. Teggart, *The Processes of History* (New Haven, 1918).

7. This does not refer to the mechanical spoken word which apparently Hitler had in mind in *Mein Kampf.* "I know that one is able to win people far more by the spoken than the written word. The greatest changes in the world have never been brought about by the goose quill. The power which set sliding the great avalanches of a political and religious nature was from the beginning of time, the magic force of the spoken word."

8. See H.M. Chadwick, *The Heroic Age* (Cambridge, 1926).

9. See Emery Neff, *A Revolution in European Poetry 1660–1900* (New York, 1940), ch. 2.

10. See Otto Jesperson, *Mankind, Nation and Individual from a Linguistic Point of View* (Oslo, 1925), 5–13.

11. Ernst Cassirer, *Language and Myth* (New York, 1946), 38.

12. Cited Jesperson, *Mankind, Nation and Individual* (Oslo, 1925), 139.

13. Herbert Spencer, *Philosophy of Style: An Essay* (New York, 1881), 11.

14. Cited Graham Wallas, *The Great Society* (London, 1914), 263.

15. For a discussion of conditions favourable to historical writing, see F.J. Teggart, *Theory of History* (New Haven, 1925).

16. See C.L. Becker, *Progress and Power* (Stanford University, 1936); see also A.C. Moorhouse, *Writing and the Alphabet* (London, 1946).

17. Edwyn Bevan, *Hellenism and Christianity* (London, 1921), 25.

18. See Christopher Caudwell, *Illusion and Reality: A Study of the Sources of Poetry* (London, 1937), 51.

2 Egypt

1. Cited Alexander Moret, *The Nile and Egyptian Civilization* (London, 1927), 375.
2. See Patrick Boylan, *Thoth, the Hermes of Egypt* (London, 1922).
3. S.H. Hooke, "The Early History of Writing" (*Antiquity*, XI, 1937, 266).
4. The dating system used herein follows Moret.
5. A.M. Hocart, *Kingship* (London, 1927), 55.
6. Naphtali Lewis, *L'Industrie du Papyrus dans l'Égypte Gréco-Romain* (Paris, 1934), 117.
7. Alfred Lucas, *Ancient Egyptian Materials and Industries* (London, 1934), 133ff.
8. Alexander Moret, *The Nile and Egyptian Civilization* (London, 1927), 457n.
9. Lynn Thorndike, *A Short History of Civilization* (New York, 1927), 37–38.
10. Moret, *The Nile and Egyptian Civilization*, 457.

    Till to astonish'd realms PAPYRA taught
    To paint in mystic colours Sound and Thought,
    With Wisdom's voice to print the page sublime,
    And mark in adamant the steps of Time.
    Erasmus Darwin, *The Loves of the Plants* (1789).

11. Cited Moret, *The Nile and Egyptian Civilization*, 270.
12. Cited V. Gordon Childe, *Man Makes Himself* (London, 1936), 211.
13. Cited T. Eric Peet, *A Comparative Study of the Literature of Egypt, Palestine and Mesopotamia* (London, 1931), 105–06.
14. Reinhold Niebuhr, *The Children of Light and the Children of Darkness* (New York, 1945), 80.
15. Cassirer has described language and myth as in original and indissoluble correlation with one another and as emerging as independent elements. Mythology reflected the power exercised by language on thought. The word became a primary force in which all being and doing originate. Verbal structures appeared as mythical entities endowed with mythical powers. The word in language revealed to man that world that was closer to him than any world of material objects. Mind passed from a belief in the physio-magical power comprised in the word to a realization of its spiritual power. Through language the concept of the deity received its first concrete development. The cult of mysticism grappled with the task of comprehending the Divine in its totality and highest inward reality, and yet avoided any name or sign. It was directed to the world of silence beyond language. But the spiritual depth and power of language was shown in the fact that speech itself prepared the way for the last step by which it was transcended. The demand for unity of the Deity took its stand on the linguistic expression of Being, and found its surest support in the word. The Divine excluded from itself all particular attributes and could be predicated only of itself.

16. Sir William Ridgeway, *The Origin and Influence of the Thoroughbred Horse* (Cambridge, 1903). On the significance of the Hyksos invasion in introducing the horse and chariot see H.E. Wenlock, *The Rise and Fall of the Middle Kingdom in Thebes* (New York, 1947), ch. 8.

17. See Herman Ranke, "Medicine and Surgery in Ancient Egypt," *Studies in the History of Science* (Philadelphia, 1941), 31–42.

18. George Thomson, *Aeschylus and Athens: A Study in the Social Origins of the Drama* (London, 1941), 121.

19. The influence of a matriarchal system probably persisted, as it has been regarded as a basis of brother and sister marriages, in which brothers obtained property of sisters. J.G. Frazer, *Adonis, Attis, Osiris* (London, 1906), 322. Sister marriage reunited matriarchal property with paternal inheritance (Flinders Petrie).

20. Lynn Thorndike, *A Short History of Civilization* (New York, 1927).

21. See G.R. Driver, *Semitic Writing from Pictograph to Alphabet* (London, 1948), 62.

22. Ibid., 139.

23. A.L. Kroeber, *Configurations of Cultural Growth* (Berkeley, 1946), 485.

24. W.M. Flinders Petrie, *The Revolution of Civilization* (London, 1922).

25. T. Eric Peet, *A Comparative Study of the Literature of Egypt, Palestine and Mesopotamia* (London, 1931), 78.

26. Ibid., 99.

27. Ibid., 129.

28. Ibid., 97.

3 Babylonia

1. *Studies in the History of Science* (Philadelphia, 1941).

2. S.H. Hooke, "The Early History of Writing" (*Antiquity*, XI, 1937, 275).

3. See C.J. Gadd, *Ideas of Divine Rule in the Ancient East* (London, 1948). For a discussion of the conflict between force and religion as the basis of law see N.S. Timasheff, *An Introduction to the Sociology of Law* (Cambridge, 1939).

4. See G.R. Driver, op. cit., 59.

5. Ernst Cassirer, *An Essay on Man* (New Haven, 1944), 47.

6. T. Eric Peet, *A Comparative Study of the Literatures of Egypt, Palestine, and Mesopotamia* (London, 1931), 26.

7. Ibid., 88.

8. T. Eric Peet, *A Comparative Study of the Literatures of Egypt, Palestine, and Mesopotamia*, 128.

9. Ibid., 97.

10. William Ridgeway, *The Origin of Metallic Currency and Weight Standards* (Cambridge, 1892), 268.

11. *Studies in the History of Science* (Philadelphia, 1941), 8.

12. Ibid., 1.

13. A.E. Cowley, *The Hittites* (London, 1920), 85.

14. D.G. Hogarth, *Kings of the Hittites* (London, 1926), 55.

15. John Garstang, *The Hittite Empire* (London, 1929), 43–44.

16. W.M. Flinders Petrie, *The Formation of the Alphabet* (London, 1912), 17–19. "A gradually formed signary, spread by traffiffic far and wide, was slowly contracted and systematized until it was reduced to a fixed alphabet." Signs, "by the systematic arrangement of some of them ... were rendered easier to learn and to remember, they supported each other to the exclusion of the unregulated signs, and so obtained a permanent preference, and lastly they were adopted as manuals, and thus they were thrust upon all the world of trade as an exclusive system." Ibid.

17. Assyrian phrase cited G.R. Driver, op. cit., 72.

18. See C.J. Gadd, *Ideas of Divine Rule in the Ancient East* (London, 1948), Lecture II.

19. "The Egyptian Origin of the Semitic Alphabet" (*Journal of Egyptian Archaeology*, III, London, 1916, 1–16) and *The Legacy of Egypt*, ed. S.R.K. Glanville (Oxford, 1942), 53–79. See G.R. Driver, op. cit., 121, for a conclusive discussion on the close relationship between Egyptian and Phoenician scripts in the absence of vowel signs, recognizably pictorial signs, direction of writing, the use of papyrus and the potsherd, and of the reed pen and ink.

20. See J.W. Jack, *The Ras Shamra Tablets, Their Bearing on the Old Testament* (Edinburgh, 1935), 43, and C.F.A. Schaeffer, *The Cuneiform Texts of Ras Shamra-Ugarit* (London, 1939).

21. Lewis, *L'Industrie du Papyrus*, 81.

22. J.H. Breasted, "The Physical Processes of Writing in the Early Orient and Their Relation to the Origin of the Alphabet" (*The American Journal of Semitic Languages and Literature*, XXXII, 230–49).

23. See *The Legacy of Egypt*, ed. S.R.K. Glanville (Oxford, 1942), 246–47, for Hebrew and Egyptian parallels.

24. C. Leonard Woolley, *The Sumerians* (Oxford, 1928), 165.

25. Morris Jastrow, *Hebrew and Babylonic Traditions* (New York, 1914).

26. See C.H.W. Johns, *The Relations Between the Laws of Babylonia and the Laws of the Hebrew People* (London, 1912).

27. *Buried Empires*, 113.

28. See A.T. Olmstead, *History of the Persian Empire* (Chicago, 1948).

29. See D. Diringer, *The Alphabet, a Key to the History of Mankind* (London, n.d.), 187.

30. Franz Cumont, *The Mysteries of Mithra* (Chicago, 1903), 7.

31. Franz Cumont, *Astrology and Religion Among the Greeks and Romans* (New York, 1912), 26.
32. Thomas Whittaker, *Priests, Philosophers and Prophets* (London, 1911), 128.
33. Ibid., 103.
34. Law closely identified with religion and dominated by belief in its divine origin implied great efforts to supply more detailed and exhaustive regulations. See Jerome Frank, *Law and the Modern Mind* (New York, 1935), 297.

4 The Oral Tradition and Greece

1. G.R. Driver, op. cit., 3.
2. "No Greek word has an exact equivalent in English, no important abstract conception covers the same area or carries with it the same atmosphere of association. Translation from one language to another is impossible, from an ancient to a modern language grotesquely impossible, because of these profound differences of collective representation, which no 'translation' will ever transfer." F.M. Cornford, *From Religion to Philosophy* (London, 1912), 45. In spite of the difficulties Gibbon described Greek as "a golden key that would unlock the treasures of antiquity of a musical and prolific language that gives a soul to the objects of sense and a body to the abstractions of philosophy." "He has erected between Euripides and the reader a barrier more impassable than the Greek language." T.S. Eliot on Gilbert Murray. "Hence the vanity of translation; it were as wise to cast a violet into a crucible that you might discover the formal principle of its colour and odour, as seek to transfuse from one language into another the creations of a poet." P.B. Shelley, *A Defence of Poetry*.
3. See Arnold Toynbee on "History" in *The Legacy of Greece*, edited by R.W. Livingstone (Oxford, 1923). See C.N. Cochrane, *The Mind of Edward Gibbon* for a reflection on the twentieth century in a reflection of the eighteenth century in *The Decline and Fall of the Roman Empire*; also the criticism of the unilateral interpretation of pre-Socratic philosophy by nineteenth-century scientism. Werner Jaeger, *The Theology of the Early Greek Philosophers* (Oxford, 1947), 195. All works of earlier periods reflections of hostility to period, i.e., Tacitus, Montesquieu, Voltaire, but in twentieth century writings reflect prejudices and avoid opposing them.
4. See George Thomson, *Aeschylus and Athens: A Study in the Social Origins of the Drama* (London, 1941); A.D. Winspear, *The Genesis of Plato's Thought* (New York, 1940); M.O. Wason, *Class Struggles in Ancient Greece* (London, 1947).
5. F.M. Cornford, *Before and After Socrates* (Cambridge, 1932), 54.
6. W.L. Newman, *The Politics of Aristotle* (Oxford, 1887), vol. I, 479.

7. See Rhys Carpenter, "The Antiquity of the Greek Alphabet" (*American Journal of Archaeology*, XXXVII, 1933, 8–29) and "The Greek Alphabet Again" (ibid., XLII, 67). Also G.R. Driver, op. cit., 176–78. Greeks probably adopted Phoenician alphabet 780–750. H.L. Lorimer, "Homer and the Art of Writing: A Sketch of Opinion Between 1713 and 1939" (*American Journal of Archeology*, LII, 1948, 11–23). See Carl W. Blegen, "Inscriptions on Geometric Pottery from Hymettos" (*American Journal of Archeology*, XXXVIII, 1934, 10–28). Argues Greeks learned writing about 750 — see Rhys Carpenter, *Folk Tale, Fiction and Saga in the Homeric Epics* (Berkeley, 1946). J.P. Haney argues for 900 BC.

8. Sir Richard Jebb, *Essays and Addresses* (Cambridge, 1907), 573.

9. See Milman Parry, "The Homeric Gloss: A Study in Word Sense" (*Transactions and Proceedings of the American Philological Association*, LIX, 1928, 233 *ff*). See Parry's proofs of oral tradition of epics in Milman Parry, "Studies in the Epic Technique of Oral Verse-Making" (*Harvard Studies in Classical Philology*, XLI, 73–148) and "The Homeric Language as the Language of an Oral Poetry" (ibid., XLIII, 1–50).

10. See M.P. Nilsson, *Homer and Mycenae* (London, 1933).

11. The manuscripts on which texts were based were probably prepared in Athens and include Attic forms very few of which were organically connected with verse.

12. See E.T. Owen, *The Story of the Iliad as Told in the Iliad* (Toronto, 1946).

13. See H.M. Chadwick, *The Heroic Age* (Cambridge, 1926), 462–63.

14. T.A. Sinclair, *Hesiod: Works and Days* (London, 1932), XXVII.

15. M.P. Nilsson, *A History of Greek Religion* (Oxford, 1925), 179 and *passim*.

16. *"Wie das Wort so wichtig dort war,*
Weil es ein gesprochen Wort war" (Goethe).

17. Werner Jaeger, *The Theology of the Early Greek Philosophers* (Oxford, 1947), 16.

18. Werner Jaeger, *Paideia, the Ideals of Greek Culture* (Oxford, 1939), vol. 1 152 *ff*.

19. F.M. Cornford, *From Religion to Philosophy* (London, 1912), 143; also idem *The Laws of Motion in Ancient Thought* (Cambridge, 1931).

20. F.M. Cornford, *From Religion to Philosophy*, 20 and *passim*.

21. Cited J.M. Robertson, *The Evolution of States: An Introduction to English Politics* (London, 1912), 39n.

22. J.L. Myres, *The Political Ideas of the Greeks* (New York, 1927), 72, also 67 *ff*. "It is strange at first sight that war, arising from luxury and self-aggrandisement, should be the point of departure for the introduction of the guardian class, and therefore of government and conscious morality. But both the theory of natural selection and the lessons of history seem to show that it is war which makes a nation." Bosanquet, *A Companion to Plato's Republic*, 85. "In the last resort in the Greek period

military ideals overlie and overrule all others." Benjamin Kidd, *Principles of Western Civilization* (London, 1902), 182.

23. See S.H. Butcher, *Harvard Lectures on the Originality of Greece* (London, 1902), *passim*.

24. Ibid., 51.

25. See J.L. Myres, *The Political Ideas of the Greeks* (New York, 1927), 212-20. For a discussion of the importance of written law to the development of vernacular literature see H.M. Chadwick and N.K. Chadwick, *The Growth of Literature* (Cambridge, 1940), 497-500. Laws first to use writing, Rhys Carpenter, *Folk Tale, Fiction and Saga in the Homeric Epics* (Berkeley, 1946), 11. Laws being written out about 650. Most inscriptions decrees of public assemblies, laws, treaties, letters to kings and others, votive offerings, statements of public accounts. E.L. Hicks, *A Manual of Greek Historical Inscriptions* (Oxford, 1882), xii.

26. "But when the laws are written, then the weak and wealthy have alike but equal right" (Euripides), cited R.J. Bonner and Gertrude Smith, *The Administration of Justice from Homer to Aristotle* (Chicago, 1930), vol. I, 68. "A written code of laws is a condition of just judgment, however just the laws may be. It was therefore natural that one of the first concessions that governments were forced to make was a written law." J.B. Bury, *A History of Greece* (New York, n.d.), 137.

27. Gregory Vlastos, "Solonian Justice" (*Classical Philology*, XLI, 69).

28. See W.J. Woodhouse, *Solon the Liberator* (London, 1938).

29. J.B. Bury, *A History of Greece*, 176–77.

30. Werner Jaeger, *Paideia, the Ideals of Greek Culture*, vol. I, 229.

31. Whitehead has pointed out that in the period from Pythagoras to Plato, as in the seventeenth and eighteenth centuries, general categories of thought were in a state of disintegration. Only in periods of disengagement from immediate pressure of circumstances and eager curiosity could the age spirit undertake a direct revision of final abstractions hidden in more concrete concepts. In these rare periods mathematics became relevant to astronomy. A.N. Whitehead, *Science and the Modern World* (Cambridge, 1926), 39, 49.

32. Jaeger, *Paideia*, vol. I, 235 *ff.*

33. See George Thomson, *Aeschylus and Athens: A Study in the Social Origins of the Drama* (London, 1941).

34. See W.M. Flinders Petrie, *The Revolutions of Civilization* (London, 1922).

35. Werner Jaeger, *The Theology of the Early Greek Philosophers* (Oxford, 1947), 155.

36. Ibid., 42.

37. P.H. Lang, *Music in Western Civilization* (New York, 1941), 5–11.

38. The secret society of Dionysus became a guild of actors. George

Thomson, *Aeschylus and Athens,* 164–73; also Sir Richard Jebb, *Essays and Addresses* (Cambridge, 1907), 146 *ff.*

39. See Werner Jaeger, *Paideia,* vol. I, *passim.*

40. Friedrich Nietzsche, *The Birth of Tragedy from the Spirit of Music,* translated by W.A. Hausmann (Edinburgh, 1923), 85. For a more conservative approach see G.M.A. Grube, *The Drama of Euripides* (London, 1941).

41. J.B. Bury, op. cit., 176–77.

42. Sir Richard Jebb, op. cit., 128 *ff;* also Werner Jaeger, *Paideia,* vol. I, 360 *ff.*

43. G.M.A. Grube, op. cit., 29.

44. *The Legacy of Greece,* 275.

45. See H. Grant Robertson, *The Administration of Justice in the Athenian Empire* (Toronto, 1924).

46. "Lycurgus is said to have banished the study of arithmetic from Sparta, as being democratic and popular in its effect, and to have introduced geometry, as being better suited to a sober oligarchy and constitutional monarchy. For arithmetic, by its employment of number, distributes things equally; geometry, by the employment of proportion, distributes things according to merit. Geometry is therefore not a source of confusion in the State, but has in it a notable principle of distinction between good men and bad, who are awarded their portions not by weight or lot, but by the difference between vice and virtue. This, the geometrical, is the system of proportion which God applies to affairs. This it is, my dear Tyndares, which is called by the names of Dike and Nemesis, and which teaches us that we ought to regard justice as equality, but not equality as justice. For what the many aim at is the greatest of all injustices, and God has removed it out of the world as being unattainable; but he protects and maintains the distribution of things according to merit, determining it geometrically, that is in accordance with proportion and law." Plutarch's Dinner Table Discussion cited in Benjamin Farrington, *Science and Politics in the Ancient World* (London, 1939), 29–30.

5 The Written Tradition and the Roman Empire

1. See Franz Altheim, *A History of Roman Religion,* translated by Harold Mattingly (London, 1938).

2. Rhys Carpenter, "The Greek Alphabet Again" (*American Journal of Archaeology,* XLII, 1938, 67).

3. Fritz Schulz, *Principles of Roman Law* (Oxford, 1936), 7.

4. It has been argued that Mediterranean influence on Roman law was slight. See Eugen Ehrlich, *Fundamental Principles of the Sociology of Law* (Cambridge, 1936), 262.

5.   For example, in intestate succession. R.W. Lee, *The Elements of Roman Law* (London, 1944), 10–11.

6.   H.S. Maine, *Ancient Law* (London, 1906), 335.

7.   Ibid., 326.

8.   Ibid., 138.

9.   Fritz Schulz, *Principles of Roman Law* (Oxford, 1936), 72.

10. G.H. Sabine, *A History of Political Theory* (New York, 1937), 161.

11. Schulz, op.,cit., 8–11.

12. Samuel Dill, *Roman Society from Nero to Marcus Aurelius* (London, 1904), 567.

13. John Edwin Sandys, *A Short History of Classical Scholarship* (Cambridge, 1915), 32. As a result of competition for manuscripts between the Ptolemies and Attalus I (241–197 BC), sellers lengthened their works in order to secure higher prices, and critical study and editing were necessary to detect forgeries. Long rolls were inconvenient and works of Greek literature were divided into a number of rolls. Philology found new scope in textual criticism. Dictionaries and grammars were produced, Greek accents were introduced.

14. Papyri of the latter part of the second century BC discovered in Egypt show the disappearance of eccentric texts and the emergence of standard texts. See *The Legacy of Egypt*, ed. S.R.K. Glanville (Oxford, 1942), 260.

15. Sandys, op. cit., 34.

16. F.P. Chambers, *Cycles of Taste* (Cambridge, 1928), 29–35.

17. E.E. Kellett, *Fashion in Literature* (London, 1931), 279.

18. Medical writings of the third century BC cited Benjamin Farrington, *Science and Politics in the Ancient World* (London, 1939), 63.

19. Gustave Glotz, "Le prix du papyrus dans l'antiquité grecque" (*Annales d'histoire économique et sociale*, January 1929, 3–12).

20. J.W. Clark, *The Care of Books* (Cambridge, 1908), 8.

21. W.W. Tarn, *Hellenistic Civilization* (London, 1941), 147.

22. Cited E.R. Bevan, *The House of Seleucus* (London, 1902), vol. I, 200.

23. Tarn, op. cit., 285.

24. In spite of a general increase in wages, those of stone letter writers declined 67 per cent in a century. At Delphi they received 9 obols per 100 letters in 340 BC, 6 obols in 335 BC, 6 obols for 300 letters in 300 BC, and the same for 350 letters in 250 BC. M.O. Wason, *Class Struggle in Ancient Greece* (London, 1947), 174.

25. G.H. Sabine, *A History of Political Theory* (New York, 1937), 150.

26. See D.R. Dudley, *A History of Cynicism from Diogenes to the 6th Century AD* (London, 1937).

27. See Tenney Frank, *Life and Literature in the Roman Republic* (Berkeley, 1930).

28. See E.V. Hansen, *The Attalids of Pergamon* (Ithaca, 1947).

29. Naphtali Lewis, op. cit., 86.

30. See A.H. Byrne, *Titus Pomponius Atticus, Chapters of a Biography* (Bryn Mawr, 1920), 14 *ff*. Egyptians used rolls of 100 feet and over in length, but the Greeks limited them to 35 feet. The papyrus sheet was generally 10 x 7½ inches and rarely over 13 x 9 inches. In Pliny's time 20 sheets constituted a roll. A roll was a cylinder from 9 to 10 inches in height and 1 to 1½ inches in diameter. In writing, the width of columns varied from a normal of 2 or 3 inches to 5 and 7 inches. A line ranged from 18 to 25 letters with 25 to 45 to a column. The recto side of papyrus was used as the pen ran more smoothly along the fibres of papyrus lying horizontally. Writing on papyrus necessitated lightness of pressure. Authors divided their works in portions conveniently contained in single rolls. It was "a common practice down to the end of Roman literary history" to publish books such as those of the *Aeneid* separately. Dill, op. cit., 162.

31. Cited Fritz Schulz, *Principles of Roman Law* (Oxford, 1936), 98.

32. C.E. Boyd, *Public Libraries and Literary Culture in Ancient Rome* (Chicago, 1915).

33. Grant Showerman, "The Great Mother of the Gods" (*Bulletin of the University of Wisconsin, Philological and Literature Series*, 1901).

34. The several grades included the *hieratica* (later called *Augusta* and *Liviana*), the best paper, 24.03 cm in size; *hieratica* of the Roman Empire, 20.33 cm; *amphitheatrica*, 16.63 cm, which was improved by Fannius apparently in charge of an entrepôt in Rome and became *Fanniana*, 18.48 cm; *sartica*, a lower grade made at Sais in the delta, 12.95 to 14.78 cm; *taenotica*, strong, thick, heavy paper; and *emporetica*, 11.09 cm, used for wrapping.

35. See A.M. Duff, *Freedmen in the Early Roman Empire* (Oxford, 1928).

36. See F.F. Abbott and A.C. Johnson, *Municipal Administration in the Roman Empire* (Princeton, 1926).

37. James Westfall Thompson, *Ancient Libraries* (Berkeley, 1940).

38. Seneca wrote in AD 49: "outlay upon studies, best of all outlays, is reasonable so long as it is kept within certain limits ... Nowadays a library takes rank with a bathroom as a necessary ornament of a house ... these productions of men whose genius we revere, paid for at a high price ... are got together to adorn and beautify a wall." Cited J.W. Clark, *The Care of Books* (Cambridge, 1901), 21. For a description of rolls and libraries see 27–30.

39. Felix Reichmann, "The Book Trade at the Time of the Roman Empire" (*The Library Quarterly*, XIII, 1938, 40 *ff*).

40. Samuel Dill, *Roman Society from Nero to Marcus Aurelius*, 160.

41. Ibid., 4.

42. See F.A. Walbank, *The Decline of the Roman Empire in the West* (London, 1946); also Gordon Childe, *What Happened in History* (New York, 1946). Early third century 1,250 [denarii] to gold pound — 301 official rating 50,000 to pound.

43. See Gustaf Hamburg, *Studies in Roman Imperial Art* (Copenhagen, 1945).

44. See W.H.P. Hatch, *An Album of Dated Syrian Manuscripts* (Boston, 1946), 4.

45. See Edgar J. Goodspeed, *New Chapters in New Testament Study* (New York, 1937); also F.G. Kenyon, *Books and Readers in Ancient Greece and Rome* (Oxford, 1932).

46. W.M. Flinders Petrie, *Egypt and Israel* (London, 1911), 141.

47. See Adolf Harnack, *The Mission and Expansion of Christianity in the First Three Centuries*, translated and edited by James Moffatt (London, 1908).

48. See Franz Cumont, *Astrology and Religion among the Greeks and Romans* (New York, 1912).

49. Cited Franz Cumont, *The Oriental Religions in Roman Paganism* (Chicago, 1911), 213; also S.J. Case, *The Origins of Christian Supernaturalism* (Chicago, 1946), 147.

50. See Vaughan Cornish, *The Great Capitals: An Historical Geography* (London, 1923), 66 *ff.*

51. See A.A.Vasiliev, *History of the Byzantine Empire* (Madison, 1928), vol. I, 174 *ff.*

52. C.K. Allen, *Law in the Making* (Oxford, 1939), 111.

53. R.W. Lee, *The Elements of Roman Law* (London, 1944), 28.

6 Parchment and Paper

1. See H. Pirenne, "Le Commerce du papyrus dans la Gaule mérovingienne" (*Académie des inscriptions et belles-lettres, Comptes rendus des séances de l'année 1928*, 178–92); also *Economic and Social History of Mediaeval Europe* (New York, 1937). The monastery at Corbie received rent including papyrus after 716. J.W. Thompson, *Economic and Social History of Europe in the Later Middle Ages, 1300–1530* (New York, 1931), vol. I, 89.

2. See H.C. Lea, *A History of Auricular Confessions and Indulgences in the Latin Church* (Philadelphia, 1896).

3. Cited J.W. Thompson, *The Medieval Library* (Chicago, 1939), 40.

4. He wrote that he felt "of all bodily tasks a perhaps not unjust preference for the work of scribes (provided they copy accurately) since by reading and re-reading Holy Scripture they gain wholesome mental instruction, and by copying the precepts of the Lord they help to disseminate them far and wide." "What happy application, what praiseworthy industry, to preach unto men by means of the hand, to untie the tongues by means of the fingers, to bring quiet and salvation to mortals, and fight the Devil's insidious wiles with pen and ink! For every word of the Lord which is copied deals Satan a wound."

5. Cited J.W. Thompson, op. cit., 109.

6. John Edwin Sandys, op. cit., 120.

7. "We declare unanimously in the name of the Holy Trinity that there

shall be rejected and removed and anathematised out of the Christian Church every likeness which is made out of any material and colour whatsoever by the evil art of painters." Cited E.J. Martin, *A History of the Econoclastic Controversy* (London, n.d.), 51; see also Edwyn Bevan, *Holy Images* (London, 1940).

8. Charles Dièhl, *History of the Byzantine Empire* (Princeton, 1925), 58.

9. Mellitus, sent to preach to the Saxons, was instructed to "keep the old temples, and, after destroying the idols they contain, turn them into churches. Keep the old festivals and allow the people to kill oxen as usual but dedicate the feast to Holy martyrs whose relics are in the Church." Cited by Françoise Henry, *Irish Art in the Early Christian Period* (London, 1940).

10. E.J. Martin, op. cit., 122.

11. See Lewis Leopold, *Prestige, a Psychological Study of Social Estimates* (London, 1913), 275.

12. See E.A. Lowe, *The Beneventan Script: A History of the South Italian Minuscule* (Oxford, 1914).

13. See T.F. Carter, *The Invention of Printing in China and Its Spread Westward* (New York, 1925).

14. See F.B. Wiborg, *Printing Ink* (New York, 1926).

15. See Lin Yutang, *A History of the Press and Public Opinion in China* (Chicago, 1936), 20.

16. See D. Diringer, op. cit., 329 *ff*; also on China, 98–110.

17. See Gerard de Gre, *Society and Ideology* (New York, 1943).

18. See G. Le Strange, *Baghdad During the Abbasid Caliphate* (Oxford, 1900); also André Blum, *La Route du Papier* (Grenoble, 1946).

19. See Robert Byron and D.T. Rice, *The Birth of Western Painting* (London, 1930), for a suggestion of discussion of the implication of the iconoclastic controversy to the history of painting.

20. See Vaughan Cornish, *Borderlands of Language in Europe and their Relation to the Historic Frontier of Christendom* (London, 1936), 47 *ff*.

21. See J.M. Hussey, *Church and Learning in the Byzantine Empire, 867–1185* (London, 1937).

22. Cited Vasiliev, op. cit., vol. II, 235.

23. See Henri Alibaux, *Les premières Papeteries Françaises* (Paris, 1926), for a concise lucid account of the spread of the paper industry; also Dard Hunter, *Papermaking Through Eighteen Centuries* (New York, 1930).

24. See *The Legacy of Islam*, ed. by the late Sir Thomas Arnold and Alfred Guillaume (Oxford, 1931), and G.E. Von Greenebaum, *Medieval Islam, a Study in Cultural Orientation* (Chicago, 1946).

25. See *The Legacy of Israel*, ed. E.R. Bevan and Charles Singer (Oxford, 1927).

26. See John Edwin Sandys, *A Short History of Classical Scholarship*, 136.

27. G.C. Coulton, *Europe's Apprenticeship, a Survey of Medieval Latin with Examples* (London, 1940), 14.

28. Ibid., 15.

29. Otto Jespersen, *Language, Its Nature, Development and Origin* (London, 1922), 23–24.

30. Gregory VII wrote in 1079: "For it is clear to those who reflect upon it; that not without reason has it pleased almighty God that Holy Scripture should be a secret in certain places, lest if it were plainly apparent to all men, perchance it would be little esteemed and be subject to disrespect; or it might be falsely understood by those of mediocre learning and lead to error," cited Margaret Deanesly, *The Lollard Bible and Other Medieval Biblical Versions* (Cambridge, 1920), 24.

31. Margaret Deanesly, *The Lollard Bible*, 31.

32. K.J. Holzknecht, *Literary Patronage in the Middle Ages* (Philadelphia, 1923).

33. See H.M. Chadwick, *The Heroic Age* (Cambridge, 1926).

34. See Steven Runciman, *The Medieval Manichae, a Study of the Christian Dualist Heresy* (Cambridge, 1947); also T.K. Oesterreich, *Possession, Demoniacal and Other, Among Primitive Races, in Antiquity, the Middle Ages and Modern Times* (London, 1930).

35. See H.C. Lea, *A History of the Inquisition of the Middle Ages* (New York, 1900).

36. See Paul Vinogradoff, *Roman Law in Medieval Europe* (London, 1909).

37. See James Bryce, *The Holy Roman Empire* (New York, 1919).

38. See H.O. Taylor, *The Medieval Mind* (London, 1925); M.L.W. Laistner, *Thought and Letters in Western Europe, AD 500-900* (London, 1931); R.L. Poole, *Illustrations of the History of Medieval Thought and Learning* (London, 1932); C.H. Haskins, *The Renaissance of the Twelfth Century* (Cambridge, 1927).

39. See Hastings Rashdall, *The Universities of Europe in the Middle Ages* (Oxford, 1895).

40. M. de Secondat, Baron de Montesquieu, translated by Mr. Nugent, *The Spirit of Laws* (London, 1752), vol. II, 322.

41. Ibid., 325.

42. See James Bryce, *Studies in History and Jurisprudence* (London, 1901), 275 *ff.*

43. C.H. McIlwain, *The Growth of Political Thought in the West* (New York, 1932), 192.

44. Ibid.

45. Cited C.H. McIlwain, *The Growth of Political Thought in the West*, 365.

46. See J.W. Thompson, The *Literacy of the Laity in the Middle Ages* (Berkeley, 1939).

47. See Margaret Deanesly, *The Lollard Bible and Other Medieval Biblical Versions* (Cambridge, 1920). "Hardly any event in English economical history has

been so full of results as the plague of 1349 was. It emancipated the serf, and it demoralized the Church. It gave occasion to the teaching of Wiklif, and assured the Reformation. Had it not been for the insurrection of 1381, and the identification of Lollardy with sedition and rebellion, the separation from Rome would have occurred in the fifteenth century. The tie which bound Western Europe to the Papacy was very slender at the Council of Constance, when John XXIII was deposed and Martin V elected. But the English rulers dreaded the Lollards, and remained orthodox and uneasy." J.E. Thorold Rogers, *The Economic Interpretation of History* (New York, 1909), 263.

48. For an interesting suggestion that *filigraines* were a type of symbolism used by papermakers and "every ream turned out by these pious papermakers contained some five hundred heretical tracts each of which ran its course under the unsuspecting nose of orthodoxy," see Harold Bayley, *A New Light on the Renaissance Displayed in Contemporary Problems* (London, 1909), 40.

49. See G.R. Owst, *Literature and Pulpit in Medieval England* (Cambridge, 1933).

50. From *Max Weber: Essays in Sociology*, translated and edited H.H. Girth and C. Wright Mills (New York, 1946), 178.

51. A.L. Smith, *Church and State in the Middle Ages* (London, 1913).

52. See Eileen Power, *The Wool Trade in English Medieval History* (Oxford, 1941).

53. P. Boissonade, *Life and Work in Medieval Europe* (London, 1927), 189–90.

54. Henry Hallam, *Introduction to the Literature of Europe in the 15th, 16th and 17th Centuries* (New York, 1887), 75.

55. See J.W. Clark, *Libraries in the Medieval and Renaissance Periods* (Cambridge, 1894).

56. J.A. Herbert, *Illuminated Manuscripts* (London, 1911), 265. See also Falconer Madan, *Books in Manuscript: A Short Introduction to Their Study and Use* (New York, 1927).

57. Ibid., 310.

58. See André Blum, *The Origins of Printing and Engraving* (New York), and Carl Zigrosser, *Six Centuries of Fine Prints* (New York, 1937).

59. D. Diringer, op. cit., 401.

60. See a suggestive discussion, J.H. Denison, *Emotion as the Basis of Civilization* (New York, 1928), 100 *ff*; also *The Legacy of India*, ed. G.T. Garratt (Oxford, 1937); L.T. Hobhouse, *Morals in Evolution, a Study in Comparative Ethics* (New York, n.d.), 525–39.

7 Paper and the Printing Press

1. See Louis Radiguer, *Maitres, imprimeurs, et ouvriers typographes 1470–1903* (Paris, 1903).

2. W.E.H. Lecky, *History of the Rise and Influence of the Spirit of Nationalism in Europe* (London, 1913), 259.

3. Deanesly, op. cit., 124–25.

4. "The invention of printing which placed within the reach of all inquirers who had a tincture of education the sacred writings for investigation and interpretation and enabled the thinker and innovator at once to command an audience and disseminate his views in remote regions ..." H.C. Lea, *History of Sacerdotal Celibacy in the Christian Church* (London, 1907), vol. II, 31.

5. Mark Pattison, *Essays*, vol. I, 187.

6. Ibid., vol. II, 227.

7. Idem, *Isaac Casaubon* (London, 1875), 511.

8. Ibid., 175.

9. *Memoirs ... of Sir James Mackintosh* (London, 1836), vol. II, 247.

10. See Vernon Hall, Jun., *Renaissance Literary Criticism, a Study of Its Social Content* (New York, 1945).

11. See Mark Pattison, *Isaac Casaubon (1559–1614)* (London, 1875), 42–43, 125–27.

12. W. Cunningham, *An Essay on Western Civilization in Its Economic Aspects* (Cambridge, 1898), 178.

13. See J.A. Goris, *Étude sur les colonies marchandes mérdionales (Portugais, Espagnoles, Italiens) à Anvers de 1488 à 1567* (Louvain, 1925).

14. A.F. Leach, *The Schools of Medieval England* (London, 1915), 332.

15. See Phoebe Sheavyn, *The Literary Profession in the Elizabethan Age* (Manchester, 1909); also M.A. Shaaber, *Some Forerunners of the Newspaper in England, 1476–1622* (Philadelphia, 1922).

16. Walter Raleigh, *Shakespeare* (London, 1907), 105.

17. "The abolition of saint-worship; the destruction of images; the sweeping-away of ceremonies, of absolutions, of fasts and penances; the free circulation of the Scriptures; the communion in prayer by the native tongue; the introduction, if not of a good, yet of a more energetic and attractive style of preaching than had existed before; and besides, this, the eradication of monkery which they despised, the humiliation of ecclesiastical power which they hated, the immunity from exactions which they resented — these are what the north of Europe deemed its gain by the public establishment of the Reformation, and to which the common name of Protestantism was given." Henry Hallam, *Introduction to the Literature of Europe in the Fifteenth, Sixteenth and Seventeenth Centuries* (New York, 1887), vol. I, 377.

18. See Albert Guerard, *Literature and Society* (Boston, 1935), 107–08, on the failure of the Bible to take root in literary soil.

19. On the limitations of the Bible as a basis of flexible political growth

essential to empires see J.B. Crozier, *History of Intellectual Development on the Lines of Modern Evolution* (London, 1901), vol. III, 204 *ff.*

20. Mark Pattison, *Essays*, vol. II, 31. "Down to the present day the peculiar nature of this structure stamps the life of the Calvinistic peoples with a unique emphasis on the cultivation of independent personality, which leads to a power of initiative and a sense of responsibility for action, combined also with a very strong sense of unity for common, positive ends and values, which are invulnerable on account of their religious character. This explains the fact that all Calvinistic peoples are characterized by individualism and by democracy, combined with a strong bias towards authority and a sense of the unchangeable nature of law. It is this combination which makes a conservative democracy possible, whereas in Lutheran and Catholic countries, as a matter of course, democracy is forced into an aggressive and revolutionary attitude." Ernst Troeltsch, *The Social Teaching of the Christian Churches* (New York, 1931), 619. "It is certain that this substratum of law in Western theology lies exceedingly deep. A new set of Greek theories, the Aristotelian philosophy, made their way afterwards into the West, and almost entirely buried its indigenous doctrines. But when at the Reformation it partially shook itself free from their influence, it instantly supplied their place with Law. It is difficult to say whether the religious system of Calvin or the religious system of the Arminians has the more markedly legal character." H.S. Maine, op. cit., 372.

21. See Ch. Enschede, *Fonderies de caractères et leur matèriel dans les Pays-Bas du XV au XIX siècle* (Haarlem, 1908).

22. G.H. Sabine, *A History of Political Theory* (New York, 1937), 478.

23. See Alexandre Beljame, *Le public et les hommes de lettres en Angleterre au dix-huitième siècle, 1660–1774* (Paris, 1883).

24. See Basil Willey, *The Seventeenth Century Background* (London, 1934), 268; also R.F. Jones, *Ancients and Moderns, a Study of the Background of the Battle of the Books* (Washington University Studies, January 1936), and R.K. Merton, "Science, Technology and Society in Seventeenth Century England" (*Osiris*, IV, 360 *ff*).

25. Vernon Hall, *Renaissance Literary Criticism* (New York, 1945), 154.

26. Arnold Toynbee, *A Study of History*, vol. III, 363.

27. C.K. Allen, *Law in the Making* (Oxford, 1939), 50.

28. Ibid., 302.

29. C.H. McIlwain, *The Growth of Political Thought in the West*, 387.

30. R. Ehrenberg, *Capital and Finance in the Age of the Renaissance, a Study of the Fuggers and Their Connections*, translated by H.M. Lucas (London, 1928).

31. Eugen Ehrlich, *Fundamental Principles of the Sociology of Law* (Cambridge, 1936), 96–98.

32. J.E. Thorold Rogers, *The Economic Interpretation of History* (New York, 1888), 86.

33. *The Economic Writings of Sir William Petty*, ed. C.H. Hull (Cambridge, 1899), vol. I, 263.

34. J.M.Yinger, *Religion in the Struggle for Power* (Durham, 1946), 94.

35. Lord King, *The Life and Letters of John Locke* (London, 1864), 204–07.

36. See B.H. Liddell Hart, *The Revolution in Warfare* (London, 1946). "Of all struggles the most appalling are the wars of religion, more especially those between religions in which the thought of a future life predominates, or in which morality is in other ways completely bound up with the existing form of religion, or in which a religion has taken on a strong national colouring and a people is defending itself in its religion. Among civilized peoples they are most terrible of all" (Burckhardt).

37. See F.P.G. Guizot, *General History of Civilization in Europe from the Fall of the Roman Empire to the French Revolution* (New York, 1843), 298–99.

38. C.M. Briquet, *Associations et grèves des ouvriers papetiers en France aux XVIIe et XVIIIe siècles* (Paris, 1897).

39. See A. Aspinall, "Statistical Accounts of the London Newspapers in the Eighteenth Century" (*English Historical Review*, April 1948, 201–32); also Stanley Morison, *The English Newspaper* (Cambridge, 1932).

40. See H.A. Innis, "The English Publishing Trade in the Eighteenth Century" (*Manitoba Arts Review*, IV, 1945, 14–24).

41. See W.T. Laprade, *Public Opinion and Politics in the Eighteenth Century England to the Fall of Walpole* (New York, 1936), and Lawrence Hanson, *Government and the Press, 1695–1763* (London, 1936).

42. See F.J. Harvey Darton, *Children's Books in England: Five Centuries of Social Life* (Cambridge, 1932).

43. John Buchan, *Sir Walter Scott* (Toronto, 1935), 287–88.

44. Amy Cruse, *The Englishman and his Books in the Early Nineteenth Century* (London, 1930), 229.

45. See A.S. Collins, *Authorship in the Days of Johnson, Being a Study of the Relation Between Author, Patron, Publisher and Public, 1726–1780* (London, 1928), also E.E. Kent, *Goldsmith and His Booksellers* (Ithaca, 1933).

46. See Dorothy Blakey, *The Minerva Press, 1790–1820* (London, 1939).

47. *Johnson's England*, ed. A.S. Turberville (Oxford, 1933), 360.

48. See C.A. Duniway, *The Development of Freedom of the Press in Massachusetts* (New York, 1906).

49. George Parker Winship, *The Cambridge Press, 1638–1692* (Philadelphia, 1945); W.C. Ford, *The Boston Book Market, 1679–1700* (Boston, 1917); L.C. Wroth, *The Colonial Printer* (Portland, 1938); Hellmuth Lehmann Haupt, *The Book in America* (New York, 1939).

50. See Sidney Kobre, *The Development of the Colonial Newspaper*

(Pittsburgh, 1944).

51. See E.C. Cook, *Literary Influences in Colonial Newspapers, 1704–1750* (New York, 1912).

52. David Ramsay, *History of the American Revolution* (Philadelphia, 1789), vol. I, 61–62, cited A.M. Schlesinger, "The Colonial Newspapers and the Stamp Act" (*New England Quarterly*, VIII, 65).

53. Philip Davidson, *Propaganda and the American Revolution, 1763–1783* (Chapel Hill, 1941).

54. Cited W.G. Bleyer, *Main Currents in the History of American Journalism* (Boston, 1927).

55. See *Political Theories of the Middle Ages*, by Dr. Otto Geirke, introduction by F.W. Maitland (Cambridge, 1900), XI.

56. See Brooks Adams, *The Emancipation of Massachusetts* (Boston, 1919); also A.M. Baldwin, *The New England Clergy and the American Revolution* (Durham, 1928).

57. John Viscount Morley, *Rousseau* (London, 1921), vol. II, 46.

58. Arthur Young, *Travels During the Years 1787, 1788, and 1789* (London, 1792), 146–47.

59. John Viscount Morley, *Diderot and the Encyclopedists* (London, 1921).

60. Serge Chakotin, *The Rape of the Masses, the Psychology of Totalitarian Propaganda* (London, 1940), 142.

61. Cited L.N. Salmon, *The Newspaper and Authority* (New York, 1923), 64.

62. See J. Bréville, *Le Centenaire de la machine à papier continu* (n.p., n.d.). Brought by Didot, invented by Louis Robert, to Fourdrinier, an English paper maker of Huguenot descent.

63. See A.D. Spicer, *The Paper Trade* (London, 1907); also H.A. Innis, *Political Economy in the Modern State* (Toronto, 1946), 35–55.

64. See C.D. Collet, *History of the Taxes on Knowledge, Their Origin and Repeal* (London, 1933); A. Aspinall, *Politics and the Press* (London, 1949).

65. The *Herald* had a circulation of 100,000 and was widely quoted and feared by northern leaders. It represented the business interests of England disturbed over the possible effects of civil war on the cotton trade and its utterances were accepted by *The Times*. W.G. Bleyer, op. cit., 205.

66. See W.C. Phillips, *Dickens, Reade and Collins, Sensational Novelists, a Study of the Conditions and Theories of Novel Writing in Victorian England* (New York, 1919).

67. See M.I. Ostrogorski, *Democracy and the Party System in the United States* (New York, 1910); also Robert Michels, *Political Parties* (New York, 1915).

68. See C.M. Briquet, *Notions pratiques sur le papier* (Besançon, 1905).

69. Elisabeth Salmon, *Die Papierindustrie des Reisengebirges in ihrer standortsmassigen Bedingtheit* (Tübingen, 1920).

70. See L. Ethan Ellis, *Print Paper Pendulum, Group Pressures and the Price of Newsprint* (New Brunswick, 1948); *Reciprocity 1911: A Study in Canadian*

American Relations (New Haven, 1939); and J.A. Guthrie, *The Newsprint Paper Industry, an Economic Analysis* (Cambridge, 1941).

71. See H.L. Mencken, *The American Language* (New York, 1936).

72. See Q.D. Leavis, *Fiction and the Reading Public* (London, 1932); also L.L. Schucking, *The Sociology of Literary Taste* (London, 1944).

73. See D.L. Cohn, *The Good Old Days* (New York, 1940).

74. E. Haldeman Julius, *The First Hundred Million* (New York, 1928). First book 1919 Omar Khayyam — gave it place in popular reading.

75. See H.A. Innis, *The Press: A Neglected Factor in the Economic History of the Twentieth Century* (London, 1948).

76. See O.J. Hale, *Publicity and Diplomacy with Special Reference to England and Germany, 1890–1914* (New York, 1940).

77. See Denys Thompson, *Voice of Civilisation* (London, 1943).

78. See Henry Avenel, *Histoire de la presse française depuis 1789 jusqu'à nos jours* (Paris, 1900); Georges Weill, *Le Journal. Origines, évolution et rôle de la presse périodique* (Paris, 1934); and E.M. Carroll, *French Public Opinion and Foreign Affairs, 1870–1914* (New York, 1931).

79. Nov. 2, 1853, *The Greville Diary*, ed. P.W. Wilson (New York, 1927), vol. II, 318.

80. "Writing political articles for newspapers has never been in England the sure introduction to political power which it formerly was in France — though, on the contrary, it has in general been found a hindrance." *Literary Studies*, by the late Walter Bagehot and R.H. Hutton (London, 1879), 387. "If the revolutions of 1848 have clearly brought out any fact, it is the utter failure of newspaper statesmen. Everywhere they have been tried; everywhere they have shown great talents for intrigue, eloquence and agitation — how rarely have they shown even fair aptitude for ordinary administration; how frequently have they gained a disreputable renown by a laxity of principle surpassing the laxity of their aristocratic and worthy adversaries." Ibid., 351.

81. See C.J. Friedrich, *Foreign Policy in the Making* (New York, 1938).

82. Compare Moritz Busch, *Bismarck: Some Secret Pages of His History* (New York, 1898), and *The Goebbels Diaries, 1942–1943* (New York, 1948). Herman Ullstein, *The Rise and Fall of the House of Ullstein* (New York, 1943). "One learns more from the newspapers than from official despatches, as, of course, Governments use the press in order frequently to say more clearly what they really mean. One must, however, know all about the connections of the different papers" (22 Jan. 1871). Moritz Busch, op. cit., vol. I, xvi.

83. See L. Dominian, *The Frontiers of Language and Nationality in Europe* (New York, 1917), and A.C. Woolner, *Languages in History and Politics* (London, 1938).

84. E.A. Freeman, "Race and Language," *Essays English and American* (New York, 1910).

85. See H.M. Chadwick, *The Nationalities of Europe and the Growth of National Ideologies* (Cambridge, 1943), 88.

86. Edmund Wilson, *To the Finland Station, a Study in the Writing and Acting of History* (New York, 1910).

87. *A Study of History* (Oxford, 1934), vol. I, 14. See also "An Estimate of the Value and Influence of Works of Fiction in Modern Times," *Works of Thomas Hill Green,* ed. by R.L. Nettleship (London, 1889), vol. III, 29–45; and H.H. Alden, *Magazine Writing and the New Literature* (New York, 1908).

88. G.C. Lewis, *An Essay on the Influence of Authority in Matters of Opinion* (London, 1849), 219.

89. R.W. Emerson, *English Traits* (Boston, 1903), 261.

90. In substance the growth of the law is legislative. Jerome Frank, *Law and the Modern Mind* (New York, 1935), 255. "The philosophical habit of the day, the frequency of legislation, and the ease with which the law may be changed to meet the opinions and wishes of the public, all make it natural and unavoidable that judges as well as others should openly discuss the legislative principles upon which their decisions must always rest in the end, and should base their judgments upon broad considerations of policy to which the traditions of the bench would hardly have tolerated a reference fifty years ago." O.W. Holmes, *The Common Law* (New York 1881), 78.

91. Charles Babbage, *Reflections on the Decline of Science in England and on Some of Its Causes* (London, 1830), 13. "By a destructive misapplication of talent which our institutions create we exchange a profound philosopher for but a tolerable lawyer." Ibid., 37.

92. Alexis De Tocqueville, *American Institutions,* translated by Henry Reeve (Cambridge, 1870), 352.

93. Ibid., 360.

94. Ibid., 364.

95. W.S. Logan, cited Benjamin Kidd, *Principles of Western Civilization* (London, 1902), 352.

96. De Tocqueville, op. cit., 353.

97. H.H. Horne, *Exposition of the Fake Medium and Barriers Excluding Men of Genius from the Public* (London, 1833), 245. The reader "pores over the gospel according to St. Criticism, and we, who are living men, with all our feelings about us, are to be crippled, bound hand and foot, hamstrung, broken upon the wheel, faced down, and melted to make candles for him to read by." Ibid., 155. See also Cyrus Redding, *Fifty Years' Recollections, Literary and Personal* (London, 1858), vol. III, 276–78, 295–97.

98. L.T. Hobhouse, *Mind in Evolution* (London, 1915), 433.

99. Bertrand Russell, *Philosophy and Politics* (Cambridge, 1947), 20–21. "The trading temper, independent and insubordinate is absolutely opposed to

the martial spirit." A.T. Mahan, *The Influence of Sea Power upon History, 1660–1783* (London, 1890), 435.

100. See E.M. Winslow, *The Pattern of Imperialism, a Study in the Theories of Power* (New York, 1948); also K.E. Knorr, *British Colonial Theories, 1570–1850* (Toronto, 1944).

101. For a discussion of artistic interest in problems of government see the remarks of Lord Milner in J.T. Shotwell, *At the Paris Peace Conference* (New York, 1937), 171–72, and Leon Trotsky, *The History of the Russian Revolution* (London, 1934).

102. See Charles Bally, *Le Langage et la vie* (Paris, 1926).

103. For a suggestion of the increase in power of the executive in comparison with the legislative branches of government following the use of the radio see Quincy Wright, *A Study of War* (Chicago, 1942), vol. II, 180 *ff* and 215.

104. J.U. Nef, *The United States and Civilization* (Chicago, 1942).

MARGINALIA

1 Introduction

pages 22–23

"It was the French culture of the English ruling caste that made England's power possible."

"Of all the Roman provincials the French have been the ones who inherited most of the [marvelous] organizing capacity of the Romans." Wyndham Lewis, *The Art of Being Ruled* (New York, 1926), 371.

page 24

a. and by the opening up of new markets

pages 30–31

Writing or separation of ideographs into phonograms the work of a highly centralized political and social organization — royal and priestly classes. Arthur Evans, *The Palace of Minos at Knossos* (London, 1921–35), vol. I, ch. 29.

2 Egypt

page 32

a. Easily controlled and regular in occurrence (?).

b. Was this to predict the floods or rather to determine the day for religious festivals [?]

On relation of pyramids to sun worship and conflict with sky religion see G.A. Wainwright, *The Sky Religion in Egypt* (Cambridge, 1938).

Conflict between oral and written traditions also [see] E. Mayer and J.H. Breasted.

page 33

c. Was this oral tradition? i.e,. followed by written.

In primitive thought spoken word universally invested with a magical power. Robert Briffault, *The Mothers: A Study of the Origins of Sentiments and Institutions* (London, 1927), vol. I, 14–23.

See W.M. Flinders Petrie, "On the Mechanical Methods of the Ancient Egyptians" (*Journal of the Royal Anthropological Institute*, XIII, 1884, 88–109) for a discussion of stone cutting before 2400 BC — performed by graving points far harder than the material to be cut, jewel points set in a bronze saw in some instances up to 8 ft in length of varying widths. In fourth dynasty tubular drills used; saws and tubular drills held down by heavy weights. Plaster extensively used by Egyptians to fill cracks. Pyramids built by labour in off seasons.

Did Egypt borrow writing from Babylonia [?].

page 34

d. Memphis with local god Ptah 25 miles from old religious capital Heliopolis. Writing prohibited migration of government or objectivity of government. Spread of writing meant change in value attached to writing. Egypt did not recover from early burden of pyramids and hieroglyphics.

Egyptians recognized first dynasty as break from prehistoric — political aspect of union of Upper and Lower Egypt — introduction of writing, large-scale use of metal tools, new modes of monumental art. Presumably did keeping of time. Henri Frankfort, *Kingship and the Gods* (Chicago, 1948), 15.

Abydos on main route to Red Sea and East — apparently centre of first dynasty.

Wealth more highly concentrated in Egypt — less scope for merchants than in Babylonia — unproductive expenditure, nobles' estates increasingly self-sufficient — aimed at political autonomy — Old Kingdom dissolved about 2475 BC.

King dreamed and depicted totem roles of clans and won immortality.

Priests of Ra (Heliopolis) overthrew fourth dynasty — Pharaoh to be bodily son of Ra.

Fifth dynasty 2750 BC residing at Memphis using name Ra. In sixth dynasty local governors more independent — fifth dynasty overthrown about 2625.

pages 35–36

e. in particular heavy emphasis on papyrus as basis of feudalism in contrast with alphabet and bureaucracy of Roman Empire.

Son of Ra in fourth dynasty superseding cult of Aten in Heliopolis. Significance of writing and art to take place of food and offerings. Pharaoh instead of temple acquired surplus products and result in monumental tombs.

By third dynasty heliacal rising of Sirius a herald of flood — bureaucracy used sidereal year. Greatest achievement — solar calendar — average interval between floods 365 days. Middle kingdom centre Thebes — pull north or south attitude of ancient Egyptians towards dead (A.H. Gardiner).

Civil service of god — perpetual corporation — script to record expenditure and receipts.

Earliest hieroglyphics accompanied by simplified cursive forms without replacing former.

Cursive signs written in ink on pottery or wood in Royal Tombs, later on papyrus. Hieroglyphics and cursive forms presumably pure ideograms — many acquired phonetic values and came to stand for consonants — used ideographic, syllabic, and consonantal signs side by side. Gordon Childe, *What Happened in History* [1964 ed., 126].

"Drawing was earlier than writing and the earliest form of writing seems to have been picture writing … When the same fixed set of pictures were used over and over again to represent not merely ideas and objects but also words and sounds." Manufacture of papyrus paper grew into "a large and flourishing industry in the Old Kingdom." J.H. Breasted, *A History of Egypt* (New York, 1912), 97.

page 37

Pictographic on wood and stone and as with Sumerians pictures given syllabic as well as word values but more used as vowels though there were 24 consonants, in contrast vowels difficult to know pronunciation used. Egyptian writing right to left but Sumerian left to right. See Adolf Erman, *Life in Ancient Egypt* (London, 1894), ch. 14 on drawing.

Preservation of bodies in dry desert sand apparently started interest in immortality.

Gordon Childe, *What Happened in History* [1964 ed., 122]. Change cult of Ra to cult of Osiris fifth dynasty started social revolution with illusory gratifications substituted for changes in social order. Abram Kardiner, *The Psychological Frontiers of Society* (New York, 1945), 427.

Cult of Osiris resisted efforts of Akhnaton to introduce monotheism. 428.

page 38

f. Moret, *The Nile and Egyptian Civilization*, 383.

g. Ibid., 403.

page 39

h. 1479(?) Breasted.

Prelogical age coming to end early second millennium — formulating of mathematics, surveying, medicine, greater attention to social justice, extension of future life to nobles and well-to-do — i.e., law — contact of religion and fame. W.F. Albright, *From the Stone Age to Christianity* (Baltimore, 1940), 138–40.

Rites for [the] masses meant rights for [the] masses. Childe, *What Happened in History* [1964 ed., 165].

pages 39–40

Papyrus for cursive writing — brush pen gave signs bolder forms. How far did spread of belief in immortality facilitate development of army to drive out Hyksos and develop empire?. Importance of belief in immortality to military power.

Middle Kingdom counts for Thebes built feudal monarchy — insubordination of vassal counts — coming of Hyksos — driving out of latter by Ahmose founder of New Kingdom using light horse-drawn chariot — formed centralized military monarchy. Childe, *What Happened in History* [1964 ed., 162].

Thutmose IV married daughter of king of Mitanni.

page 41

i. 1350 BC. Breasted.

"Monotheism was imperialism in religion" (Breasted).

Akhnaton not founder of Aten cult — this developed about 1400 BC. In Egypt idea of potency of divine name assumed gigantic dimensions. Liturgies of more advanced peoples — idea of prayer gains potency from solemn utterance of true divine name — especially Mediterranean and India. L.R. Farnell, *The Evolution of Religion: An Anthropological Study* (New York, 1905), 184–88.

pages 41–42

Decline of Egypt under Rameses III, 1198–1167. Rameses I about 1320 BC.

Cult of Sut, enemy of Horus.

Cursive form developed to hieratic — in seventh century demotic writing — hieratic became priestly class script — demotic used to end of fifth century contributed to Coptic. D. Diringer, *The Alphabet, a Key to the History of Mankind* (New York, 1948), 64–67.

Divine worship of mortal abhorrent to Judaism and not accepted by severer Zoroastrianism but part of state system of Egypt — finally imposed on Greco-Roman world. Farnell, *The Evolution of Religion*, 76.

page 43

j. Also substituting more lifelike representation for standardized canons of proportion. Hogarth claims art reaches highest point in oligarchy or monarchy and that destruction of latter leads to developed best artisan work for people. D.G. Hogarth, *The Twilight of History* (London, 1926), 27.

See W.F. Albright, *The Vocalization of the Egyptian Syllabic Orthography* (New York, 1934).

pages 43–44

k. They provided a scaffolding for social organization and science but delayed an understanding of nature. Science made possible the urban revolution but was exploited by superstition and magic.

Puns and word play regarded as efficacious in establishing real relations between objects involved because of belief in marvellous power of words. H. Frankfort, *Kingship and the Gods* (Chicago, 1948), 124.

Writing an abstruse mystery not combined with manual avocations. Clerks became officials or stewards — schools maintained by treasury for security of officials.

On law see T.E. Peet, *The Great Tomb Robberies of the Twentieth Egyptian Dynasty* (Oxford, 1933); W. Spiegelberg, *Studien und Materialien zum Rechtswesen des Pharaonreiches der Dynast XVIII–XXI (c 1500–1000)* (Hanover, 1892).

pages 44–45

Probably punches of hard copper or bronze in Egypt and Babylon. Cut stone — wastage — need for constant resharpening.

Theriomorphism — divinity as animal becomes inadequate and leads to questioning and mysticism — in Egypt development of Logos — divine reason. L.R. Farnell, *Greece and Babylon: A Comparative Sketch of Mesopotamian, Anatolian and Hellenic Religions* (Edinburgh, 1911).

3 Babylonia

page 46

a. Flooding irregular and incalculable.

On clay see F.G. Kenyon, *Ancient Books and Modern Discoveries* (Chicago, 1927), 18–27.

pages 47–48

b. Administrators wrote on ledgers all at one time.

c. Angle changed 90 degrees and perpendicular columns turned so that characters on their sides and scribe reading left to right — shift from space to time arrangement.

Accounting — pictures of products brought with numbers to indicate quantity — in bureaucracy sound values given to various pictures. Writing monopoly of few — emergence of cuneiform.

pages 49–50

Literate city life persisted after disruption of empire. Resistance to aggression favoured new industries — new centres of civilization in cities.

Sargon, conquering king, personal legislation constituted fiat, overrode custom. Sargon and sons first to create vast military empire — kings of Akkad brought vast booty — forcible distribution of wealth spread purchasing power. Middle class profited from imperialism — spread of money economy — trade in metals an imperial monopoly. King made himself a god in empire. Childe, *What Happened in History* [1964 ed., 144–51]. By 3000 BC three civilizations (India, Sumer, Egypt) dependent on uncommon and socially expensive metals — state organization based on residence instead of kinship, abolished blood feuds, great increase in population. Copper or bronze too expensive to replace stone. Superiority and cost of metal equipment favoured monopoly of pharaoh, king, and city governor. Childe [138–40].

page 51

d. This not true according to Frankfort, *Kingship*, 225. But Gadd *Ur* holds

226

divine kings in second and third dynasty to Hammurabi when deification died out. [C.J. Gadd, *History and Monuments of Ur* (New York, 1929), 123.]

State organization disintegrated around 2500 BC. Barbarians from Gutium — temple libraries and schools continued as invaders needed clerks and sciences. Enormous increase in writing in third dynasty. Childe [159]. Kings of Ur reunited rival cities of Sumer and Akkad — by 2100 Sumerian monarchs dominated Elam and Assyria but collapsed about 2000 BC. About 1800 BC Amorite dynasty in Babylon consolidated new kingdom civil service of governors and judges — heavy solid wheels replaced by spoked wheels, asses by horses. Childe [160].

Tendency to place Hammurabi dates later 1728–1686. W.F. Albright, *From the Stone Age to Christianity: Monotheism and the Historical Process* (Baltimore, 1940), 10.

Elaborate canal system demanded unification in Babylonia. G.A. Barton, *The Origin and Development of Babylonian Writing* (Baltimore, 1913).

pages 51–52

See J.S. Newbury, "The Prehistory of the Alphabet" (*Harvard Studies in Classical Philology*, XLV, 1934, 105–56).

page 53

e. At head of pantheon with Kassites not Hammurabi.

f. Code extremely brutal to our standards but that of highly civilized and commercialized state based largely on earlier Sumerian laws.

Anu, sky. Enlil, storm. Ninkhursag and Enki, the earth.

page 55

Difficulties of writing — limited number of scribes and consequent extensive use of seals.

pages 55–56

g. S. Casson, *Progress and Catastrophe* (London, 1937), 132.

Peake and Fleure argued great crisis fifteenth and thirteenth centuries due to arrival of horse and sword from central Asia [H.J.E. Peake and H.J. Fleure, *The Horse and the Sword* (Oxford, 1933)].

Mursilis Hittite King destroyed Babylon about 1600 BC. Albright [*From the Stone Age to Christianity*, 113].

Kassites about 1740 to 1169 BC. Peake and Fleure [*The Horse and the Sword*, 3].

Kassites changed system of counting years and used year of reign to indicate the date of events. Early growth of private enterprise evident in engraved seal stones — but community never forgotten.

Hittites = Anatolians.

pages 56–57

h. Protection against common foe.

i. Rameses II exhausting Egypt with colossal building enterprises — reflecting supreme influence of religion and priesthood. Mitanni princesses married pharaohs three successive reigns. Peake and Fleure, *Merchant Venturers in Bronze* (Oxford, 1931).

Iron mentioned in Amarna letters fourteenth century, wrought iron hatchet found Ras Shamra fifteenth to fourteenth centuries. Rameses II asked Hattusil for smelted iron. H.H. Rowley, *From Joseph to Joshua* (London, 1950), 22.

Mitanni in diplomatic confederation used script and language of Akkadians.

Hittites persisted with stone and not as Assyrians adopt brick structures after 2400 BC.

Hittites probably had monopoly of iron to 1250 BC. Peake and Fleure, *The Horse and the Sword*, 54.

Breasted — daughter of Hittite king married Rameses II 1259.

Chariot consolidated authority — stability of empires Assyria, Hittite, Egypt due to sole command of mobile arm to be despatched quickly and to speed conferred on officials and overseers. After fourteenth century horse training in north Syria — chariot races.

Light horse-drawn chariots reduced journeys. Childe [182–83].

Aryans and Hittites learned secret of iron — with iron, commoner could meet bronze age knight. Bronze age ended about 1200 BC. Childe [191–94]. 1500–1400 horse-drawn chariot appears — wheeled cart about 2000 BC. Childe [169].

page 57

j. 1280 (?) This date regarded as worthless by Burn.

k. Arameans (?) Hittites captured Carchemish early fourteenth century — latter in turn captured by Assyrians end of eighth century and followed by emergence of Phrygian power. D.G. Hogarth, *Ionia and the East* (Oxford, 1909).

Mitanni and Aryan chiefs about 1450 BC adopted equipment and organization, cuneiform script, and Akkadian language of earlier civilization. Hittite chiefs invaded Babylonia about 1595, borrowed theology, law, poetry, science, writing materials, and characters from Mesopotamia. [Childe, 170–71.]

Hittite empire finally disappeared possibly 1115 BC. Peake and Fleure, *The Horse and the Sword*, 66–67.

Assyria declined slowly after Tiglath-Pileser 1113–1074. Substantial achievements of bronze age saved. Expansion of Asiatic military empires on Akkadian model — colonizing of Phoenicians, Greeks, Etruscans.

Bronze age collapse left small partially barbarized communities — reorganized as imitations of bronze age — theocratic states Palestine, Phrygia, Medes, Lydia. Assyria reduced these economically interdependent units followed by Medes and Persians.

page 58

l. Vannic language persisted to eighth or seventh century.

m. First mention of organized cavalry under Ashur-nasir-pal.

page 59

n. Had Enlil been replaced by Marduk and in Assyria Marduk by Assur?

Among Oriental autocracies instinctive bias is religious — kingship of divine type. In Babylon the king and the god were together joint source of law and order. L.R. Farnell, *Greece and Babylon*, 119–20. Legal contracts in Babylon show law had freed itself from religion — judge a secular authority since drawing up contracts [by] professional notary and with no necessary connection with temples. Farnell, 132.

Nabu the scribe — writer and keeper of Doomsbook of Heaven. Babylonian deities as arbiters of destiny. In Babylon power of spoken word great in magic — the word exalted to great cosmic divine agency. Farnell, 174–76. In Babylonian religious phraseology god becomes mystified — retires into hazy conception of an all-pervading spirit — his *word* becomes active agent. Farnell, 56.

Esarhaddon attempted to hold subject peoples by conciliation. Cumberland Clark, *The Art of Early Writing* (London, 1938), 103.

page 60

o. His position was parallel to that of Rome faced by the literary achievements of Greece.

p. Ethiopia driven from Lower Egypt 661 BC.

page 62

q. Even in Egypt in the eighteenth dynasty laws were written on forty rolls of leather.

Decline of Egyptian and Minoan sea power gave the advantage to the Phoenicians on the Mediterranean.

page 63

r. Hyksos movement may have induced a rural population to create a "non-monopolistic" means of communication. D. Diringer, *The Alphabet*, 215.

s. Decline of Hittite and Mitanni led to minor Aramean states — wave of

Aramean migration to north Syria twelfth and eleventh centuries. Diringer, 253.

Also T.J. Meek, "The Beginnings of Writing" (*University of Toronto Quarterly*, XI, October 1941, 15–24).

Evans argues alphabet from Crete to Cyprus and to Palestine (Philistines). A. Evans, *The Palace of Minos*, introduction. See J.R. Newbury, "Prehistory of Alphabet." North Semitic alphabet probably emerged in Hyksos period 1730–1580 BC.

page 64

t. Long slashing swords with weight in blade rather than hilt. Cremation accompanied iron age. Writing in Mycenean times to keep official records.

Ras Shamra script to bridge gap between alphabet and cuneiform — alphabet represented by sign of wedge-shaped lines on clay. ["The Beginnings of Writing"], 23. Papyrus imported by Phoenicia, twelfth century system of writing accompanied papyrus and displaced clay tablet — before tenth century alphabet of consonants developed in relation to demands of trade. Breasted, 484. Papyrus supplementing clay in Syria.

page 65

u. Probably from Cyprus — brought cremation and iron age created Hebrew state.

Lack of vowel sounds among Semites permitted diffusion of alphabet and rapid adaptability. Writing an attempt to represent speech accurately but number of letters too small. Phonetic system of any language too complicated to be expressed by small group of symbols. Permanent values attached to consonantal sounds but not to vowels. Diringer, 217–18.

page 66

v. Particularly important as Moses probably carried Egyptian elements of monotheism from Egypt and in escape revolted against iconography — need for religion carried with individual. W.F. Albright, *From Stone Age to Christianity*, 206.

Hebrews rejected highest values recognized by culture of Egypt and Mesopotamia. Absolute transcendence of God — foundation of Hebrew religious thought — transcendentalism prevented kingship assuming profound significance in Egypt and Babylonia. In Hebrew religion alone ancient bond between man and nature destroyed. Frankfort, *Kingship*, 343.

Jews used skins for sacred writing. Sir G.M. Thompson, *An Introduction to Greek and Latin Palaeography* (Oxford, 1912), 27.

pages 66–67

w. Customary law reflected in patriarchal stories of Genesis — suggest Hebrews originally from northern Mesopotamia. Albright, *From Stone Age to Christianity*, 180.

x. See Albright, 193, on writing.

Saul, 1020–1000; David, 1000–960. Albright, 222.

Lavish expenditure of Solomon 960–925 followed by rebellion of north.

Followed by reaction and destruction — Solomon's temple — Ark of Covenant and heir to Tabernacle at Shiloh. Jeroboam 1 to offset influence had new sanctuaries at Bethel and Dan. Albright, 223, 228.

David and Solomon brought tribes together in political unity based on common worship of Jahweh. Rowley, 262.

David made Jerusalem capital — beginning of urbanization.

Palestine a buffer between Egypt and Babylonia developed a literature that reflected a deep religious faith and a lofty monotheism.

Story of Moses probably added to epic nucleus after conquest of Canaan and combined narrative recited by Levites or rhapsodists until break-up under Philistines in eleventh century followed by J invasion (south) and E (north) and written down before 750 BC — combined in JE in eighth or seventh century. Albright, 190.

pages 67–68

y. Sennacherib destroyed local sanctuaries 701 BC facilitated centralization. Provincialism broken by necessity of going to Jerusalem three times a year. Secularizing of rural populations.

Palestine part of Babylonian empire under code of Hammurabi (2123–2083 BC). Brief concise character of Decalogue reflects lapidary style — engraving on stone tablets. Covenant code drew heavily on code of Hammurabi — revised and expanded in Deuteronomic code probably seventh century — required public worship and sacrifice at central shrine in Jerusalem — reformation of Joshua 621 BC. Deuteronomic code made tithing legal. See Solomon Gandz, "Oral Tradition in the Bible," *Jewish Studies in Memory of George A. Kohut 1874–1933*, ed. S.W. Baron & A. Marx, 248–69.

Priestly code 400–350 BC. Translation of code of Hammurabi, see J.M.P. Smith, *The Origin and History of Hebrew Law* (Chicago, 1931), 181–222.

pages 68–69

Assyrians and Persians organized communication — modified version of government of bronze-age monarchies.

Tyre captured by Nebuchadnezzar 573 BC.

Cyprus took over throne culture from Assyria and Babylonia. Cyrus victory over Nabonidus 539 BC. Albright, 250, 327.

In seventh century sanctuaries put out completely recast version of Mosaic tradition — becoming book of Deuteronomy — reflects claim of Jerusalem sanctuary and priesthood to primacy over northern Samaritan priesthood and sanctuary. After fall of Samaria priests of Jerusalem attempted to capture leadership previously held at Shechem. Power of memorization and schematic form — probably committed to writing middle of ninth century. F.V.Winnett, *The Mosaic Tradition* (Toronto, 1949), 160–62, 167.

pages 69–70

z. Great King single master dominated Persian cultural life — Persian art composite of royal fancy reflecting copies of omnipotent dilettante with love of size. Columns give perpendicular in architecture.

Under Darius Aramaic alphabet used to write Persian. Olmstead, 116. Attempt to write Persian in cuneiform alphabet failed. Aramaic never dominated Asia Minor where nationalistic feeling retained. Lydian and Lycian characters and languages for inscriptions. A.T. Olmstead, *History of the Persian Empire* (Chicago, 1948), 480–81.

Pahlavi [alphabet] derived from Aramaic writing — natural development of local cursive Aramaic scripts. Diringer, 306.

Papyrus used by Persians especially after conquest of Egypt, 525 BC.

pages 70–71

aa. 345 (?).

bb. Albright, 276.

Cyrus assisted Jews in completing temple in 536 BC. Xenophon with Greek mercenaries under Cyrus attacked Babylon 401 BC. Burning of Persepolis brought age of independent oriental empires to an end.

Semitic influence less evident among magi who had been tribe of Medes specializing in knowledge and practice of certain ritual — bodies buried after torn by bird or dog — continued by Parsees.

pages 71–72

cc. Darius and successors (522–405) about 400 BC. Artaxerxes II lists gods Ahura Mazda, Mithra, Anahita.

Apparently discovering that moon returned to original position with reference to sun in 19 years — i.e., eclipses 18 years 11 days apart.

Greeks intercalated only 7 months in each cycle of 19 years — beginning of year kept not too far from summer solstice. W.S. Ferguson, *Athenian Tribal Cycles in the Hellenistic Age* (Cambridge, 1932), 5.

pages 72–73

Destruction of national dependence brought change from Hebraism to Judaism.

Absence of metallic money in Babylonia, Assyria, Egypt. Emphasis on law in Babylon compared with Egypt.

High spiritual concept of purity of Mazdean religion never escaped bondage to ritual as in case of Judaic and Hellenci. Farnell, *Evolution of Religion*, 131.

Eternal antagonism between prophet and ritual priest, Christ and Pharisee, result of idea that only evil will and evil thoughts can defile heart and soul. Farnell, 123.

page 74

dd. According to J.M.P. Smith, 400–350 BC.

The Old Testament carries dividing line between ancient and modern world, i.e., writing and alphabet.

Ezra pointed way to salvation of Judaism — abandonment of nationalistic hopes, reconciliation to foreign rulers and loyalty to them. Full acceptance of position of Jew as guardian of God's moral law — introduction of the law the great work of Ezra. Olmstead, 307.

Covenant between God and people of Israel rendered human monarchy a substitute — obedience to God and his laws inseparable from idea of unity and community — authoritarian principle impossible. V. Ehrenberg, *Aspects of the Ancient World* (Oxford, 1946), 95.

Early Aramaic ninth to seventh century golden age — after latter date Arameans lost independence. Duel between cuneiform complicated theocratic system and simple democratic system. Palestinean Jewish script from second to first centuries BC. Diringer, 257–61.

Holiness Code compiled after 570 BC. The Hebrew prophets threw down the barriers of tribal limitations to the jurisdiction of the deity.

Mencken's "luscious prose" of religion.

4 The Oral Tradition and Greek Civilization

page 75

Knossos-Cretan-Minoan civilization built up bureaucracy — vast archives — became most vulnerable of political organizations and collapsed. Sea checked tendencies of Egypt in monumental architecture and sculpture.

Greeks probably introduced stone under influence of Egypt to replace wood and brick in architecture in seventh century and later. D.S. Robertson, *A Handbook of Greek and Roman Architecture* (Cambridge, 1943), 5. Use of stone an indication of concern with time.

page 76

a. Law, lapidary style, decalogue, simplicity in contrast with other media. Contrast between stone and clay writing see F. Murceau-Dargin, *Recherches sur l'origine de l'écriture cunéiforme* (Paris, 1898).

How far horse introduced in Egypt handicapped by collar adapted from ox-yoke and consequently more used for light vehicles such as chariots.

pages 79–80

b. See Macaulay on Milton.

c. Aristotle's house known as "house of the reader," "much learning produces much confusion" (Aristotle). S.H. Butcher, *Some Aspects of the Greek Genius* (London, 1891), 190.

See Aristotle's comments on Empedocles (lecture notes 5). Plato and Aristotle — written tradition — Plato wrote for paternal [indecipherable] dogmatism (excluded Homer) basis of Medieval Catholic state and Inquisition — Renaissance return to oral tradition. [See Eric A. Havelock, *Preface to Plato* (Cambridge, Mass., 1963).]

pages 80–81

d. This apparently used by Akkadians speaking Greek, displaced by Dorians and based on Minoan system. Carpenter suggests alphabet introduced to Greece in eighth century. Carpenter, 91. Evans thought

Cypriote syllabary a modification or adaptation of Minoan to Greek and that second modification in Syria the basis of Phoenician alphabet. Evans suggests alphabet in Greece before 900 BC. Arthur Evans, *The Palace of Minos at Knossos* (London, 1921–1935), vol. IV, ch. 112.

Plato deliberately attacked poetry to break up rhythm and favoured classification. Plato opposed Heraclitus with his universal flux by doctrine of Ideas *not* subject to flux through sensible things subject to flux. See *Ion* of Plato for account of rhapsodist reciting Homer. "At the tale of pity my eyes are filled with tears, and when I speak of horrors my hair stands on end and my heart throbs." Rhapsodists "very precise about the exact words of Homer, but very idiotic themselves" (Euthydemus).

Dynasty at Mycenae shortly before 1600 BC — after fall of Knossos, Mycenae became political and cultural centre of Aegean world. Thebes one of the wealthiest cities in the world in fourteenth century. G. Thomson, *Studies in Ancient Greek Society* (London, 1949), 371–78.

pages 81–82

The Greeks with Canaanite Phoenician script "breathed into its consonantal skeleton the living flesh and movement of the vowels." Cadmus writing. Myres, 339.

Greek epics beginning in the Mycenean age were produced by minstrels who were among the retinues of an aristocratic or feudal organization with centres of wealth and power.

Poetry was linked to the oral tradition of Greek feudalism. Language tended to become archaic but was rejuvenated by poets speaking the language of the age.

page 82

e. See T.W. Allen [*Homer: The Origins and the Transmissions* (Oxford, 1924), 225 *ff*]. Also Hesiodae.

Childe holds divine kingship withered away in Greece in the iron age. Gordon Childe, *Social Evolution* (London, 1951), 126–27.

Creation of new art of rhythmical speech — transformation of dance step to verbal music. Poetry wedded to music — elimination of dance brought song — music as form developed from poetry as content of music. Thomson, *Studies*, 451. Poet not divided from audience by barrier of literacy. Ibid., 454. Parry gave proof of *Iliad* and *Odyssey* as oral literature.

Greek literature was the natural heritage of a Greek-speaking population. F.G. Kenyon, *Books and Readers in Ancient Greece and Rome* (Oxford, 1932), ch. 1. All Greek literary growth sprang from natural powers of expression.

Homeridae at Sparta eighth century, Argos eighth and seventh, Kyrene end of seventh acquired place in Delian festival of Apollo — at Delos minstrels raised art to pitch of excellence. Thomson, *Studies*, 563. Opulent patronage of merchant princes brought art of epic which had grown out of court life into its own. Ibid., 568.

Homeridae prevented Greek epic being committed to writing. (Did tyrants flourish with writing?) Ibid., 575.

pages 83–84

f. *Works and Days* beginning of eighth century reference to Arcturus astronomically belongs to this date.

All culture started with the creation of an aristocratic ideal and the cultivation of an aristocratic ideal appropriate to a nobleman and a hero (Jaeger). As the first work of the Panhellenic spirit it left its stamp on the civilization of Greece and of the West. The pervasive influence of a medium developed in the oral tradition was widened in the history of Greek literature and in Western civilization. The aristocracy assumed that mastery of words meant intellectual sovereignty. Homer's attitude towards gods that of men engaged in dangerous warfare — dangerous occupation the most blasphemous.

Homer without religion — courage the love of power realization that arouses the common lot (Burn).

Flexibility of oral tradition to meet demands of working people. Carpenter suggests Hesiod-written literature in contrast with Homer [Rhys Carpenter, *Folk Tale, Fiction and Saga*, 16] but Parry thinks *Theogony* follows oral tradition. [M. Parry, "Studies in the Epic Technique of Oral Verse-Making" (*Harvard Classical Studies*, XLI, 1930, 73–147, 90–91.]

pages 84–85

Fall of Minoan civilization and fall of Rome — advanced effete society collapsed under barbarian invasions — both absorbed culture of conquered and evolved epic but Germanic nation adopted Latin language, whereas Achaeans preserved theirs and imposed it on the conquerors. G. Thomson, *Studies in Ancient Greek Society* (London, 1949), 431.

Hesiod described pressing social needs of people, cherished old moral code based on unchanging wisdom of farmer and daily toil. "Work is no disgrace but idleness is."

Sappho and Alcaeus influenced by oral tradition. M. Parry, "The Homeric Language as the Language of an Oral Poetry" (*Harvard Studies in Classical Philology*, XLIII, 29).

Hogarth, *Ionia and the East*, argues that influence from Mesopotamia through Hittites, Phrygian, and Lydian an important factor in blossoming of Ionian culture rather than decline of Phoenicians.

Homeric verse, dactylic in Attic becomes trochaic — factor in decline of hexameter — loss of dactylic meant loss of vitality of metre and new metre closer to speech. Thomson, *Studies*, 476. Lyric in seventh century probably also reflected collapse of heroic poetry and aristocracy.

page 85

Beginning of vowel shift possibly result of upheaval created by Dorian invasion. Ibid., 522.

Ionian mercenaries returned from assisting Psammetichus I in 663. Papyrus probably introduced first from Phoenicians, i.e., use of word Biblos — possibly preceding foundation of Naucratis a shortage of papyrus developed and Ionians used skins for writing. Lorimer, 21. Carpenter (97) argues for 625 or 600. See E. Gjerstad (*Annals of Art and Archeology*, XXI, 1934, 67–84).

Papyrus used in Ionia by Greeks by 500 and in Athens by 400 BC. W.H.P. Hatch, *The Principal Uncial Manuscripts of the New Testament* (Chicago, 1939), 5.

pages 86–87

g. See Albright, *From Stone Age to Christianity*, 285.

h. See H.F. Cherniss ["The Characteristics and Effects of Presocratic Philosophy" (*Journal of the History of Ideas*, XII, June 1951, 319–45)]. Ideas essential category of man's understanding of the universe.

Oral tradition linked to homosexuality — male society — declines with rise of women.

page 87

Anaximenes of Miletus. Anaximander held underlying substance could not be either air, water, earth, fire and must be unlimited. Concerned with problem of many out of one. He saw the sum of wrongs to be expiated in the plurality of things that have become. Truth became a universal category to which every personal preference must yield.

pages 88–89

A.H.M. Jones, "Economic Basis of the Athenian Democracy" (*Past and Present*, no. 1, February 1952, 13–31), great majority of Athenians owned no slaves. See *Athenian Studies Presented to W.S. Ferguson* (Cambridge, Mass., 1940) on size of slave population [451–70].

page 91

i. Was Solon of the family of Medontidae who had held the kingship? M.O. Wason, *Class Struggle in Ancient Greece* (London, 1947), 65, 76.

Propitiation for bloodshed emerges after eighth century and becomes important at Delphi and Crete. L.R. Farnell, *The Evolution of Religion* (London, 1947), 133–34.

Solon and Theognis used oral tradition in iambic poetry but writing known as a means of preserving. M. Parry, "The Homeric Language as the Language of an Oral Poetry" (*Harvard Studies in Classical Philology*, XLIII, 29).

pages 91–92

Solon brought together state and spirit, community and individual and aimed for a just medium between excess and deficiency, excessive power and helplessness, privilege and serfdom. (But this destroyed by money economy.)

Oral tradition permits painters on vases to attempt to show several scenes at once but written tradition compels a concern with time and painters use scenes with fixed space and time. Dominance of scribe over painters corresponds in development with drama in fifth century, using scenes of fixed space and time. Drama also dialogue an attempt to find compromise between oral and written tradition. Oral tradition depends on memory and use of repetition to give sense of time and continuity. Written tradition accentuates continuity and time. K. Weitzmann [*Illustrations in Roll and Codex* (Princeton, 1947)].

pages 92–93

j. Olive trees required 16–18 years.

Merchant princes and money made kings seize the royal power. Merchants of cities in trans-Aegean trade routes became support of tyrants. Geometric period 900–700 BC dominated by Athens and Attic power. Last quarter of seventh century Corinthian potters lowered standards to meet huge demands of foreign merchants — in first half of sixth century Attic wares seriously competing with Corinth export trade and virtually having a monopoly after 550 and Corinthian becoming local industry. Red figure style invented between 530 and 520. "Classical type" emerged 480–450 BC. Uniform conception of ideal beauty replaced livelier characterization of individual differences. Arthur Lane, *Greek Pottery* (London, 1948).

Athens in sixth century probably beginnings of Orphian [religion]. W.K.C. Guthrie, *Orpheus and Greek Religion* (London, 1935), 129. Aristotle regarded Onomakritos one of commission of four appointed by Peisistratos for recensing of Homeric poems as editor or author of Orphic literature. Ibid., 14.

pages 93–94

k. 566 BC. Probably begun about 550 by Peisistratos and completed by son Hipparchus. Hippias driven out 510 BC.

Collections of religious literature in late seventh and sixth centuries —

Egypt, Babylonia, Phoenicians, Greeks. J.H. Oliver, *The Athenian Expounders of the Sacred and Ancestral Law* (Baltimore, 1950), 1–3.

City Dionysus celebrated first about 53 BC.

Orpheus writings.

Dramatic performances part of Dionysian festivals encouraged by tyrants. See T.W. Allen, *Homer: The Origins and the Transmissions* (Oxford, 1924), also J.A. Scott, *The Unity of Homer* (Berkeley, 1921). Quadrennial Panathenaic festival established 566 BC. Introduction of vine brought dominance of Dionysus — new type of agriculture. J.E. Harrison, *Prolegomena to the Study of Greek Religion* (Cambridge, 1908), 424.

Greek art, science, and thought stimulated by contact with Semitic and Egyptian civilizations. Culture flourished with multiplication of free contacts among trading communities and their colonies.

Hogarth emphasized Asia Minor.

pages 94–95

Time more thought of as a god by the Greeks except in the Orphic tradition. Guthrie, *Orpheus*, 85. With philosophy time became abstract and lost mythological dress [Ibid.], 90. Orphism probably from Crete. Tyrants edited, compiled, and revised Orpheus and Homer — Orpheus sought spiritual ecstasy — abstinence and rites of purification — believed in future life. Harrison, *Prolegomena*, 472–76.

Cardinal conviction of religion of Dionysus that worshipper can become and be his god — basis of development of drama — impossible for Olympians as no one believed he could become them. By attaining divinity man could attain immortality. Ibid., 568–70.

World of divine origin but with rational mathematical explanation — Pythagoras. Guthrie, *Orpheus*, 218. Most important commandment to abstain from eating meat. Ibid., 196. Pythagoras revived custom of burial in contrast with cremation. Harrison, *Prolegomena*, 599. Achaeans not Orpheus introduced dark disgrace of eternal punishment to religion. Ibid., 612. Mysticism gave preeminence to individual and was a protest against particularism in religion. See F.M. Cornford on Pythagoras and numbers: "The Invention of Space," *Essays in Honour of Gilbert Murray* (London, 1936), 215–35.

page 95

l. Four principal notes
6:8:12
octave   12:6
fifth   12:8
fourth   8:6

Orphic Bible a collection of books varying greatly in spiritual content. Guthrie, *Orpheus*, 159. Orphic teacher had mass of books — significance revealed in sacred writings. Ibid., 155. Orphic had dogma set and hardened in mould of mass of religious poetry. Orphism founded on collection of sacred writings, 10. Dionysus the god of Orphic religion. Orpheus preached and reformed religion of Dionysus. Delphi completed work of joining Apollo and Dionysus in the sun (Helios). Guthrie, 41–43. Orphism did nothing without a warrant from books. Dependent on sacred literature containing precept and dogma. Ibid., 202–06. Orphic religion height of individualism after fourth century decay of city-state and growth of individualism gave individualistic religions free play. Ibid., 201. Orphism addressed to every individual as an individual, 249.

page 96

System of kinship controlled by aristocratic class replaced by a system which ignored the class but preserved the principle of kinship. A new tribal system and a new calendar supported the demands of a new middle class.

Cleisthenes admitted large number of metics and strangers as citizens — ten new tribes named for popular heroes — blow at family influence. B.R. English, *The Problem of Freedom in Greece from Homer to Pindar* (Toronto, 1938), 102–03. Cleisthenes assumed contract to complete second temple of Apollo at Delphi after defeat of Athenian democrats in 513 BC to win support of priesthood. W.B. Dinsmoor, *The Architecture of Ancient Athens* (London, 1950), 91.

page 97

Democratic institutions followed by patriotic feeling.

After 499 BC Athens absorbed Ionian culture. In fifth century absorbed Ionian philosophy but little interest in science.

There exists only the eternal unity. The one in the many. A continual sway of homogeneous justice was bound by eternal laws. "Much learning does not instruct the mind — the only wisdom is to know the reason that reigns over all" (Heraclitus). "Men pray to these images; this is like trying to converse with the walls of a house." Heraclitus. Edwyn Bevan, *Holy Images* (London, 1940), 65.

page 98

m. Introduced logic as third basic form to systems of Thales and Anaximander.

n. According to Aristotle a scientist writing in epic form of verse.

Heraclitus opposed Pythagoras ideal as harmonious, all goodness, all health, all plenty, static world. Guthrie, *Orpheus*, 252. Fire a symbol of ever-changing universe. "The learning of many things teacheth not understanding." Guthrie, 225–26. Suggested supreme mind intervening only once to bring order out of chaos — disastrous to progress of thought — taken up by Plato. Parmenides held predecessors confused "starting point of becoming with the permanent ground of being." Guthrie, 231. Empedocles escaped Parmenides's conclusion that evidence of sense perception out of touch with reality. Guthrie, 232. Atomists took theory of void from concern of geometry with infinite space. F.M. Cornford, "The Invention of Space," *Essays in Honour of Gilbert Murray*, 215–35.

page 99

o. See note 25, page 67.

p. Covered period before and after invasion of Xerxes.

Punch is used from 650 for two centuries — gave way to flat chisel after 450; latter used on flat relief — frieze of Parthenon and tombstones — commercialized output until 300 or until year 450. S. Casson, *The Technique of Early Greek Sculpture* (Oxford, 1933), 176–81. Bronzework a finished art by early fifth century. Ibid., 117. Drill used after 530–525 and intensively 510–500 — declined after 500. Ibid., 148–66. Athens starved into submission 404 by Persians cutting off supplies of grain. Large stone statues essentially cut in age of iron. Casson, 66. Importance of athletics to rise of individualism.

page 100

q. Sung by full chorus of fifty.

r. Weakening position of lyre. See Kathleen Schlesinger, *The Greek Aulos* (London, 1939), claiming this preceded string instruments.

Greek tragedy connected with mimetic dance in expressing weakness in face of nature and will to master it. Greek thought in tragic age pessimistic or artistically optimistic (Nietzsche).

Thespis in 534 combined actor with chorus meant addition of satyrs and tragedies with Dionysian festival. Theognis iambic poetry — oral verse mastery but writing down for preservation. M. Parry ["The Homeric Language as the Language of an Oral Poetry" (*Harvard Studies in Classical Philology*, XLIII, 1–50, 29)]. Also wrote for merchant princes of Aegina opposed to democratic tendencies. Pindar chose his own words — relatively free from oral tradition.

A kindred group was united by common blood, a magical society by men. The externalization of collective power over one class became power at first daemonic and then personal, not ourselves. From the collective life of the many emerges the one, a magical society assumed that to know names was to have power over souls. To classify things is to name them. The name of the thing is its soul. Cornford, 141.

Drama also favoured by older cults — impersonation of gods by priests — performance of suggestive rites by bards or choruses. E.S. Holderman, *Study of the Greek Priestess*, 1913.

pages 100–101

s. Clash of wills possible, state and spirit coalesced and became a perfect unity.

t. 458 BC.

u. Central lesson of Aeschylus — man is master of his own destiny.

Aeschylus held sin a curse which runs in families — *Oresteia* suggests solution in dissolving old family ties in new and wider unit of city-state. Guthrie, *Orpheus*, 235.

Mystic tradition of philosophy favoured drama. Dionysian ritual and tragedy had functions similar to those of initiation. Drama with form of epic — see Carpenter, *Folk Tale*, 78–79.

[Sophocles] began to exhibit plays 468 BC. In *Antigone* religious duty to family triumphs over claims of civic obedience. Drama unique Greek creation fusing lyric and epic. Aeschylus influenced most by epic poems — "gathered Crumbs from Homer's table." Susan B. Franklin, *Traces of Epic Influence in the Tragedies of Aeschylus* (Baltimore, 1895), 2, 81. Aeschylus in *Eumenides* reconciled old order of vengeance with new law of mercy. Harrison, *Prolegomena*, 252. Aeschylus used painted scenery in later days. See A.W. Pickard-Cambridge, *The Theatre of Dionysus in Athens* (Oxford, 1946), 31.

In period after Protagoros and Anaxagoras brought philosophy to Athens or after 450 BC when Athens fighting for empire tragedy killed and philosophy replaced it — in this period old comedy flourished, rationalism and individualism conquered man and state. V. Ehrenberg, *The People of Aristophanes: A Sociology of Old Attic Comedy* (Oxford, 1943), 12–13.

pages 101–102

v. Attack on Socrates probably helped to condemn him.

w. Oral tradition persisted in assembly and limited possibilities of written law. Prose was literally created as there were no foreign models on which it might be based.

x. Hecateus elaborated map of world drawn by Anaximander.

Age of Euripides calculating, businesslike, concerned with profit and loss. Vehicle for sublime free thinkers. From Euripides birth of Hellenistic Greek from pangs of dying poetry and stricken city-state. Supremacy of tragedy for over a century coincided with rise, greatness, and decline of secular power of Athens. Euripides influenced by Peloponnesian War.

As a product of democratic free speech rise and fall of comedy coincided with Athenian democracy. Democracy not designed for scattered groups unable to meet in an assembly but for one community. Atmosphere of oral discussion and convocation.

Athenian ideal found place for fundamental political values.

Aristophanes apparently first to have play written before performance — with place of comedians suggested, people no longer able to follow play as dealing with new material with which they were not familiar and needed a preliminary description.

pages 102–103

y. Preserved genuine folk art — "the art of the Logos, the thing said, transmitted and augmented." Moses Hadas, *A History of Greek Literature* (New York, 1950), 111.
Allen claims recension did not take place at Athens.

Havelock argues development of alphabet reduced number of letters and made possible teaching of youth to point of developing schools 410–405 — implied a fundamental diffusion of people. Ionic alphabet officially reorganized 403 BC. Twenty-four letters instead of 21. With dominance of Attic, gulf between spoken Greek and book language gradually widened.

Herodotus drank "at the Homeric cistern till his whole being is impregnated with the influence thence derived." George Rawlinson [*The History of Herodotus* (New York, 1860), vol. 1, 6].

Epic, lyric, drama correspond to early monarchy, aristocracy, democracy. Thomson, *Studies*, 404. Choral lyric characteristic of aristocracy. Ibid., 480. Thucydides followed drama. F.M. Cornford, *Thucydides Mythhistoricus* (London, 1907).

pages 103–104

z. 451 BC [?].

Narrow policy of Athens in granting citizenship one of the chief reasons for decline. V. Ehrenberg, *Aspects of the Ancient World* (Oxford, 1946), 65. Mining conducted by slaves — prosperity coincided with increase in use of silver. G.M. Calhoun, *The Business Life of Athens* (Chicago, 1926). Rise of contempt for labour probably result of industrial development of tyrants — i.e., more exacting industry and culture. P.N. Ure [*The Origin of Tyranny* (Cambridge, 1922), 19]. See G.B. Grundy [*Thucydides and the History of his Age* (London, 1911)], 193, date of 5 years truce with Sparta.

Thucydides recreated past through speeches but claiming they are not strictly historical.

Delian league 477 BC after battle of Salamis.

How far corrosion of anti-Persian confederacy in Athenian empire and development of slave labour relieved class tension. Liberty under Pericles maintained at home by suppression abroad, checked by Persians in East and Carthage in West — city-state found closing paths of internal development.

pages 104–105

With emphasis on intellectual qualities, ethical qualities fell into the background. Humanism subordinated technical efficiency to culture and distinguished between technical knowledge and power and true culture. W. Jaeger, *Humanism and Theology* (Milwaukee, 1943). See H.T. Wade-Gery, "The Peace of Kallias," *Athenian Studies Presented to William Scott Ferguson* (Cambridge, 1940), 121–56.

Peace treaties with Persia and other Greek states beginnings of recognition of importance of writing in binding people. Peloponnesian war great loss to country — destroying olive trees. Citizenship — Athenians greatest glory simplicity in the home, splendour in the city that was the principle. Inspiration given to all art and thought by the idea of the state. Following common effort against Persia, democracy limited to reforms of Aristides and Pericles. Freedom and victory were bonds between Solon's faith in justice and new democracy. Under Pericles numbers of individuals had economic independence and personal political freedom. Independent of superiors Athens offered conditions favouring free political life of individuals.

Athenian empire ended with navy. Grundy, *Thucydides*, 314.

Protagoros embodiment of sophistry, Gorgias set tone of last 30 years of fifth century in rhetoric. Like its rival philosophy it sprang from poetry.

Seventh-century Sparta convinced that aesthetic culture could form whole character of citizens. Women were freer in public and private life in Sparta than in Ionia. Constitution of Athens imposed political equality on social inequality. In cities other than Sparta tyranny victorious over aristocracy and followed by plutocracy.

pages 104–105

aa. Battle of Mantineia 362 overwhelming importance of oral tradition in Athens — juries became serious obstacle in efficiency of courts in handling disputes of Athenian empire and weakened its federal possibilities.

See Werner Jaeger, *Demosthenes, the Origin and Growth of His Policy* (Berkeley, 1938).

Socrates followed Euripides in contributing to growth of individualism. The political life of Athens was moulded on the Ionian pattern, the Spartan ideal was reborn in the realm of the intellect through the aristocratic influence of Attic philosophy.

5 The Written Tradition and the Roman Empire

pages 106

a. Jupiter optimus maximus Minerva Juno

b. Liber Roman name for Dionysus; Demeter, goddess of fertility; Dionysus, Iacchus; Kore, daughter of Demeter.

The Greek alphabet was divided between eastern and western, the latter spreading to Italy in the ninth and eighth centuries and becoming the source of the Latin alphabet. J.B. Carter, "The Reorganization of the Roman Priesthood at the beginning of the Republic" (*Memoirs of the American Academy in Rome*, I, 1912, 9–17).

page 107

c. in 471 BC. IV by 449 BC. Inviolability of plebeian magistrates not legally recognized until 449 BC.

Papyrus used in Rome after 250 BC. W.H.P. Hatch, *The Principal Uncial Manuscripts of the New Testament* (Chicago, 1939), 5.

Ceres introduced with importation of large supplies of grain from Sicily and Cumae — oldest Greek cult, Greek functions, language, style. Temple dedicated 493 BC, i.e., Ceres, Liber, Libria apparently represent Eleusinian, Demeter, Kore, and Iacchus.

Etruscan sea power broken at Cumae 474 BC by Hieron of Syracuse —
patron of Pindar — and by Romans 310 and way open for Rome's
expansion. Influence of Etruscans in building up city, i.e., walls, military
organization.

Iron age — cremating — Latium — Sabines inhumation — Etruscans
checked Sabines and brought restoration of cremation. Inez G. Scott,
"Early Roman Traditions in the Light of Archeology" (*Memoirs of the
American Academy in Rome*, VII, 1929, 7–116).

page 108

d. Numbers increased of augurs and pontiffs to 9 each and 4 augurs and
5 pontiffs plebeian.

Terentilian law *de legibus conscribendis* 462 BC led to Twelve Tables. Roman
plebs seceded to Sacred Hill 494 BC. Plebs power to finally defeat measures 339 BC. J.L. Strachan-Davidson, "The Growth of Plebeian Privilege
at Rome" (*English Historical Review*, I, 1886, 209–17).

Priestly college open to plebeians 300 BC. Sutherland, 33. First time two
consuls were plebeians in 172 BC.

Board of moneyers about 289 BC. Silver coinage necessary to trade in
Greek cities of Campania and South Italy and overcame disadvantages of
reliance on large *aes* coins. C.H.V. Sutherland [*Coinage in Roman Imperial
Policy 31 B.C.–A.D. 68* (London, 1951), 2]. Denarius introduced about 187
BC. See A.H.J. Greenidge (*Legal Procedure of Cicero's Time* (Oxford, 1901)]
on problem of oral and written tradition.

page 109

e. 269 according to Sutherland.

page 110

f. See Pollock.

Adoption principle helped to make problems of dynasties. Central dilemma
of adapting the constitution of the city-state to the government of a great
empire failed in Athens but assumed by Macedonia and Rome. Greek conception of *process* and *formulation*, of *physis* was never translated into Roman

law with its notions of origin and substance. *Origin* and *contract* were imposed on Greek *process* and *formulation* and brought confusion for 1500 years. J.L. Myres, *Political Ideas of the Greeks* (New York, 1927), 385–89.

pages 111–112

g. Constructed for consuls 498 BC.

h. King worship entered Greek world with Alexander. "March divided, fight united."

First Punic War to battle of Actium (31 BC) Romans enriched by booty from other nations.

Epameinôndas Theban general against Spartans first to formulate consciously principle of superiority of force at decisive point — not necessarily over whole field of operation.

Philip and Alexander used these principles in having an army strong in cavalry. A.R. Burn, *Alexander the Great and the Hellenistic Empire* (London, 1947), 33–35.

pages 112–113

i. This new text, which monopolized market, had 24 divisions for each poem.

See F.G. Kenyon, *The Text of the Greek Bible* (London, 1949), 25, i.e., with apocrypha.

Translation of Pentateuch changed meaning of Jewish words in Greek — opened way to Greek philosophy. E.R. Goodenough [*By Light, Light: The Mystic Gospel of Hellenistic Judaism* (New Haven, 1935), III, ch. 3].

pages 113–114

j. Opening of Gospel of St. John —- Essene view of new doctrine of the way. W.M. Flinders Petrie, *Egypt and Israel* (London, 1911), 116.

Septuagent — translation into Greek for Jews in Alexandria illustrates decline in influence of Hebrew as sacred language and determination of Jews to understand Bible in their own language. Pentateuch probably completed early in third century.

Rise of wisdom literature about 200 BC succeeded Hermetic books. Influence of Orphism in Protagoras and Plato evident in Philo-Hellenistic Judaism sect — see Goodenough, *By Light, Light*, 2–3, 7.

Decree of 239 or 238 to have fixed solar year with one day added every four years. Later abandoned but returned to and fixed by Romans. J.G. Frazer, *Adonis, Attis, Osiris, Studies in the History of Oriental Religion*, vol. 5–6 of *The Golden Bough* (London, 1907), 281.

page 114

Unnatural dualism of Orphics contributed to separation of lower world of *sensa* from heavenly world of ideas of Plato. Guthrie, *Orpheus*, 157. Platonic concept of theory of ideas possible only because Plato had continually in mind static shapes discovered by Greek mathematics — geometry adapted Plato's manner of thinking and success crowned in Euclid. Plato concerned with Being — Platonic dualism offset by Aristotle's concept of nature. Plato's problem of being or Aristotle's problem of becoming — influence of geometry evident in idea. Plato venerated geometry as, more than other disciplines, the speculative thought which brought nothing material. Julien Benda, *The Great Betrayal* (London, 1928), 121.

Geometry — offspring of Egyptian mind — astronomy and astrology children of Babylonia. Wm Ridgeway, *The Origin of Metallic Currency and Weight Standards* (Cambridge, 1892), 251. Egyptians used decimal system. Greek art of coining introduced to Egypt under Ptolemy Lajos. Egyptians behind Babylonians in arithmetic — more accurate in geometry — used formulae for volume of truncated pyramid.

page 115

Possibly better kind of parchment produced at Pergamum under Eumenes II. W.H.P. Hatch, *Principal Uncial Manuscripts of the New Testament* (Chicago, 1939), the invention of vellum regarded as inferior to papyrus, which was used for literary works. Stoic school of learning at Pergamum.

pages 116–117

k. i.e., second Athenian confederacy.

See E.R. Bevan, "Rhetoric in the Ancient World," *Essays in Honour of Gilbert Murray* (London, 1936), 189–214. Intimate association of chorus with action of play weakened — audience concentrated on actors — consequent raising of stage to improve vision especially of more remote seats. High stage in Hellenistic theatre at Athens about middle of second century BC. A.W. Pickard-Cambridge, *The Theatre of Dionysus in Athens* (Oxford, 1946), 268–69.

pages 117–118

l. Dramatic performances introduced 361 BC. E.N. Gardiner, *Athletes of the Ancient World* (Oxford, 1930), 119. Gladitorial show 264 BC following Etruscan funeral games.

Individual writer in Rome created epic — also in England — but epic of Greece in oral tradition.

pages 118–119

m. Probably 159 — broke his leg while in Rome and lectured during his convalescence.

Keeping of account books to indicate rights of Senate and of generals in Italy by 190 BC.

page 121

Breakdown of stichometry with increased interest in reading aloud — interpunction and colometry. J. Rendel Harris, *Stichometry* (London, 1893).

page 122

n. i.e., Pompeius see A.H.J. Greenidge, *Legal Procedure of Cicero's Time* (Oxford, 1901), 476.

See Laura Robinson, *Freedom of Speech in the Roman Republic* (Baltimore, 1940); also Kenneth Scott, "Octavian's Propaganda and Antony's *De Sua Ebrietate*" (*Classical Philology*, XXIV, April 1929, 133–41). Problem of interference of *dies nyasta* reduction in number of days in which court could be held to 45, traditional emphasis on writing. After 200 BC Italians emigrated — place of Italian stock filled by alien stock unfamiliar with republican traditions. M.E. Park, *The Plebs in Cicero's Day* (Cambridge, 1918).

Alexandrian library founded when Caesar burned his ships in its harbour, Mark Antony transported Pergamum library to Alexandria, scattered by Theophilus 392 and destroyed by Arabs after 642. W.A. Mason, *A History of the Art of Writing* (New York, 1920), 392, 397–98.

pages 122-123

o. Worship of Asklepios introduced Athens 421 BC from Epidaurus. J.E. Harrison, *Prolegomena*, 344.

p. Suppression in Italy in 186.

Temple of Phoebus Apollo with library completed and dedicated 28 BC. Arminius AD 9 defeated Roman legions and blocked civilizing of German tribes. Choice of Rhine and Danube as defensible boundaries — depth of rivers —lack of frost in winter.

pages 123–124

Official recognition of Caligula of Isis, her consort Serapis, and son Horus. A.D. Nock argues ruler worship not Oriental but Greek but could only develop after decline of Delphi by 400 which checked worship of rulers. A.D. Nock (*Harvard Studies in Classical Philology*, XLI, 1–62). See L.R. Taylor, *The Divinity of the Roman Emperors* (Middletown, Conn., 1931). See especially W.S. Ferguson, "Legalized Absolutism en route from Greece to Rome" (*American Historical Review*, XVIII, October 1912, 29–47).

Triumviri decided on building a temple to Serapis and Isis 43 BC. G.W. Botsford, *The Roman Assemblies from Their Origin to the End of the Republic* (New York, 1909), 459.

Bloodless gods in Roman panopticon arranged according to number. Romans knew neither divine images nor temples, not interested in marriage or genealogy of gods as with Greeks. H. Wagenvoort, *Roman Dynamism* (Oxford, 1947), 78.

Emperor Gaius changed princeps to autocrat.

Civil war after murder of Commodus — Septimius Severus winner rewarded army — raised pay — promoted soldiers to administrative posts, militarized government. Citizenship given to Italians and inability to attend assemblies in Rome favoured demagogues fighting for popular support with backing of army — leading to principate [over] Liberties as a political idea at Rome.

page 125

q. 2?

r. End of term "Roman" publicly.

page 126

Augustus imposed inheritance tax on Roman citizens — Caracalla, 212, made free inhabitants citizens and exposed them to inheritance taxes. *Fiscus* of Augustus and successors became indistinguishable from *aerarium* by AD 68. C.H.V. Sutherland, "*Aerarium* and *Fiscus* During the Early Empire" (*American Journal of Philology*, LXVI, no. 262, 1945, 151–70). Claudius's reign witnessed rise to prominence and power of freedmen. M. Hammond, *The Augustian Principate in Theory and Practice During the Julio-Claudian Period* (Cambridge, 1933), 126. Augustus reforms in administration introduced profound change in concept of public service. Ibid., 192. In 23 BC high command finally separated from civil government important advance in constitutional history. Ibid., 44. Army's power to determine succession irresistible by AD 69. M. Hammond, 154. Economy measures of Augustus — long terms of service, low pay, frontier camps for army had no difficulties for Tiberius. Ibid., 48.

Separation between emperor and Senate emphasized by rise of imperial civil service. Ibid., 193.

page 127

s. Also suggests sacred character of writing.

After Augustus, knights in civil offices required to hold preliminary military position — Hadrian admitted knights to civil service without military service. Training for procuratorships in various offices. Military training not a satisfactory background for civil affairs. Hadrian employed knights instead of freedmen in all higher administrative positions. R.H. Lacey, *The Equestrian Officials of Trajan and Hadrian* (Princeton, 1917), 38.

Domitian began substitution of direct for indirect collection of duties and this given strong impetus under Hadrian. Ibid., 42.

Tabularium — record office finished at Rome 78 BC. 230 x 144 ft — used concrete vaulting. D.S. Robertson, *Handbook of Greek and Roman Architecture* (Cambridge, 1943), 240.

pages 127–128

See M.R. Cagnat, "Les Bibliothèques municipales dans l'empire romain," *Memoires de l'Institut national de France* (Paris, 1909). Tryphon sold Martial's first book of Epigrams at a profit of 2 denarii, Martial, Epigrams, vol. XIII, epigram 3 — selling at 5 denarii but this high — far more than a day's pay for most. M.P. Charlesworth, *The Roman Empire* (Oxford, 1951), 103. Aeneas a Trojan in *Aeneid* to offset Greek Homer (Livy). See Gaston Boissier, *Cicero and His Friends* (London, n.d.).

Druids with oral tradition but apparently used Greek letters — probably gained power over administration as priesthood which founded on oral tradition yet added use of writing. N.K. Chadwick, *The Druids* [Cardiff, 1966, 42–43].

pages 128–129

Ultimate stagnation in part due to growth of governmental caste more concerned with preservation of administrative machine on which its existence depended than with real needs of people. M. Hammond, *The Augustan Principate* (Cambridge, 1933), 193.

Domitian restored Delphic temple AD 84.

Hadrian started fashion of emperor with beard of Greek philosopher — idea of best man — Hellenic as emperor — selected according to philosophical and moral principles rather than political ideas and interest of state. Process of Hellenization of Principate — change concerned at least in theory exclusively with personality of individual princeps. Irony that Marcus — philosopher conqueror — had to abandon idea of succession of "the Best" and accept dynastic idea. V. Ehrenberg, *Aspects of the Ancient World* (Oxford, 1946), 210–12.

page 130

t. Also before [Vespasian] see C.H.V. Sutherland, *Coinage in Roman Imperial Policy 31 BC–AD 68* (London, 1951).

u. Earliest important use late second century.

Emphasis on space — i.e., Roman army based on limited interest in time — absorption of Greek deities — lifeless character — equally false, equally true, equally useful. Greeks — sculpture historical but Rome influenced by linear and narrative — showing groups and neglecting sculpture and individual. Principle of annual coinage established with Vespasian. Ibid., 180.

Aes produced more regularly.

[Theodore] Birt held that column reliefs had origin in triumphal paintings rather than rolls. See K. Weitzmann, *Illustrations in Roll and Codex* (Princeton, 1947), 125.

page 131

Conflict between nationalism and universalism led to divorce between Judaism and Christianity. Individualism meant sharper distinction between soul and body — struggle of man against disease a contest with malevolent spirit. Sheol, a general gathering place, became place for wicked in New Testament. Judaism sharply distinguished between Jew and non-Jew; Christianity, between Heaven and Hell.

Talmud includes Mishna compiled at end of second century AD and comments on Mishna and Gemora.

On Gnostic Christianity see S.G. Rylands, *The Beginnings of Gnostic Christianity* (London, 1940), especially on influence of Jews and Greeks.

Great demand for scriptures after end of persecution probably brought revolution in book production and substitution of vellum for papyrus. F.G. Kenyon, *The Text of the Greek Bible* (London, 1949), 120.

pages 131–132

Eucharist entered on new development which finally separated it from local Jewish religion and association with Jewish meals in second century. Communion feast of early apostolic days divorced from setting in a common meal and took on character of more formal act of worship. J.H. Srawly, *The Early History of the Liturgy* (Cambridge, 1947), 38.

Gospel of John written in first century and latest of gospels. W.F. Albright, *from Stone Age to Christianity*, 380–81.

Alexandrian school founded by Pentaenus then Clement and Origen. M.L.W. Laistner [*Christianity and Pagan Culture* (Ithaca, 1951), 57–61]. Origin of codex about AD 100. Codex predominant and roll abandoned between fourth and fifth centuries. K. Weitzmann, *Illustrations in Roll and Codex* (Princeton, 1947), 70–73.

Butler argues St. Matthew had originality and Luke and Mark linked to it and that it was translated from Aramaic or written by an Aramaic — hence earlier than AD 70.

pages 132–133

v. Completed about 245 colossal work and hence did not survive.

Jerome produced gospels 384 and remaining books probably 391 — whole work completed 404 — became Vulgate and included Apocrypha — books excluded from Hebrew canon. Latter finally fixed about AD 100 after Jerusalem destroyed and Hebrews decided authoritatively on contents.

page 134

w. In 332 Constantine ordered copies of scripture made for new churches.

309 Constantine stabilized currency, created solidus — 72 to gold pound, partly based on confiscated pagan gold temple treasures. Nomination of successors and co-regents alone foiled ambitious aims and intentions of usurpers — success of camp followers made difficult. V. Ehrenberg, *Aspects of the Ancient World* (Oxford, 1946), 216. Monarchy became dyarchy or triarchy because emperors could no longer master tasks (220).

page 135

x. Acacius excommunicated [Patriarch of Constantinople 484–519]. Reunion with Rome under Justin 519.

y. Persecution of Monophysites began 527 year Justinian came to throne — probably included Constantinople intended as Christian city and a break with pagan past. Library opened about 354 BC at Constantinople by Emperor Constance.

Worship of Isis outlawed 391 — came to end at Philae under Justinian — 527–65. Attempt of Christians to secure control over feast days — circuses, games prohibited on Sunday, April 17, 312. No spectacles of any sort on Sunday, August 27, 399, also 425. M.L.W. Laistner, *Christianity and Pagan Culture* (Ithaca, 1951), 8. Olympian festival abolished by decree of Theodosius AD 393. Arcadians demolished Delphic temple.

pages 135–136

About AD 350 papyrus books replaced by vellum copies in damaged library of Pamphilus at Caesarea. W.H.P. Hatch, *The Principle Uncial Manuscripts of the New Testament* (Chicago, 1939), 8.
Council of Ephesus 431–51. Supremacy of Alexandria but latter disappeared with Council of Chalcedon 451.

page 137

Parchment apparently not used in Constantine's time or in his bureaucracy. R.L. Poole, *Lectures on the History of the Papal Chancery Down to the Time of Innocent III* (Cambridge, 1915), 148–49.

John I went to Constantinople 526 and papacy divided by Constantinople to last Greek pope Zacharias 741–52. Edessa captured by Persians 609. Peace between Romans and Persians 562 — Christians allowed exercise of religion in Persia but forbidden to proselytize.

6 Parchment and Paper

page 138

Privilege granted by Benedict III to abbey of Corbie on papyrus roll 22 ft, 6 in. long. L.R. Poole, *Lectures on the History of the Papal Chancery* (Cambridge, 1915), 197. Papyrus superseded by parchment under Benedict VIII (1020–22). Ibid., 37. Parchment used earlier but papyrus persisted to 1050 and occasionally used under Gregory IX and Victor II. Ibid., 59, 197. As long as papyrus used, Pope's subscription used and took the form *Benete valete* written in full. Ibid., 47.

page 139

a. Rule of Pachomios followed by St. Martin of Tours — also St. Ninian of Pictish church in Scotland. Was this rule used by St. Patrick and St.

Columba? Apparently followed by St. Columbanus founder of monastery of Luxeuil. Did it accompany missionary zeal?

St. Patrick spread papacy.

See Harry Bresslau, *Papyrus and Parchment*. Also "Rapport de M. Delisle sur une communication de M. Brutails," *Bulletin du Comité des Travaux historiques et scientifiques* (Paris, 1884), 157–63.

page 140

b. See C.E. Stevens, *Sidonius Apollinaris and His Age* (Oxford, 1933).
c. former?

page 141

d. St. Columbanus (Bobbio) St. Gall (St. Gall), Pictish scholars educated at Bangor in Ulster under St. Comgall. A.B. Scott, *The Pictish Nation: Its People and Its Church* (Edinburgh, 1918), 41.

e. St. Wilfrid insisted on Easter Sunday after 15th opposed Celtic system which allowed Easter to be kept on 14th and calculated moon on cycle of 84 years. R.L. Poole, *Chronicles and Annals: A Brief Outline of Their Growth* (Oxford, 1926), 24. From time of Bede year reckoned from Incarnation of Lord in England — taken by missionaries to East Frankish [dominions] and official [until] 839 — with influence of Otto the Great the Rome date accepted 963 in Papal Chancery. Ibid., 25–26.

Easter Table of Dionysus Exiguus constructed at Rome 525 — experimented at Whitby. Ibid., 24. Beginning of the year in Middle Ages.

Celtic church in Scotland not brought into line until influence of English clergy in twelfth century. A.C. Poole, *From Domesday Book to Magna Carta* (Oxford, 1951), 267.

Concern of church for control over time at Easter.

Alcuin probably had little influence on French writing.

Boniface first Transalpine Bishop to swear obedience to Pope.

Did spread of writing kill poetry — Alcuin to Bishop of Lindisfarne —

"When the priests dine together, let the words of God be read. It is fitting on such occasions to listen to a reader, not a harper, to the discourses of the Fathers, not the poems of the heathen. What has Ingeld to do with Christ?" G. Thomson, *Studies in Ancient Greek Society* (London, 1949), 577.

f. Biscop brought pictures from Rome for churches in Wearmouth and Jarrow for those unable to read — first gospels and Apocalypse, later Old and New Testament.

Power of oral tradition in Ireland — see Solomon Gradz ["Oral Tradition in the Bible," *Jewish Studies in Memory of George A. Kohut 1874–1933*, ed. S. W. Baron and A. Marx, 248–69].

page 143

g. Anointed with oil at hands of clergy, ceremony repeated by Pope Stephen 754.

h. Last Greek pope — papacy diminished by Byzantine empire after 526.

Vellum manuscripts in uncial, i.e., capital letters fourth to ninth century — in ninth century size of volumes necessitated by uncial cumbrous and new style minuscule used for documentary writing instead. F. G. Kenyon, *The Text of the Greek Bible* (London, 1949), 37.

Imperial year at Constantinople and Indiction apparently used after 537 and a general practice after 530 — neither used after 781. R. C. Lane, *Lectures on the History of the Papal Chancery* (Cambridge, 1915), 38. Pontifical year substituted probably 781. Ibid., 20.

page 144

i. In this he apparently failed — i.e., unable to abolish anointing. See Gerald Ellard, *Ordination Anointings in the Western Church Before 1000* AD (Cambridge, Mass., 1933).

See A. Goldschmidt, *German Illumination* (New York, n.d.) — development of painting under Charlemagne — influence of Irish and Anglo-Saxon. Independent development with use of pen especially in Initials.

See F. G. Kenyon, *Ancient Books and Modern Discoveries* (Chicago, 1927).

Contributions of Charlemagne to monetary system of Europe — $1\pounds$ = 20s 240 d. argent.

Curial hand corruption of ancient cursive — affinity with Beneventan script — persisted in papal chancery to beginning of twelfth century — gradually defeated by minuscule. R.L. Poole, *Lectures on the History of the Papal Chancery* (Cambridge, 1915), 58. Minuscule invaded chancery in eleventh century. Ibid., 136. Notary named Lanfranc invented beautiful minuscule 1093. Curial borrowed from minuscule and minuscule from cursive. Ibid., 73–74.

page 145

j. Otto I anointed and crowned at Aachen 936 as German king. Henry I refused to be anointed.

k. Not an order but reformed Benedictines with reorganization under Abbot of Cluny (1073–85) (Gregory VII).

Success of Charlemagne in Europe in conquests turned Scandinavians towards England. See A. Goldschmidt, *German Illumination* (New York, n.d.), vol. II. Ottoman period showing Byzantine influence in illumination — independence from England and France.

page 146

See B. Karlgren, *The Chinese Language* (New York, 1949).

page 147

l. Buddhist King, 259–222 BC.

m. And of Buddhism — two or three centuries after AD 62.

A.F.Wright, "Fu I and the Rejection of Buddhism" (*Journal of the History of Ideas*, XII, 1951, 33–47).

In India the spoken word exalted even above the might of the gods themselves.

"I" derived from concrete, purely sensory beginnings and when finally coined gave religion a new category. Transformation of objective existence into subjective being elevated the Deity to the "absolute" realm. The notion of Being and the notion of self combined in Indian speculation which took its departure from the "Holy Word," the Brahma. All Being must submit to the power of the Holy Word. E. Cassirer, *Language and Myth* (New York, 1946), 76–77. Step to the idea of true monotheism.

page 148

n. M. Rubens Duval, "Historie politique, religieuse, et littéraire d'Edesse jusqu'à la première croisade' (*Journal Asiatique*, XVIII, 8th series, 1891, 432–33).

School probably opened 363.

Paper known in West long before 751. Bagdad as metropolis accompanied by expansion of trade — Persian Gulf, India, and China by sea. (Homani), 53. Papyrus continued to be used in Egypt apparently until after AD 950. W.H.P. Hatch, *The Principal Uncial Manuscripts of the New Testament* (Chicago, 1939), 5. Paper used by Arabs in Egypt in eighth century. Ibid., 9. Great linen industry of later Babylonia. A.T. Olmstead, *History of the Persian Empire* (Chicago, 1948), 80.

Nestorianism officially condemned at Ephesus 431.

Mohammedan oral tradition written down under Haroun al Raschid to preserve purity.

S. Gandz ["The Dawn of Literature, Prolegomena to a History of Unwritten Literature," *Osiris*, vol. VII (Bruges, 1939), 261–515, 476].

page 149

See J.H. Freese, *The Library of Photius* (London, 1920). Basilian monasteries in southern Italy (Calabria) centre of influx of classical Greek learning in twelfth and thirteenth centuries. Revival of twelfth and thirteenth century a turn from arts to great authors. W. Jaeger, *Humanism and Theology* (Milwaukee, 1943), 25–29.

pages 150–151

Eastern church more Platonic, western more Aristotelian — Eastern Europe no reformation or renaissance.

Parts of Europe in Latin Empire largely Catholic, Teutonic Christians accepted Reformation, Poland, Ireland outside influence of Rome remained Catholic chiefly for political reasons. In reformation reformers reverted to Hebraism — book religion, Sabbatarianism, legalism. W.R. Inge, *Diary of a Dean* (London, 1950), 164.

page 152

Fall of Bagdad meant stimulus to paper-making in Italy and Europe as supplies cut off.

pages 152–153

Al-Khwarizmi translated by Robert of Chester at Segovia 1145 and algebra introduced to West. Hindu Arabic numerals introduced by translation of Al-Khwarizmi arithmetic. Not frequently used before 1550 nor generally used before 1700. A.C. Poole, *From Domesday Book to Magna Carta* (Oxford, 1951), 245. Gibson argues [Aquinas] did for mind what Martel did for force in helping to escape from Arabian civilization and Mohammedanism — see Étienne Gilson, "St. Thomas Aquinas" (*Proceedings of the British Academy*, XXI, 1935, 29–45).

page 154

0. Influenced by Bogomils. N.H. Baynes and H. St. L.B. Moss, ed. [*Byzantium: An Introduction to East Roman Civilization* (Oxford, 1948), 354].

page 156

Bull of 1301 led Philip IV to summon first meeting of Estates General. In turn Boniface called synod and issued *Unam Sanctam*. Nogaret sent by Philip IV to arrest Boniface. Absolute power of papacy leading to reliance on democracy or rationalism. The mania for centralization and government regulations dates from the time when jurists began to take a share in the government in the time of Philippe le Bel. *The Recollections of Alexis de Toqueville*, ed. J.P. Mayer (New York, 1949), 94.

Becket — struggle between king and church — power under Clarendon constitutions insisting on trying clergy guilty of crime. Avignon not in France with Provencal speech but dominance of French cardinals. See V.H. Galbraith, *The Literacy of the Medieval English Kings* (London, 1936). English prose continued through Conquest as did Anglo-Saxon illumination, F.

Wormald ["The Survival of Anglo-Saxon Illumination After the Norman Conquest" (*Proceedings of the British Academy*, XXX, 1944, 127–45)].

Fourteenth century Registers of curia, thirteenth century great papal formula books, public notary formulary part of main development but later and belongs to fourteenth century and to early years at Avignon. Reflect enormous administrative and legal centralized bureaucracy at Avignon. G. Barraclough, *Public Notaries and the Papal Curia* (London, 1934), 122–31. See R.V. Rogers, "Law Reporting and the Multiplication of Law Reports in the Fourteenth Century" (*English Historical Review*, LXVI, October 1951, 481–506). Also see Bollard.

pages 156–157

Novel disseisin gave speedy remedy to man rejected from freehold, introduced by Henry II. "One of the most important laws ever issued in England." A.C. Poole, *From Domesday Book to Magna Carta* (Oxford, 1951), 407.

Jury system used by Carolingian emperors to obtain information on oath in ninth century — passed to Normandy and to England. Ibid., 405. Magna Carta an assertion of existing law and custom — how far was it a protest against John placing England and Ireland under a bond of fealty and homage to pope in 1213. On significance of English law see V.H. Galbraith, *The Literacy of the Medieval English Kings* (London, 1936). Domesday Book and Magna Carta landmarks in transition from oral society to written society.

page 158

p. Flying buttress overcame weakness of cement in carrying side thrust and increasing height and in turn pointed arch, tall thin columns.

pages 158–159

Franciscans revived interest in Virgin Mary, partly result of increased pretensions of Papacy — Gregory VII —Vicar of St. Peter. Innocent, vicar of Christ — consequent interest in Virgin Mary in intercession. Attempt of Franciscans to bridge gap with vernacular particularly in relation to women. Troubadours (1071–1294) and ladies of Middle Ages developed concept of romantic love — also Crusades [?] and illegitimacy.

Struggle with Becket led to recall of English students from Paris 1167 associated with Oxford. A.C. Poole, *From Domesday Book to Magna Carta* (Oxford, 1951), 237–38.

On extent of influence of Imperial bureaucracy on papal bureaucracy see R.L. Poole, *Lectures on the History of the Papal Chancery* (Cambridge, 1915).

page 161

q. Vespasiano di Bisticci, *Vite de Uomini Illustrie* (Milan, 1951). To 1498 he helped form three libraries — Laurentian in Florence, Vatican, Federigo duke of Urbino — latter bought by Pope Alex VII for Vatican. H.J. Wheatley, *Prices of Books* (London, 1898), 64.

pages 162–163

Writing in India in Harappa period 3000–2400 BC confined largely to seals.

Proscription against monks in China removed in 335 — rapid spread of Buddhism. Seat of patriarch of Buddhism moved from India to Peking in 526.

page 163

See Wu Ta-k'un, "An Interpretation of Chinese Economic History" (*Past and Present*, I, February 1952, 1–12). Period (1) to Ch'in dynasty 221 BC and (2) to 1840. Wittfogel over-emphasizes irrigation factor. H.G. Creel, *The Birth of China* (London, 1936). H.G. Creel, *Studies in Early Chinese Culture* (London, 1938). Present China — industrial bourgeoisie and urban proletariat, peasants and petit bourgeoisie form contrasts — bureaucratic monopolists and great landlords dispossessed.

7 Paper and the Printing Press

page 164

Fall of Constantinople 1453 followed by attempts of Rome to recapture position, i.e., building of St. Peter's, Vatican Library, work of Michelangelo — emphasis on St. Peter's and drain on funds through sale of indulgences led to revival of concept of dualism in England — Henry VIII — and in Germany to reformation — interest in scriptures in Hebrew and Greek and emergence of sacred word in uniform German. End of Byzantine empire 1453 left church in stronger position and probably accentuated intolerance, which led to revolt of Protestantism.

page 165

Prohibition in Venice 1441 of imports of cards from Germany, i.e., woodblocks obviously — Italy and Germany (Koch).

pages 167–168

a. "The just shall live by faith," Romans 1:17 discovered by Luther 1508 or 1509.

Luther used Hebrew canon of Old Testament and followed by English — other books in Apocrypha. Estienne's Bible 1550 — the common Byzantine text in its latest form, i.e., of Eastern church and became received text before Revised version 1881. Froben urged Erasmus to complete Greek Testament before completion of Cardinal Ximenes in Spain — *Complutensian Polyglot* completed in 1517 in 5 volumes issued 1522.

pages 168–169

Jesuit support of tyrannicide (Juan de Mariana, *De rege et regis institutione*, 1599) comparable to that of anarchists — drove terror into minds of political and economic rulers. See A. Growoll, *Three Centuries of the English Booktrade* (New York, 1903), bibliography.

Bible a divisive force making languages sacred and emphasizing Puritanism — break of N. England in Brooks Adams, *The Emancipation of Massachusetts* (Boston, 1919), break in England — revolution under Cromwell.

J.W. Adamson, "The Extent of Literacy in England in the 15th and 16th Centuries" (*The Library*, Series 4, vol. x, 1929, 163–93).

page 171

Contrast between Byzantine Empire and Tudorism — Caesaropapism of church, woman on the throne. Disappearance of Constantinople led to renaissance of England and reformation.

E. Heawood, "Sources of Early English Paper-Supply" (*The Library*, series 4, vol. x, 1929–1930, 282–307, 427–54. See J. Walker, "Censorship of the Press during the Reign of Charles II" (History, xxxv, 1950, 219–38. See *Collected Papers of Henry Bradshaw* (Cambridge, 1889), for annotated references to day book of John Dorne, Oxford bookseller in 1520, 427–50.

page 174

b. Laud.

c. Levellers almost alone in advocating free press — authors opposed monarchical publication. 1586 Bishops given important place in censorship under Elizabeth to check criticism of Anglican church.

page 175

d. On Galileo see E.A. Moody, "Galileo and Avempace" (*Journal of the History of Ideas*, xii, April and June 1951, 163–93, 375–422).

page 178

"The privilege of the stationers is, in my opinion, a very great hindrance to the advancement of all human learning." Hobbes in 1679.

pages 179–80

e. How far did it improve the writer's bargaining power?

f. First notable English novel of sentimental analysis — advent of everyday manners and common people to artistic acceptance. L.F. Cazamian, *History of English Literature* (London, 1926–27), vol. ii.

Addison and Steele bridge gap between Puritanism and monarchy — i.e., Shakespeare and Cromwell. *Spectator* said to have increased 3000 to 30,000 in 20 months.

page 185

V. Kiernan, "Evangelicalism and the French Revolution" (*Past and Present*, no. 1, February 1952, 44–56). Significance of Wilberforce, British and Foreign Bible Society, 1814. See R. Coupland, *Wilberforce* (Oxford, 1923).

page 189

W.L. George, *Caliban* (New York, 1926), centring around life of Northcliffe.

page 190

Irene Fozzard, "The Government and the Press in France 1822 to 1827" (*English Historical Review*, January 1951, 51–66).

page 192

g. A retreat from Augustine's original sin and contributing to success of Marx. Oxford movement followed logically by Manning's interest in papal infallibility.

page 195

See *The Letters of Ezra Pound, 1907–1941* (New York, 1950) — criticism of monopoly of W.H. Smith and Co. in England say 1912–14 to 1932 — effective attack on economic system — concerned with social credit.

"Commerce is the cure for the most destructive prejudices — wherever we find agreeable manners, there commerce flourishes — wherever there is commerce there we meet with agreeable manners." (Montesquieu) quoted in E.M. Winslow, *The Pattern of Imperialism* (New York, 1948), 15. See Frederick Greenwood, *Rewards* (1892).

Cleon — Comment on impossibility of Athens being a democracy and an empire (Thucydides).

SUGGESTED READING

The following bibliography is not meant to be all-inclusive. Instead, it is a selection of Harold Innis's own works and secondary sources about Innis and the communications field. More extensive bibliographies can be found in Alexander John Watson's Innis biography, *Marginal Man: The Dark Vision of Harold Innis*, and in Paul Heyer's Innis study, *Harold Innis*.

Acland, Charles R., and William J. Buxton. *Harold Innis in the New Century.* Montreal and Kingston: McGill-Queen's University Press, 2003.

Angus, Ian. *A Border Within: National Identity, Cultural Plurality, and Wilderness.* Montreal and Kingston: McGill-Queen's University Press, 1997.

Babe, Robert E. *Canadian Communication Thought.* Toronto: University of Toronto Press, 2000.

Carey, James W. *Communication as Culture.* New York: Routledge, 1992.

Cassirer, Ernst. *Language and Myth.* New York: Dover, 1946.

Cayley, David. "The Legacy of Harold Innis." Transcript of CBC Radio program. Toronto: CBC RadioWorks, 1994.

Christian, William, ed. *The Idea File of Harold Innis.* Toronto: University of Toronto Press, 1980.

_____. *Innis on Russia: The Russian Diary and Other Writings.* Toronto: Harold Innis Foundation, 1981.

Creighton, Donald. *Harold Adams Innis: Portrait of a Scholar.* Toronto: University of Toronto Press, 1957.

Crowley, David, and Paul Heyer. *Communication in History: Technology, Culture, Society.* Boston: Allyn and Bacon, 2003.

Crowley, David, and David Mitchell, eds. *Communication Theory Today*. Stanford, CA: Stanford University Press, 1994.

Czitrom, Daniel J. *Media and the American Mind: From Morse to McLuhan*. Chapel Hill: University of North Carolina Press, 1982.

Deibert, Ronald. *Parchment, Printing, and Hypermedia: Communication in World Order Transformation*. New York: Columbia University Press, 1997.

Drache, Daniel, ed. *Staples, Market, and Cultural Change: Harold Innis*. Montreal and Kingston: McGill-Queen's University Press, 1995.

Drucker, Johanna. *The Alphabetic Labyrinth: Letters in History and Imagination*. London: Thames & Hudson, 1995.

Grant, George. *Technology and Empire*. Toronto: House of Anansi Press, 1991.

Hardt, Hanno. *Social Theories of the Press*. Lanham, MD: Rowman & Littlefield, 2001.

Harold Innis Research Foundation. *Innis Research Bulletin*. Eds. Mel Watkins and Roger Riendeau. Toronto: Innis College, 1994–95.

Havelock, E.A. *Harold A. Innis: A Memoir*. Toronto: Harold Innis Foundation, 1982.

Heyer, Paul. *Harold Innis*. Lanham. MD: Rowman & Littlefield, 2003.

____. *Communications and History: Theories of Media, Knowledge, and Civilization*. Westport, CT: Greenwood, 1988.

Innis, Harold A. *The Bias of Communication*. Toronto: University of Toronto Press, 1995.

____. *Changing Concepts of Time*. Lanham, MD: Rowman & Littlefield, 2004.

____. *The Cod Fisheries: The History of an International Economy*. Toronto: University of Toronto Press, 1978.

____. *Essays in Canadian Economic History*. Ed. Mary Quayle Innis. Toronto: University of Toronto Press, 1956.

_____. *The Fur Trade in Canada: An Introduction to Canadian Economic History.* Toronto: University of Toronto Press, 2001.

_____. *A History of the Canadian Pacific Railway.* Revised ed. University of Toronto Press, 1971.

_____. *Peter Pond: Fur Trader and Adventurer.* Toronto: Irwin and Gordon, 1930.

_____. *Political Economy in the Modern State.* Toronto: Ryerson Press, 1946.

_____. *The Press: A Neglected Factor in the Economic History of the Twentieth Century.* New York: AMS Press, 1978.

_____. *Problems of Staple Production in Canada.* Toronto: Ryerson Press, 1933.

_____. *The Strategy of Culture.* Toronto: University of Toronto Press, 1952.

Innis, Harold, and A.R.M. Lower, eds. *Select Documents in Canadian Economic History.* Philadelphia: Porcupine Press, 1977.

Innis, Harold, and A.R.W. Plumtre, eds. *The Canadian Economy and Its Problems.* Toronto: Canadian Institute of International Affairs, 1934.

Innis, Mary Quayle. *An Economic History of Canada.* Toronto: Ryerson Press, 1943.

Kroker, Arthur. *Technology and the Canadian Mind: Innis/McLuhan/Grant.* New York: St. Martin's Press, 1985.

McLuhan, Marshall. *The Gutenberg Galaxy: The Making of a Typographic Man.* Toronto: University of Toronto Press, 1968.

_____. *The Mechanical Bride: Folklore of Industrial Man.* Corte Madera, CA: Gingko Press, 2006.

_____. *Understanding Media: The Extensions of Man.* Cambridge, MA: MIT Press, 1994.

Melody, William, Liora Salter, and Paul Heyer, eds. *Culture, Communication and Dependency.* Norwood, NJ: Ablex Publishing, 1981.

Neill, Robin. *A New Theory of Value: The Canadian Economics of H.A. Innis.* Toronto: University of Toronto Press, 1972.

Ong, Walter J. *Orality and Literacy*. London and New York: Routledge, 1988.

Owram, Doug. *The Government Generation: Canadian Intellectuals and the State 1900–1945*. Toronto: University of Toronto Press, 1986.

Patterson, Graeme. *History and Communications: Harold Innis, Marshall McLuhan, and the Interpretation of History*. Toronto: University of Toronto Press, 1990.

Postman, Neil. *Amusing Ourselves to Death*. New York: Penguin, 1986.

_____. *Technopoly: The Surrender of Culture to Technology*. New York: Knopf, 1992.

Rogers, Everett M. *A History of Communication Study: A Biographical Approach*. New York: The Free Press, 1994.

Rowland, Wade. *Spirit of the Web: The Age of Information from Telegraph to Internet*. Toronto: Thomas Allen, 2006.

Stamps, Judith. *Unthinking Modernity: Harold Innis, McLuhan, and the Frankfurt School*. Montreal and Kingston: McGill-Queen's University Press, 1995.

Starr, Paul. *The Creation of the Media: Political Origins of Modern Communications*. New York: Basic Books, 2004.

Watson, Alexander John. *Marginal Man: The Dark Vision of Harold Innis*. University of Toronto Press, 2006.

INDEX

CPSIA information can be obtained
at www.ICGtesting.com
Printed in the USA
JSHW021808080223
37465JS00001B/3